BUYING PRIVATE COMPANIES
AND BUSINESS ASSETS

BUYING PRIVATE COMPANIES AND BUSINESS ASSETS

Published by ICSA Publishing Ltd
16 Park Crescent
London W1B 1AH
www.icsapublishing.co.uk

First published 2004

Designed and typeset in Sabon by Paul Barrett Book Production, Cambridge

Printed and bound in Great Britain by TJ International Ltd., Padstow, Cornwall

British Library Cataloguing in Publication Data

A catalogue record for this book is available from the British Library.

ISBN 1-86072-246-6

Contents

Preface

This book aims to help busy people in the world of business to understand better the key legal issues involved in selling or buying privately owned companies based in England and Wales. That will include legal and accountancy practitioners, company secretaries, funding professionals, finance directors, and other managers who have had some experience of corporate transactions but would like to know more about this stimulating (and often quite exciting) process.

Gateley Wareing is a commercial law firm, based in the Midlands, which deals with a large number of these corporate transactions each year. Our ten corporate partners act for a variety of clients, including owner managers, publicly quoted companies, banks and venture capitalists. Whatever economic trends may be reported in the press, sales and disposals of private companies and businesses remain at the heart of corporate activity and of our business. Business owners will continue to retire, emigrate or just want to 'get out'; corporate buyers will seek growth through acquisition; banks and venture capitalists will have monies to invest; and managers will want to seize the opportunity of business ownership.

It is challenging, to say the least, to put together a work such as this, whilst acting for clients on actual corporate transactions. The good news is that I am probably in the same boat as you, the reader. When I want information, it needs to be concise and relevant, as well as accurate. This book has been written so that the reader can dip into a chapter or perhaps just one paragraph that will help with their thinking. At the same time, it is hopefully short enough to permit even busy people to read and digest.

As a result, what it does not do is go into depth on legal issues or dwell on academic arguments. There are heavyweight reference works that do this. Neither is it a do it yourself work enabling someone without experience of corporate transactions to deal with the matter without professional advice from a practitioner experienced in the field.

Overall, I hope it provides a practical and straightforward guide to a wide range of legal issues involved in share and business acquisitions. It aims to set out the critical path from initial planning to completion celebrations and beyond. Because the field is not an exact science, some practitioners may disagree with the matters of opinion and approach set out in this book, but hopefully they will find some of the comments and suggestions useful.

Commentary on the major issues involved in buying and selling a business is to be found in the first half of the book, and a selection of key sample documents required in the transactions discussed is located towards the back of the book.

I would like to thank my colleagues for their assistance in compiling this book, including Clare Bates, Ruth Andrew, Michael Cummins and Kirstin Roberts; Kerry Harrison for her exceptional word processing skills and Lisa Rooks for her support in the process.

Companies House forms are Companies House-Crown Copyright and are reproduced with permission of the Stationery Office Limited.

AUSTIN MOORE

Acronyms and general terms

Acronyms

AIM	The AIM Market of the LSE (previously the Alternative Investment Market)
AIM Rules	The rules applicable to AIM as issued by the LSE
CA	Companies Act 1985
CC	Competition Commission
CGT	Capital gains tax
EIS	Enterprise Investment Scheme
EMI	Enterprise Management Incentives
FA	Finance Act (with the year it was enacted)
FSA	Financial Services Authority
FSMA	Financial Services & Markets Act 2000
IA	Insolvency Act 1986
IPR	Intellectual property rights
IR	The Inland Revenue
IT(EP)A	Income Tax (Earnings & Pensions) Act 2003
JVCo	A limited company formed as the vehicle for a corporate joint venture
Listing Rules	The rules applicable to companies listed on LSE as issued by the FSA
LLP	Limited liability partnership
LSE	London Stock Exchange plc
NDA	Non-disclosure agreement
Newco	New limited company
non-QCB	Non-qualifying corporate bond
OFT	Office of Fair Trading
PAYE	Pay As You Earn
p/e	Price/earnings ratio
QCB	Qualifying corporate bond

SAR	Substantial Acquisition Rules
SDLT	Stamp duty land tax
TOGC	Transfer of going concern for VAT purposes
TUPE	Transfer of Undertakings (Protection of Employment) Regulations 1981
UKLA	UK Listing Authority, currently part of the FSA
VAT	Value added tax
VC	Venture capitalist
VCT	Venture capital trust

General terms

Acquisition	The acquisition of the shares of a limited company or a business, as described in Chapter 1.
Articles	The articles of association of the company as adopted and filed at Companies House.
BIMBO	A buy-in management buy-out, as described in Chapter 2.
Completion	The point at which the acquisition is completed and finalised.
Connected persons	The meaning given in Section 346 CA, broadly the close family of an individual, family trusts and companies in which he or she has at least a 20% interest.
Distributable profits	Those profits available for distribution under Section 263 CA; further explanation is given in Chapter 8.
Due diligence	The process of examining the affairs of the target, as described in Chapter 6.
Financial assistance	The giving of financial assistance by a company for the purchase of its own shares as defined in Section 151 CA, as described in Chapter 9.
IBO	An institutional buy-out, as described in Chapter 2.
MBI	A management buy-in, as described in Chapter 2.
MBO	A management buy-out, as described in Chapter 2.
Ordinary resolution	A resolution of the shareholders of a company passed by a simple majority (more than 50%).
P2P	A public to private transaction, as described in Chapter 2.
Pre-emption	The right of existing shareholders, where shares are to be issued or transferred, to be offered those shares before third parties.
Purchaser	The individuals or entity which is acquiring the target.
Special resolution	A resolution of the shareholders of a company required under CA or its articles to be passed by a 75% majority.

Target	The company or the business which is the subject matter of an acquisition.
Vendor(s)	The shareholders of the target in the case of a share sale and the owner of the business in the case of a business sale.
Warranties	The contractual representations and warranties given to the purchaser on an acquisition regarding the legal, financial, commercial and taxation position of the target.
Whitewash	The process of approving financial assistance given by a private company under Section 155 CA, as described in Chapter 9.

Introduction

CHAPTER

1

1.1 Scope

1.1.1 This book deals with key legal issues arising on two types of acquisition, namely:

- **share purchase**, where the purchaser acquires all of the shares, or sufficient shares to gain control, of a limited company;
- **business purchase**, where a purchaser acquires the assets and undertaking of a business entity, as a going concern.

1.1.2 These transactions could be between private individuals or publicly quoted companies. The defining feature is the subject matter or target of the acquisition. This book does not cover the takeover of public companies themselves. Although many of the legal rules and principles apply equally to them, the investment exchange on which the shares are dealt imposes special rules and practices to such acquisitions. In addition, the parties will need to consider the City Code on Takeovers and Mergers. In short, it is a specialist area beyond the scope of this book. Chapter 13 does however deal with the specific legal issues arising where either the vendor or the purchaser is a quoted company.

[handwritten margin note: Doesn't cover takeover of publically quoted companies]

1.1.3 This book only comments on matters of English law. Practically speaking, this means it deals with companies incorporated in England and Wales and businesses which have a base there. Even if the vendor or purchaser is based in another territory, the law governing the acquisition will usually reflect the domicile of the target. In any event, the parties should choose the governing law and clearly express it in all relevant agreements. Failure to do this can lead to unwanted effects and disputes, since the laws on jurisdiction are not straightforward. Also, whatever law is chosen by the parties to apply to the acquisition itself, rights of third parties (such as employees, creditors, customers and landlords) are likely to be governed by the laws of the country where the target is based. This will usually necessitate the use of local lawyers and professionals.

[handwritten margin note: Can choose law for acquisition but rights of 3rd parties governed by local law]

1.1.4 The mechanics of an acquisition are based on the law of contract and also (where the target, vendor or purchaser is a company) company law. A basic understanding of the principles of contract will be assumed in this book. By way of a very crude recap on these principles, the essential requirements to formation of a contract are set out below.

ESSENTIALS OF A CONTRACT

Capacity

- There can be no contract with an individual who is a minor (under 18) or is mentally incapable.
- A company's capacity is no longer limited, as regards third parties, by its memorandum of association, under s.35 CA.
- Where a transaction is approved by the board of directors of the company, a third party dealing in good faith is not concerned with any limitation on their powers under s.35A CA.

Offer and acceptance

- In the case of an acquisition this will usually be satisfied by a written contract between the vendor and the purchaser.
- An oral contract for sale of shares or the sale of assets (other than property) can be binding.
- Pre-contract communication should be made expressly 'subject to contract' to differentiate between an offer, which will lead immediately to contract on acceptance, and negotiations.

Consideration

- This refers to a commercial benefit from the arrangement, such as payment of a price to the vendor and a detriment to purchaser.
- Consideration need not be 'commercially sufficient' for the contract to be binding.
- Consideration is presumed where a document is entered into as a deed (which should be expressly stated in the document).

Intention to create legal relations

- No contract will be created unless the parties intended that their acts should have legal effect or such intention can be presumed.
- This intention will usually be presumed to exist where business people are communicating with each other.
- Letters of intent or heads of agreement will not be legally binding if it is made clear that they are only an expression and record of the purpose and intention of the parties, and are not intended to be legally binding.

1.1.5   There are a number of other areas of law relevant to acquisitions. These depend on the assets and activities of the target, but commonly include:
- property – see paragraph 7.9;
- employment – see chapter 10;
- pensions – see paragraphs 3.8, 7.14 and 11.10 and chapter 12;
- taxation – dealt with in various sections of the book;
- environmental issues – see paragraph 7.12.

1.1.6   This book addresses the key issues encountered in most acquisitions. Each target is different and its particular circumstances will require more detailed consideration of relevant legal issues than the size of this book permits.

1.2 Perspective

1.2.1 Although concerned with the legal aspects of the process, this book attempts to look through the eyes of the vendor and the purchaser, rather than the advisor standpoint. Clearly, the vendor and the purchaser have different perspectives and one of the keys to successful negotiation and effective communication is to understand the perspective of each.

1.2.2 At a basic level, the objectives of a vendor in the acquisition process are likely to include:

- maximising the consideration for the sale;
- minimising risks associated with the consideration, for example where it is not paid in cash on completion;
- mitigating the tax effects of the transaction on the vendor and persons connected with the vendor;
- managing risk arising under any obligations to the purchaser, such as warranties and any retained liabilities;
- limiting future restrictions and obligations, for example restrictions on future competition;
- certainty as to the legal, accounting and tax effects of the acquisition;
- completing the transaction within an agreed acceptable timescale.

1.2.3 The basic objectives of the purchaser are partly a reverse of these and could be listed as:

- minimising the consideration payable, or at least maximising the value derived from that consideration;
- if possible, deferring payment of the consideration to reduce funding costs and assist cash flow (deferred consideration);
- if consideration has regard to future or unproven performance of the target, making at least part of it subject to performance criteria (contingent consideration);
- mitigating the tax effects of the acquisition on the target and the purchaser;
- understanding the business and financial position of the target, through due diligence;
- managing any risk that might affect the value of the target, by having legal redress against the vendor for matters not properly disclosed;
- obtaining funding from third parties for the acquisition, where necessary;
- certainty about the legal, accounting and tax effects of the acquisition;
- completing the transaction within an agreed timescale.

1.2.4 The key common objective is certainty, not just about the effects on the parties and on the timescale but, critically, as to whether the transaction will deliver their expectations of value. This is why the legal process of an acquisition is basically concerned with examining, recording and implementing exactly what the parties intend to be the position between them.

1.2.5 Wherever the purchaser has to obtain funding for the acquisition, there is a third party who needs to be satisfied with the process. Venture capitalists

3

(VCs) and banks that deal with acquisition finance on a regular basis will usually have had more experience of deals than the parties themselves and so will be a useful source of advice and common sense on the process. However, there are often occasions when the purchaser is willing to proceed but the funder is not satisfied with the terms of the deal. This may be due to gaps in due diligence or matters revealed which have not been fully explored. It could also relate to the amount or terms of the consideration. The purchaser is caught between the vendor and the funder and may become involved on negotiations on two fronts. From the vendor's perspective, this is a 'purchaser issue' although the vendor needs to appreciate that the deal will not happen if it cannot be funded.

1.3   Regulation

1.3.1   As noted above, there is relatively little legislation that has specific application to the transfer of ownership of private companies and business.

1.3.2   The marketing and promotion of shares and other securities in private companies is, however, subject to regulation. This is currently contained in the Financial Services and Markets Act 2000 (FSMA). FSMA will have an impact on the marketing of shares; this is dealt with in paragraph 5.6. In the case of private company acquisitions, the key issue will be to obtain exemption from the restrictions on 'financial promotions' under s.19 FSMA.

1.3.3   Perhaps the greatest area of regulation relevant to company sales and business sales relates to taxation. However, this is not a book on taxation and the reader is referred to specialist works including the *ICSA Tax Guide*. Anyone engaging on a corporate transaction is advised to obtain tax advice from a specialist in the field. This book does however comment on particular tax issues as they arise.

1.4   Alternative methods

1.4.1   Chapter 2 describes different types of business and share acquisitions. Chapter 3 compares key features of each. One common feature is that acquisitions have a relatively low rate of success. 'Success' in this context means that the acquisition achieves the objectives set for it by the purchaser. Common reasons for failing to do this are set out below.

CAUSES OF FAILURE

■ Lack of planning, to ensure that the acquisition is the appropriate step for the purchaser at that time.

■ Inadequate due diligence, so that a problem issue is not discovered or not fully appreciated.

■ Financial performance of the target not being sufficient to justify the purchaser's financial commitment (including additional costs of servicing debt).

- Management failing to understand or cope with new responsibilities.
- Insufficient working capital to run the business.
- Failure to integrate the target's existing management and employees (or, depending which way you look at it, their failure to integrate with the purchaser).

1.4.2   There are other methods of combining business activities, which may reduce the risk of full acquisition. Joint ventures are mentioned in Chapter 2. Where the purpose of acquisition is to gain use of intellectual property rights (IPR) (such as brand names, particular technology or know how) it is possible, as an alternative, to enter into a licence agreement with the owner of that intellectual property. The mechanics and legal issues arising from licensing are beyond the scope of this book but it is possible to make the following basic comparisons with acquisition:

- there may be no capital sum paid to 'acquire' the IPR and all payments can be geared to the purchaser's use and reward;
- both purchaser and vendor retain their identities and independence, although contractual restrictions on their future activities may be agreed;
- the purchaser does not pick up unwanted assets or liabilities (although consider the relevance of TUPE if there is, in reality, a transfer of business activities);
- although a properly negotiated licence agreement should be created, costs are likely to be lower than for an acquisition.

1.4.3   Franchising is another alternative to acquisition. In most cases, it comprises a licence to use the franchisor's brand name, 'get up' and know how plus support for the franchisee in establishing a business in a given location. It is therefore similar to licensing, with some of its advantages. However, in the experience of many, payments to the franchisor for those rights and for ongoing support have proved expensive, and its popularity (with a few high profile exceptions) has reduced over the last few years.

1.4.4   The stark alternative to acquisition is start-up and/or organic growth. Many businesses start with a determined individual or team of individuals and a good idea. This is particularly true of technology businesses where the principal asset may be IPR developed by the founders. However, start-ups will usually require years of very hard work on low remuneration to build up the business and many end in business failure.

1.4.5   The attraction of business and share acquisitions has and will continue to be the immediate access to the business' revenues, customers, assets and skills base, which is not just conceptual but is a working example of the business opportunity open to the purchaser.

CHAPTER 2

Specific Transactions

2.1 Asset sales

2.1.1 Business acquisitions are often referred to as 'asset sales'. Where tangible assets (for example plant and equipment) are sold without the purchaser acquiring a going concern, this is merely a contract for the sale of goods, which is not what this book is about. However, even if the vendor does not expressly agree to sell goodwill or transfer ongoing contracts, there may still be the transfer of a going concern if in fact the purchaser will use the assets acquired to carry on a business activity that is a continuation of the vendor's activity. The distinction is relevant to, in particular, whether employees will transfer to the purchaser under the Transfer of Undertakings (Protection of Employment) Regulations 1981 (TUPE) and whether the transfer of assets is treated as a transfer of going concern (TOGC) for VAT purposes. The key point is that the parties' description of the transaction may not cover all its legal effects.

2.1.2 The opposite also applies, in that a business sale need not involve any transfer of tangible assets. A classic example of this is the transfer of goodwill to a competitor where the vendor is ceasing its business activities in that field. A sole practitioner (for example, an accountant) may be retiring from practice and agree to hand over client connections to another practice. The consideration may include a fixed sum based on the recurring fee income of the vendor's practice, but is also likely to include an element based on future fees generated from the vendor's clients in the period following completion. Even if no tangible assets are transferred (office equipment is likely to have little value and the computer system is likely to be redundant), this should be regarded as a going concern transfer. Accordingly:

- employees of the vendor's practice are liable to transfer to the purchaser under TUPE;
- due diligence should be carried out on the financial performance of the vendor's practice and the contracts and relationships with clients.

This will help the purchaser gain a proper view on the value of goodwill and the resources necessary to service those clients.

2.2 Insolvency sales

2.2.1 An insolvency practitioner will not transfer the share capital of a company that is in receivership or administration. The business (or 'assets' as the insolvency practitioner will usually refer to them) may be transferred as a going concern. A receiver's power to sell the business will be governed by the charge under which the receiver is appointed, although an administrative receiver will have that power under statute if not under the terms of the charge. An administrator is appointed by the court. Whether the administrator has the power to sell the business should be ascertained by checking the terms of the court order. This may include limitations. In either case, the basic mechanics of sale are the same as for any business disposal, namely defining what assets are being sold under the sale agreement and reviewing what liabilities and responsibilities will pass to the purchaser. These include those passing by operation of law (for example transfer of employees under TUPE) in addition to the terms of the contract.

2.2.2 An increasingly common type of transaction on corporate insolvency is the 'pre-pack receivership'. This describes the situation where an insolvency practitioner is appointed, having already reached an understanding that all or part of the business will be acquired by a new company, very often controlled by existing management. There is no separate legal basis for this transaction, but it has particular features. The business will be sold within a very short period after appointment and before any meeting of creditors (or indeed full investigation of the creditors) has taken place. Commonly, the purchaser would be expected to assume all ongoing obligations of the business. Such arrangements are usually entered into in close consultation with the principal secured creditor(s).

2.2.3 A liquidator is not empowered to continue trading activities of the target following the order or resolution for winding up. It is therefore less likely that the business will be transferred as a going concern. However, if a purchaser is ready to take on the business as a going concern at or very shortly following the appointment of a liquidator, the liquidator will sell the assets used in that business as a going concern. Again, this will be a business transfer for the purposes of TUPE.

2.2.4 A key feature of an insolvency sale is that the receiver, administrator or liquidator will not offer any warranties regarding the target company. The risk of purchase is left entirely with the purchaser. Some of those risks are highlighted below. The ability of the purchaser to mitigate this risk will depend on whether the purchaser has existing knowledge of the business or has the opportunity to carry out due diligence on the assets (whether by physical checking or by enquiries of third parties). For this reason, existing management will have an advantage over outside parties.

RISKS ON RECEIVERSHIP SALE

- The vendor has no title to the assets (for example, the assets are subject to retention of title or hire purchase).
- Third parties have rights over the assets (for example, liens, charges and tenancies).
- The assets do not exist (for example, an asset list is wrong or the items have been stolen or destroyed).
- The condition of the assets (for example plant and equipment is not working or is unsafe).
- Defects in manufacture (for example stock is defective and the purchaser sells it to customers who can claim against the purchaser).

2.2.5   The rationale for insolvency practitioners refusing to give warranties is basically twofold. First, they have only recently been involved in the business and have very restricted knowledge of its affairs. The persons with knowledge, namely the company's directors and/or shareholders, have no motivation to give warranties themselves. Warranties given by the company would be worthless, since it is insolvent and liable to be wound up and dissolved in due course. Secondly, the insolvency practitioner is involved in order to carry out a particular process, namely:

- in the case of a receiver, to realise assets as agent of the company in order to satisfy amounts due to the secured creditor who has appointed the receiver;
- in the case of an administrator, to carry out the terms of the court order;
- in all cases, to administer the affairs of the company in accordance with insolvency legislation.

The insolvency practitioner recovers fees for carrying out this process, but is not otherwise entitled to benefit from the sale. For the insolvency practitioner to accept liability under warranties would not be a commercial proposition. A minor exception is that insolvency practitioners will usually be prepared to warrant that neither they nor their firm have created third parties' rights over the assets being sold. This is a warranty they can give, because it relates to their own acts.

2.2.6   An insolvency sale contract will invariably provide that the receivers enter into the contract without personal liability. Quite apart from the lack of warranties, this means that any obligations in the contract for sale will be enforceable only against the company (which is insolvent, making them almost worthless). Where the purchaser manages to negotiate an obligation on the part of the receiver, clear words are needed to ensure that this is enforceable against the receiver and not just against the vendor company. Note that an obligation to discharge a liability that the contract states to be 'as an expense of the receivership' does not impose any personal liability on the receiver. It does however mean that the receiver is confirming that that liability will be discharged out of the proceeds collected from disposal of the floating charge assets before the receiver's own fees are paid out.

2.2.7 It will be apparent from the list above that the insolvency sale process does not give any warranty of good title to the assets being purchased. The purchaser is acquiring 'such right, title and interest as the vendor company may have' in those assets. Third party rights will include any finance company that has supplied the relevant assets on hire purchase or lease. Those assets will be owned by the finance company and it may retrieve them from the purchaser. The purchaser will have no claim for reimbursement of the price paid from the receiver. Indeed, the receiver will look for an indemnity from the purchaser for any liability or expenses incurred by allowing the purchaser to take possession of the asset. Another example would be retention of title rights of an unpaid supplier. Where there is doubt as to ownership of the assets that cannot be clarified before completion, it would be preferable for the price relevant to those assets to be held in a specified account (often referred to by lawyers as 'held in escrow') for a set period to allow for third party claims to be made. In practice, receivers will be reluctant to agree this. If so, the purchaser has to decide whether the price it is paying for the assets reflects that risk.

2.2.8 Any bank or other creditor having a charge over the assets of the company should be required to give a release of the assets from the charge at completion. Even when purchasing assets from a receiver appointed by a bank, the purchaser should obtain a release from the bank itself.

2.3 Joint ventures

2.3.1 There is no legal definition of a 'joint venture'. It is an expression used to describe participation between two or more entities to achieve a common purpose. Usually that will be where the parties wish to exploit an opportunity or expand an area of their current activities, but lack particular resources to do that effectively. Rather than buy those resources (assuming they are for sale), they contract with each other to provide them in consideration of shared rewards. Those resources could be:

- intellectual property and know how;
- a skilled workforce;
- specialist equipment that is not fully utilised;
- customer connections or access to a particular market;
- business opportunities open to them, but which they cannot fulfil alone;
- local knowledge or residency;
- cash resources or access to finance.

2.3.2 A successful joint venture requires necessary resources to be matched so that each joint venture partner 'brings something to the party'. It will be clear from the above list that joint ventures can often be achieved without any acquisition, for example:

- licensing of rights, so that the licensee can carry on the activity in exchange for royalties;
- a contractual arrangement, for example to hire premises, equipment or people;

- sharing of information and rights so that both parties carry on the activity, perhaps in different markets.

2.3.3   In many cases however, a joint venture will be achieved through a new company formed by the parties as a vehicle for the joint venture (JVCo). JVCo will acquire part of the undertaking of one or more parties and this transaction should be looked at as a business acquisition, subject to most of the principles outlined in the rest of this book. For example:

- the transaction should be documented as a purchase by JVCo from each relevant party, with the same care as to the definition of assets and liabilities being transferred;
- as an investor in JVCo, each party should carry out due diligence on the business assets being transferred to JVCo;
- the parties should consider warranties being given not just to JVCo but to them independently to back up their investment in JVCo;
- the parties should expect to be restricted from future competition with JVCo, particularly with regard to business activities they are transferring to JVCo;
- the implications of TUPE as regards any changes to the workforces of the parties need to be considered carefully;
- the accounting and tax implications of the transaction need to be considered and agreed.

2.3.4   The parties to the joint venture will be co-shareholders in JVCo and will therefore usually enter into a shareholders' agreement (usually called a joint venture agreement) to regulate their rights as shareholders. These issues are considered at paragraph 2.4.5.

2.3.5   Competition law issues can be particularly relevant to joint ventures, whether or not they involve the creation of a joint venture company (see Chapter 8).

2.4   Minority shareholdings

2.4.1   References in this book to share purchase relate primarily to the acquisition of the entire issued share capital of a company. This is the most straightforward type of acquisition, resulting in the purchaser having full control of the share rights and thus the board of directors of the target company. Where the purchaser will acquire less than 100 per cent of the target share capital, the following issues arise:

- whether to acquire an interest in the target company by acquisition of shares from the existing shareholders or by subscription for new shares;
- existing shareholders' rights;
- the rights attaching to the shares which are acquired, particularly when these comprise a minority shareholding.

2.4.2   In crude terms, whether the purchaser acquires existing shares or subscribes for new shares depends on who is to receive the consideration for the acquisition. A subscription for new shares is an investment in the company with no immediate return to the existing shareholders. The corresponding advantage to the existing shareholders is that the target company has greater resources: they have to weigh up whether the increased value and opportunities of the target company outweigh the dilution of their share capital. If not, or if the intention is for the existing shareholders to extract value from the transaction, the purchaser will be expected to buy existing shares.

2.4.3 As well as this obvious commercial distinction, there are also taxation considerations. A sale of shares by existing shareholders would involve a disposal subject to capital gains tax (CGT), whereas a subscription for new shares has no direct tax effect on them. If the purchaser is looking to acquire a holding of less than 30 per cent in the target company, a share subscription may allow the purchaser to benefit from Enterprise Investment Scheme (EIS) relief, brief details of which are given below.

[handwritten margin note: Disposal of shares subject to Capital Gains Tax]

ENTERPRISE INVESTMENT SCHEME

[handwritten margin note: relevant to UK only]

Key conditions
- The purchaser must be an individual (note that an analogous regime – corporate venturing relief – applies to companies).
- The purchaser subscribes for new shares (not the acquisition of existing shares).
- The purchaser and connected persons do not between them hold more than 30 per cent of the target's equity share capital or voting rights.
- The shares held by the purchaser are equity shares without preferential rights to dividends or capital.
- The target carries on a 'qualifying activity', basically meaning that it is a trading company not engaged in certain specified non-qualifying activities, such as property development, nursing homes, hotels and guest houses, farming and money-lending.
- The target must be unquoted (although for this purpose companies on AIM are not quoted).
- The activities of the target are carried on wholly or mainly in the United Kingdom – the Inland Revenue will review all relevant practices to decide this, the key issue being where the company's principal place of business is, by reference to its employees, capital assets, manufacturing and marketing operations.
- If the investor will be a director or work in the target company, any remuneration must be 'reasonable'.

Basis of reliefs
- Investment limit of £150,000 in any single tax year (in one or more companies).
- Income tax relief for higher rate tax payers is equivalent to 20 per cent of the amount invested (in other words, one-fifth of the amount invested is returned as an income tax rebate).
- Subsequent disposal of the shares will be exempt for CGT provided they are held for at least three years and the target company has in the meantime maintained its qualifying status.
- Deferral of CGT arising on the disposal of other assets may be obtained by subscribing for qualifying EIS shares.

2.4.4   Assuming the purchaser acquires a stake in the target company with the agreement of the existing or remaining shareholders, the parties would usually agree a shareholders' agreement to regulate the company's affairs and to set out shareholders' rights. This reflects the fact that company legislation and the 'standard' set of regulations for private companies referred to as Table A are unlikely to protect them adequately. A shareholder holding less than 50 per cent of the voting shares will not be entitled to appoint a director (unless the articles provide otherwise), nor is a shareholder entitled to access to the target company's premises or accounting records. The rights of such a minority shareholder are limited to receiving the annual accounts and notices of shareholders' meetings. Thus, a purchaser taking a strategic stake should seek a shareholders' agreement and appropriate articles by a negotiation.

minority shareholding rights

2.4.5   Each shareholders' agreement is specific to the circumstances of the parties, but would deal with the issues set out below. A joint venture vehicle would usually have a shareholders' agreement dealing with similar issues. Venture capitalists (VCs) will invariably seek a shareholders' agreement with additional protection for the VC, as described in Chapter 9.

COMMON PROVISIONS IN SHAREHOLDERS' AGREEMENTS

+ for JVs as well

- Rights of the shareholders to be, or to appoint, directors and/or a chairman/woman and to remain involved in management of the target company.
- A list of matters that can only be transacted with the approval of all or of a specified majority of shareholders.
- Restrictions on the disposal of shares and future issues of shares (or at least pre-emption rights).
- Where the shareholders are individuals, options for the sale of shares on their death, bankruptcy or cessation of employment.
- Drag-along clauses as referred to in paragraph 2.5.6.
- Restrictions on shareholders' present and future business activities.

2.4.6   As well as a shareholders' agreement, the parties may also agree to adopt new articles of association of the target company. Some of the provisions of the shareholders' agreement can (and indeed should) be dealt with in the articles of association. These include any rights attaching to shares. However, the parties often prefer to include matters in a readable agreement rather than in the articles, which are often seen as legalistic.

2.4.7   Where the purchaser and the existing shareholders will have separate rights (for example special voting or dividend rights), the share capital of the target company will be divided into different classes. The rights attaching to those separate classes will be set out in the articles of association. For example, the articles could contain A and B shares having the following rights:

A & B shares

- both A and B shares carry the rights to appoint an equal number of directors;
- A shares carry the right to appoint the chairman with a casting vote (this assumes an intention that the A shareholders would be able to outvote the B shareholders);
- A shares carry a preferential right to dividends equal to x per cent per annum or perhaps y per cent of profits (note that such special rights would prevent the A shares qualifying for EIS reliefs);
- on a sale or return of capital, the A shares would have rights to the first z pounds.

2.5 Dissenting shareholders

[handwritten: Ways in which existing shareholders may block acquisition of shares by a purchaser.]

2.5.1 Existing shareholders who were not in agreement with the acquisition of shares by the purchaser may be able to block the acquisition in a number of ways. The purchaser (and those shareholders supporting the acquisition) should take these into account at the outset. The legal bases are set out in the next four paragraphs.

2.5.2 If it is proposed that the purchaser would subscribe for new shares, the requirements would be:
- sufficient authorised but unissued share capital to cover the share issue, failing which the target company would need to pass an ordinary resolution (more than 50 per cent of shareholders' votes in favour) to increase it under s.123 CA;
- authority for the directors to allot those shares, if not contained in the articles of association of the target company, given by an ordinary resolution pursuant to s.80 CA;
- dis-application of pre-emption rights (where those arise under the articles or under s.89 CA) which may require a special resolution (75 per cent of shareholders in favour) under s.95 CA;
- approval of the board of directors to the issue, which will require a majority of the directors to be in favour.

2.5.3 If it is proposed that the purchaser would acquire existing shares from some but not all of the shareholders, the issues to be dealt with are:
- the articles of association of the target company may contain pre-emption rights on transfer of shares, which would mean that the selling shareholders would have to offer their shares to the other existing shareholders before the purchaser;
- if those pre-emption rights exist, they could be overridden by a special resolution, but see paragraph 2.5.5;
- if the articles contain a discretion for the directors to refuse to register a share transfer, approval of the majority of the directors will be required to obtain full legal title to the shares.

2.5.4 Apart from the specific rights under the articles and statute outlined above, the purchaser should investigate whether there are any contractual rights as between the shareholders. For example, a shareholders' agreement may provide a restriction on sale of the shares or a right of pre-emption (whether or not this is contained in the articles). There may be options granted over the shares, exercisable on a shareholder ceasing to be employed by the target company or attempting to dispose of his or her shares outside of the articles.

2.5.5 Lastly, a minority shareholder may petition the court under s.459 CA if the affairs of the target company are being conducted in a manner that is unfairly prejudicial to the interests of some of its members. This is a wide ranging right, entitling any shareholder to complain to the court if they can show unfair treatment to them in their capacity as shareholder. Thus, even if the purchaser will acquire sufficient shares to pass ordinary and special resolutions as above, regard should be had as to whether the minority shareholders could complain at the treatment. In fact, s.459 CA cannot easily be invoked on an acquisition if the articles of association provide a clear procedure for share transfers. The most likely remedy for a shareholder who successfully invokes s.459 is an order that his or her shares be purchased at their full market value without any discount for the shares being a minority holding. Therefore, an offer to purchase those shares at such a value (particularly if this is backed up by an independent valuation) is a practical method of dealing with the issue.

2.5.6 The preceding paragraphs deal with a situation where the purchaser wants to acquire some but not all of the shares. If the purchaser wants to acquire all the shares but some shareholders are reluctant to sell, the purchaser's options are fairly limited. The articles of association of the target company may contain a provision entitling the majority to force the minority to sell. This is known as a 'drag-along' or 'come-along' clause. Even when this right exists, it is in practice difficult to force dissenting shareholders to sell. The only statutory assistance is provided by s.429 CA, but with a rather cumbersome procedure. This clause applies where the purchaser makes a 'general offer' to acquire all the shares in the company (or all shares of a particular class). This envisages a formal offer document, similar to those used on public company transactions. If such an offer is made and is accepted by at least 90 per cent of the shareholders of the company, there is a procedure to require the remaining 10 per cent to sell at the same price. In practice this procedure is rarely implemented in private company transactions.

2.6 Management buy-outs

2.6.1 A management buy-out (MBO) describes the situation where existing employees of the target company acquire control through acquisition. This may be an acquisition of the shares or the business of the target company. It may also arise through a receivership sale. A key feature differentiating MBOs from other corporate acquisitions is that management rarely has the financial resources to fund the transaction itself and therefore relies almost entirely on banks, VCs, asset funders and deferred consideration. The issues surrounding these are dealt with in Chapter 9. That funding is serviced and repaid from the profits of the target company and the funding will invariably be secured against its assets.

2.6.2   The structure of an MBO will usually involve establishing a new limited company (Newco), which will acquire the target. In the case of share purchase, it thus becomes the holding company of the target. The principal reason for this step is to facilitate the arrangements to fund the Newco. As noted above, the MBO will usually be funded by equity funding and loans secured on the assets of the target company. The principal borrower of these loans is Newco (which avoids individual managers from being personally liable for the whole amount of the borrower). Creation of Newco also provides the vehicle in which venture capitalists can make equity investments. The nature and terms of those investments is a subject in itself, but in basic terms the VC is protecting its position as a shareholder of Newco, in much the same way as described in 2.4. Commentary on the terms of equity funding is given in Chapter 9.

2.6.3   As well as the classic MBO, other transactions involving management teams and VCs have become prevalent and each has spawned its own acronym, some of which are described below. In particular, the IBO has been a significant feature of the corporate finance market for several years as VCs become increasingly proactive in sourcing, originating and leading buy-outs of private companies.

BUY-OUT ACRONYMS

- **MBO** – existing managers of the target acquire control through acquisition.
- **MBI** – a management buy-in, led by entrepreneurs who intend to manage the target but are not currently employed in it.
- **BIMBO** – a buy-in management buy-out, where the management team will consist of existing managers and managers from outside.
- **IBO** – institutional buy-out, where the acquisition is sourced and led by an institution such as a VC, that engages management usually with a small equity stake.
- **P2P** – a public to private transaction, where a publicly quoted company is acquired by private owners, usually through an IBO or MBO.

2.6.4   Most buy-out transactions are leveraged, meaning that the amount of outside funding is high in comparison with the level of assets of the target. This can arise because the value of a target is based on a multiple of its current and anticipated profits and/or because the buy-out team must compete with trade buyers with greater resources and strategic reasons to make the acquisition. The late 1980s and 1990s saw an increasing number of buy-outs and, as this boom grew, an increasing number of 'highly leveraged' transactions in the UK and the US. Many of these involved VC backing for technology businesses, where investment was based almost entirely on future prospects. It has been more difficult, during the last few years, to attract VC funding for technology-based business or, indeed, to find support for a highly leveraged opportunity.

2.6.5   However, it is still the case that most buy-outs are funded well beyond the security value of the purchaser's assets. Banks lend against business plans showing profit and cash generation, which is referred to as 'cash flow lending'. It follows that the bank funding these transactions is more directly concerned with the whole process of due diligence and warranty protection, in addition to its own lending terms.

2.6.6   Another key feature of MBOs is that the vendors will often be reluctant to provide any commercial warranties on the sale. The arguments on this are dealt with in more detail in paragraph 3.5.

2.7   Employment related securities

2.7.1   The Finance Act 2003 introduced a new regime for the charging of income tax to the extent that an individual receives any benefit whatsoever from shares acquired 'by reason of their employment'. This has particular significance for MBOs, where existing employees acquire shares (which includes shares in Newco). The income tax charge is equally capable of applying on an MBI, since the test of whether shares are acquired by reason of employment includes proposed employment. To complete the picture, the charge applies not just to employment but also to the holding of an office, so that even an existing or proposed non-executive director could be caught by the charge. In short, any individual who is a director or proposed director or employee or proposed employee of the target or a holding company or subsidiary of the target, should consider the provisions of Sch. 22 FA 2003 (Schedule 22) before subscribing for shares.

2.7.2   The essential aim of Schedule 22 is to tax a benefit that may derive from:
- the acquisition of shares at an undervalue;
- an increase in market value as a result of the lifting or variation of restrictions attaching to the shares;
- the conversion of low value shares into more valuable shares after an acquisition has been carried out.

2.7.3   The 2003 changes go further than any former piece of legislation to tax these potential benefits. Previous planning included management subscribing for shares in Newco before the acquisition was completed so that they were investing in the target business as founders rather than in their capacity as employees. This planning measure will no longer suffice.

2.7.4   There are in essence two potential events that could give rise to an income tax charge:
- the acquisition of shares, by reason of employment;
- the lifting of restrictions attaching to the shares.

2.7.5　A straightforward situation arises where a manager acquires shares at less than their market value. The definition is the same as for CGT purposes, namely the value a prudent third party purchaser would pay. Management will often pay fairly nominal value for their shares in Newco, since most of the funding of the acquisition will come from third parties. In providing the shares in Newco, regard should be given to the fact that Newco has incurred those borrowings and so it is perfectly possible to come to the conclusion that Newco's shares have nominal value at the outset because of the debt burden. A well-advised management team will however take steps to record how the shares in Newco have been valued and consider whether there is an undervalue. If there is, the correct course would be to declare this as a benefit on which income tax is paid. At this stage, it may be possible to declare a fairly modest undervalue and accept the charge to tax. If the matter is not addressed and Newco is sold some years later at a significant profit, the Inland Revenue would have the benefit of hindsight in arguing that the value of shares in Newco was significantly undervalued.

2.7.6　The charge to tax based on the lifting of restrictions is equally open ended. The definition of restriction is wide and covers any contract, arrangement, agreement or condition that provides for:
- the potential transfer of shares for less than market value;
- a restriction of freedom to dispose of or retain the shares;
- the disposal or retention of the shares resulting in a disadvantage to the holders.

2.7.7　Typical restrictions included in the articles of association of Newco would thus include:
- pre-emption rights on transfer, whereby any shareholder must offer shares to the other shareholders before selling to a third party;
- good/bad leaver provisions, whereby a shareholder who ceases to be employed by the company must offer the shares for sale;
- a set period during which the shares cannot be sold.

2.7.8　All these provisions are quite common in the articles of Newco. Schedule 22 allows for an exception where an employee shareholder is required to offer his or her shares if dismissed for misconduct. However, good/bad leaver provisions usually go beyond this and, for example, provide for compulsory transfer if the employee shareholder leaves voluntarily.

2.7.9　There would only be a relevant restriction if the value of the shares were reduced by the restriction. Thus, pre-emption provisions on transfer arguably do not decrease the value of the shares because they apply to other shareholders as well so arguably they represent a protection as much as a restriction for shareholders. Also, the charge to tax on lifting of the restriction relates only to the increase in value by reference to that restriction so there may be no increase to tax.

2.7.10　The Schedule 22 regime allows management to make an election at the time when the shares are acquired which may mitigate these tax effects. The election is irrevocable and must be made within 14 days of the original acquisition, jointly between the manager and the company of which he or she is an employee or director (which will either be the target company or Newco). There is more than one possible election, but most common is likely to be that all restrictions attaching to the shares should be ignored and that the manager wishes to pay tax on the unrestricted value. If the manager has paid what is considered to be full market value for the shares and expects high growth in the future, this election would be beneficial in that little or no tax is payable immediately and no further tax or national insurance contributions will be due when the restriction is lifted. This election also ensures that the manager's base cost for CGT purposes is the full, unrestricted value.

2.7.11   The company is entitled to claim a tax deduction for an amount equal to that on which the employee is taxed by acquiring the shares. Such a corporation tax deduction is only allowed on fully paid, non-redeemable ordinary shares and, except in the case of a listed company, where the company is not under the control of another company.

2.7.12   A particular problem arises on buy-outs backed by VCs where there is a 'ratchet'. This is a provision that allows management to become entitled to a greater stake in the business if certain conditions are fulfilled. These might relate to future profitability or sale of the target, or onward sale of the target where the price exceeds specified sums. The ratchet can be achieved in the articles by enhancing the effective voting or capital rights attaching to the shares held by management (or those held by the VC, in the case of a 'reverse ratchet'). Such a ratchet arrangement would fall within the definition of a restriction attaching to the shares. Thus, the basic position of Schedule 22 is that a charge to income tax will arise on the uplift in value of the shares when the ratchet operates. This could be a very significant sum, which will be chargeable to income tax.

2.7.13   The difficult and somewhat uncertain position arising on buy-outs (particularly those with ratchets) led the British Venture Capital Association (in effect the VCs' trade association) to reach an understanding with the Inland Revenue on the income tax treatment of the equity investments by managers in companies backed by venture capital and private equity. This is recorded in a memorandum of understanding dated 25 July 2003, which has become a key document in deciding whether a charge to income tax and national insurance contributions (NICs) is likely to hit management on buy-out transactions. The terms and effect of the memorandum cannot be fully summarised here, but the broad principles are set out in the following points.

2.7.14   If no ratchets are in place, the Revenue accepts that the price the managers have paid for their shares is the full unrestricted market value, where the following conditions are met:

- managers' shares are ordinary shares;
- any leverage provided by the holders of ordinary shares, particularly the VC, is on commercial terms (meaning that the expected rate of return on those shares is commercially set and would, for example, exceed the highest returns paid on debt);
- the price paid by the managers is not less than that paid by the VC for shares of the same class/rights;

- managers acquire their shares at the same time as the VC;
- managers' shares have no features that are not available to other holders of ordinary capital;
- managers are fully remunerated via salary/bonus through an employment contract.

If these conditions are met, no income tax/NIC liability arises in connection with the shares, either now or in the future.

2.7.15   If ratchets are in place, the following additional conditions must be met for there to be no income tax/NIC liability:

- the ratchet is an arrangement whereby the participation of the ordinary shareholders might vary with the performance of the company or the VC's rate of return;
- the ratchet exists at the time the VC acquires its ordinary shares;
- managers pay a price that reflects the maximum economic entitlement at the time of acquisition.

The Revenue also accepts that, provided the above conditions are met, the existence of forfeiture conditions, drag or tag-along rights will not result in a tax exposure.

2.7.16   Note that the tax effects under Schedule 22 could apply on a business purchase as well as a share purchase, since management will still be subscribing for shares in Newco. Also, whilst Schedule 22 has been dealt with under the heading of MBOs, it also applies where a director or employee (or proposed director or employee) becomes a shareholder. This could apply where a corporate purchaser seeks to involve employees more closely in the business through share participation. In such cases, it will usually be more tax efficient for the company to grant share options to those individuals, including Enterprise Management Incentives (EMI) options with the tax benefits that come with them.

2.8   Other methods of share purchase

2.8.1   By far the majority of share purchases are concluded by the transfer of shares between the parties, using the usual form of share transfer. There are limited other methods of transferring ownership of a company, dealt with below.

2.8.2   It is possible to change ownership of a company by means of a scheme of arrangement under s.425 CA. This enables a company to reach a compromise with its shareholders, which is then approved by the court. This arrangement is quite commonly used on the takeovers of public companies. It is particularly useful where the company has a large number of small shareholders, where many of them might not respond to a takeover document and thus a purchaser would find it difficult to acquire 90 per cent acceptance for a takeover offer. There is nothing in the legislation to prevent the procedure being used for private companies, even when they have relatively few shareholders. The cost of an application to the High Court and complying with the conditions of Part XIII CA would usually deter purchasers from following this route, particularly as the court has discretion to refuse to approve the scheme. However, it can and has been used on the acquisition of private companies and has one quite significant advantage over the normal method of share purchase, in that stamp duty is not payable on the transfer of ownership under such a scheme.

2.8.3   Takeover of a business may involve some form of reconstruction where, for example, the parties want to complete a share purchase but the target company contains an asset to be retained by the vendors. In such a case, that asset may be extracted by one of the following methods carried out prior to the sale:

- a dividend in specie of the relevant asset (a dividend satisfied by the asset and not in cash), if the target company has sufficient distributable profits to match the value of the asset being extracted;
- a statutory demerger which requires sufficient distributable profits and that the assets to be extracted comprise a trade;
- a reconstruction under s.110 IA, whereby the target company (or a new holding company installed above it) is placed into members' voluntary liquidation and the assets of the target company are then distributed by the liquidator to new companies owned by the existing shareholders.

2.8.4   These reconstructions permit segregation of assets, but require careful consideration of the taxation implications and legal issues.

CHAPTER 3

Share Sale or Business Sale

3.1 Introduction

This chapter compares the two main methods of selling a commercial enterprise, namely a sale of assets or a sale of shares. An attempt is made to look at this from both the vendor's and the purchaser's perspective. The two do not always coincide and which prevails will be a matter for negotiation. That negotiation requires understanding the costs and risks involved, but will also be affected by the parties' relative bargaining positions.

3.2 Necessity

3.2.1 Where the business is unincorporated, there is no choice but to sell the assets which make up that business. This applies not just to a sole trader or sole practitioner, but also to a partnership. Even though a limited liability partnership (LLP) takes on some of the attributes of a corporate body (including, in particular, limited liability status) it remains a partnership and thus can only be 'sold' by a transfer of the assets and (to the extent agreed) assumption of liabilities of the partnership.

3.2.2 Often the target business will be a division of the vendor. A division has no separate legal entity and merely means an identifiable part of the business. In this case, the most straightforward transaction would be a business sale of the assets of that division. Other factors may prevail, such as a major contract or licence held by the vendor company that is vital to the continuation of the target business but which cannot be transferred, or the vendor's wish to avoid double taxation. In such cases, the alternative would be for the remaining divisions to be transferred to the vendor or to another subsidiary. This is likely to have tax implications and thus some form of reconstruction may be necessary (see paragraph 2.8).

3.2.3 If some of the target's shareholders are opposed to the sale and it is not possible to compel them to sell under a drag-along clause (see paragraph 2.5.6) the only solution may be a business sale. This would require the consent of the board of directors of the target company but not necessarily of its shareholders, since the decision to sell assets is a board decision. There are certain

21

exceptions to this, where consent of the dissenting shareholders may be required:

- where the articles of association of the target or a shareholder's agreement provide a veto on the sale in favour of the dissenting shareholders;
- where any director of the vendor company is connected with the purchaser, in which case, under s.320 CA, approval of the shareholders by ordinary resolution (more than 50 per cent) will be required;
- where the dissenting shareholders could argue that the transaction was unfairly prejudicial to them under s.459 CA (see paragraph 2.5.5).

3.2.4   Where the target business is in receivership or administration, as noted at paragraph 2.2, this will limit the choice to a sale of assets only.

3.3   Continuity

3.3.1   Sale of the share capital of the target does not affect its status. All contracts with customers, suppliers and employees are unaffected. An important exception is where contracts are terminable on a 'change of control'. This is dealt with in more detail at paragraph 4.5.4.

3.3.2   By way of contrast, a business sale involves a transfer of the assets and potentially the agreement to discharge certain liabilities of the target. The target company's legal identity is unchanged and the purchaser is a new owner. This is so, even where the purchaser takes on the corporate name of the vendor company on the day of completion. This will however assist with business continuity and is achieved by arranging for the shareholders of the vendor company to pass a special resolution to change its corporate name. This allows the purchaser to pass a special resolution to change its own corporate name and file both resolutions together at Companies House. The name swap may be carried out as a 'same day name change' by paying an additional fee to Companies House.

3.3.3   This change of ownership on a business sale will necessitate assignment of any uncompleted contracts and re-establishment of credit terms with suppliers. Many commercial contracts contain restrictions on assignment (for example under standard terms and conditions). The request for consent to assign the contract may be refused or result in renegotiation and have an adverse effect on the continuity of the business. Where the purchaser of the business is a Newco, it will have no existing credit rating and will not inherit this from the vendor. It may be necessary to take steps to establish a rating with the credit reference agencies.

3.3.4   Regulatory licences and approvals obtained by the target company are usually personal to it, so that a business sale may require the purchaser to reapply or at least go through a further approval process. Note, however, that such licences and approvals are sometimes terminable on change of control in any event. Certain licences and approvals depend on the continued involvement of named individuals, who have certain skills or who have undergone training or approval processes. In this case, a share sale or business sale will not be the key issue: it will be a matter of ensuring that the relevant individual will be involved in the business.

3.4 Liabilities

3.4.1   On a share sale, all the target company's liabilities will remain with it. This is often unattractive to the purchaser, who is then relying on due diligence, warranty cover and insurance to cover any problems.

3.4.2   For the same reason, a share sale is attractive to the vendor because the vendor has no continuing responsibility for those liabilities, except under any guarantees given by the vendor and under warranties. The share sale is thus more likely to give the vendor a 'clean break'. This contrasts with a business sale whereby the vendor company retains primary liability for all debts and liabilities, even where the purchaser has agreed to assume and discharge them.

3.4.3   On a business sale, the purchaser will only become responsible for liabilities assumed under the sale contract. There are some limited exceptions, the prime one being that responsibility for employees engaged in the business passes to the purchaser under TUPE. Another example relates to environmental liabilities, where the new owner will have responsibility for historic contamination of land if they knew about the contamination.

3.5 Warranties

3.5.1   Because there is less risk of assuming unknown liabilities on a business sale, warranties required by the purchaser are likely to be more limited both in their scope and as to the potential liabilities. For this reason, a business sale may be attractive to the vendor as well as to the purchaser because many vendors are concerned about the potentially onerous nature of warranties.

3.5.2   The purchaser will be equally aware of the difficulties in enforcing warranties in practice and therefore may also find the business sale more attractive if there are areas of risk which cannot be fully quantified.

3.6 Mechanics of transfer

3.6.1   Apart from warranties, the documentation on a share transfer can be quite straightforward. A transfer of the shares will be sufficient to pass ownership of the company and thereby effectively to pass all the assets of the company into the control of the purchaser.

3.6.2   Contrary to popular perception, it is less straightforward to document the transfer of a business because the contract must clearly identify all the assets to be transferred and must be sufficient to vest title in the purchaser. There will therefore be specific documentation to transfer freehold and leasehold property, intellectual property rights and contracts.

3.6.3   As noted above, assets to be excluded from the sale can more simply be dealt with on a business sale (simply by excluding them from the assets sold under the contract). On a share sale, some form of transfer or reconstruction is needed.

3.6.4   Assuming that the finance for the purchase is to be secured on the assets of the target business, this is straightforward in the case of a business sale (subject to obtaining third party consents from, for example, the landlord of leasehold premises). In the case of a share sale, granting security over assets of the target company would amount to financial assistance, requiring a whitewash procedure to be followed (see paragraph 9.9).

3.7   Tax considerations – General observations only in this section.

3.7.1   The tax implications of the transaction are likely to have a major effect on how it is structured. The level of the effect depends on the specific circumstances, in particular the base costs and capital allowances position in relation to the target business' assets. It is thus necessary to look at each case using specialist tax advice; the comments below are general observations.

3.7.2   In the case of individual vendor(s), the preference will usually be for a sale of shares to avoid 'double taxation' of the proceeds. This could arise on a business sale, because the target company sells assets and is thus potentially liable to corporation tax on its gain and/or claw back of capital allowances. The extraction of the net proceeds is then subject to tax in the hands of the vendors. By contrast, a sale of shares will be subject to tax only on the proceeds of that sale.

3.7.3   Furthermore, the proceeds of a sale of shares will be subject to capital gains tax (CGT), usually with the benefit of taper relief. This will reduce the effective rate of tax to 10 per cent for most vendors. In addition to the potential for double taxation on a business sale, the extraction of value by the individual shareholders would usually be by dividend from the vendor company, at a rate of tax higher than 10 per cent. CGT treatment of the proceeds of sale may however be obtained through liquidating the vendor company following the sale.

3.7.4   A corporate vendor is less likely to be hit by double taxation. Dividends paid by the subsidiary should be tax neutral. If the purchaser wishes to buy the assets of a member of a group of companies, the group will need to consider whether any rollover reliefs will be available to offset gains on the assets sold. The position on a share sale is however clearer. Under the Finance Act 2002, a disposal of a substantial shareholding (meaning a holding of 10 per cent or more) in a trading company by a UK company will be exempt from corporation tax.

3.7.5   One of the purchaser's objectives may be to utilise trade losses accrued by the target. In broad terms, this is more easily achieved on a share sale, in that the losses remain with the target. Thus, they should usually be available in the target company and may be surrendered to other members in the purchaser's group. Note however that anti-avoidance legislation restricts the set-off of losses incurred before the target company entered the purchaser's group.

3.7.6 Stamp duty is payable on a sale of shares at 0.5 per cent of the consideration. By contrast, stamp duty is no longer payable on the transfer of other assets. Stamp duty land tax (SDLT) is payable on the transfer of freehold property. Since the rate of SDLT can be as high as 4 per cent, a business sale may incur a higher stamp duty cost than a share sale if the target holds significant property interests.

3.8   Employees

3.8.1 Employees' rights are unaffected by a share sale as their employer remains constant. On a business sale, their employment will transfer to the purchaser under TUPE, achieving broadly the same result.

3.8.2 Because TUPE does not apply on a sale of shares, employee issues are actually more straightforward and certain difficult areas are avoided. For example, any dismissal in connection with the transfer of an undertaking is automatically unfair (unless the economic, technical or organisational (ETO) defence is shown – see paragraph 10.3). If a dismissal is made immediately following a share purchase, the usual rules about whether that dismissal was unfair will of course apply, but there is no presumption that the dismissal is unfair.

3.8.3 Obligations to inform and consult with employees arise under TUPE (see paragraph 10.7). On a share sale, there is no obligation to inform and consult in advance of the transaction, other than where this would be necessary anyway because of planned redundancies or changes to terms and conditions of employment.

3.9   Pensions

3.9.1 In broad terms, rights under occupational pension schemes do not transfer automatically under TUPE. However, the 'pensions promise' (namely the expectation of benefits from the pension fund and/or contributions by the employer) may be incorporated into the contractual terms of employment if that is the correct interpretation of those terms and other communication between employer and employee. In short, therefore, the purchaser of a business as a going concern has to consider what rights the employees have to benefit from the existing pension scheme and/or a pension scheme offering equivalent benefits. Whilst a share sale is not a transaction caught by TUPE, the same point applies, ie the right to benefit from a pension scheme may be a contractual term which the purchaser must continue to honour.

3.9.2 Where an occupational scheme relates only to the target company, there should be little complication on a sale of shares. (The obvious exception would be any changes to appointed trustees.) On a business sale, the position is likely to be more complicated. If the purchaser is to 'take over' the whole scheme, this would usually involve changes to those responsible as employers under the scheme.

3.9.3   On a business or share sale where an occupational pension scheme covers the vendor's other companies or other employees, this may result in a transfer of part of the fund to a new scheme set up by the purchaser, which will require specialist advice and actuarial valuation.

3.9.4   If a pension scheme deficit is identified, this could amount to a very significant liability or potential liability. This could itself make a share sale impossible as the target company is likely to be one of the persons liable to contribute to the deficit.

3.9.5   The benefits of each method of selling a commercial enterprise are shown below.

KEY ADVANTAGES OF EACH METHOD

Share sale	Business sale
No double taxation	Avoid unwanted assets
Continuity	Restrict exposure to liabilities
Avoid TUPE issues	Avoid financial assistance issues

4

Vendor Preparations

4.1 Overview

4.1.1 Like so many things, the key to a successful sales process is advance planning. This may start months or even years before the sale takes place. Any owner of a business should have a plan, whether this is to achieve rapid growth and sell the business within three years or, at the other extreme, to provide a good income for the vendor and the vendor's family over a much longer period. The wish to hand ownership of a business down from generation to generation is less prevalent now than in earlier times. There is increasingly less chance that the next generation will want to follow in the same footsteps, plus it should not be assumed that they will have the right skills to do so. Thus, a handover of ownership is likely to involve a sale, whether to the managers and/or a venture capitalist (VC) through a buy-out or to a trade buyer.

4.1.2 Some typical objectives of vendors were noted in Chapter 1. For the purpose of planning for sale, these could be encapsulated in the following four areas:

- increasing the attractiveness of the target;
- maximising the value of the business;
- minimising the tax payable in respect of the sale;
- anticipating problems in the sales process.

Vendor objectives

4.1.3 A thorough review of the business of the target should be undertaken in the light of the vendor's objectives and the timescale in which a sale is anticipated. The sales process may not be totally within the control of the vendor. It may be necessary to sell the business quickly, due to circumstances beyond the vendor's control, such as illness or loss of a major income stream. The sale may be initiated by an approach from a purchaser which is attractive and may not be repeated. Therefore, at the risk of stating the obvious, maintaining a consistent financial performance and keeping the legal and contractual affairs of the target in good order are important goals.

4.2 Financial grooming

4.2.1 This book does not cover business planning to increase the attractiveness of the target, nor how this can be affected by economic trends. This very important area is a major part of the role of the vendor's accountancy advisors. The specialists in this field (ranging from corporate finance boutiques to global accounting firms) will endeavour to add to the value of the business significantly by analysing its financial and trading performance and then assist the vendor to implement measures such as those listed below. Which measures are most relevant depends entirely on the business and how it has been run up to that point. However, the key indicators of value will be the level of profit the target can generate for its owners in the future and how consistent and 'robust' that profit generation is.

MEASURES TO ENHANCE VALUE

- Increase revenues from profitable business activities, for example through better marketing.
- Increase profit margins, for example by raising prices to customers where this is economically possible.
- Reduce costs, for example through changes to the workforce.
- Discontinue unprofitable activities or products, after considering the effects on related activities.
- Dispose of non-essential assets (or plan to extract them before completion of the sale).
- Make strategic acquisitions, such as businesses that are complementary to the existing business and intellectual property rights (IPR).
- Create a structured and balanced management team.
- Reduce reliance on the vendor as an executive member of the management team.

4.2.2   In many cases, the value of the business is based on a multiple of its annual profits. The applicable multiplier (or price/earnings ratio – p/e) has regard to the sector, maturity and quality of the business as well as the general economic climate and is not a scientific calculation. However, to demonstrate the importance of profit generation, if the appropriate multiplier is ten, adding £100,000 to the net profit figure increases the value of the business by £1 million.

4.2.3   Two more quick points on multipliers. First, when referring to values of privately owned companies, a multiplier will usually be applied to profits before taxation. The justification would be that tax on a privately owned company may be seriously affected by planning measures or other factors. Multipliers relating to listed companies (as quoted in daily newspapers) are based on post-tax profits. There is however no rule on which approach is correct for private companies, so care should be taken to ensure that the parties are talking to each other on the same basis. Secondly, profits used in the calculation of value should be adjusted to take into account abnormal factors. This would include remuneration paid to the vendors that exceeds the cost of replacing them as this would have the effect of deflating profit. Increasingly, under a tax regime that significantly favours the payment of dividends over salary and bonus to business owners, vendors may receive less remuneration than it would take to replace them, possibly meaning that the profits should be adjusted downwards to reflect the ongoing costs of employing management. Other adjustments would include discounting profits that have been affected by an abnormally lucrative contract or other non-recurring income.

4.3 Tax planning

4.3.1 This was looked at briefly in the comparison between selling shares and assets in Chapter 3. Broadly speaking, most vendors of companies will be looking to utilise taper relief by selling their shares in the company. This will be subject to capital gains tax (CGT) and is likely to give them an effective rate of tax of 10 per cent. At this relatively low rate, the motivation to carry out tax planning measures is greatly reduced.

4.3.2 This book is not a tax work and any vendor should seek specialist tax advice tailored to their particular circumstances. At a very basic level, the sale of shares in a company will be subject to CGT. There is one key exception, where a company purchases its own shares under the procedure set out in Ch. VII CA 1985. The amount paid to a shareholder by the company to purchase those shares will be taxed as a distribution (in other words a dividend), unless certain conditions are met. The main condition is to establish that the payment is for the benefit of the company's trade; it is possible to obtain advance clearance from the Inland Revenue (IR) for this.

4.3.3 As with any disposal subject to CGT, the amount charged to tax is calculated according to the gain made. The chargeable gain is the price the shareholder receives or is deemed to receive for the shares less the indexed base cost. This is the original cost of acquisition by the shareholder (or the shares' value in 1982, if held since then) plus indexation allowance to reflect the increase in value due to inflation for periods up to April 1998.

4.3.4 Individuals are entitled to an annual exemption from CGT (£8,200 for the tax year 2004/05). Trustees also have an annual exemption (£4,100 for 2004/05). Subject to this and taper relief (dealt with in the next paragraph), the net chargeable gain is subject to CGT at marginal income tax rates for interest income (in other words 10 per cent, 20 per cent and 40 per cent). Thus, a taxpayer who has income exceeding the lower and basic rate bands (£31,400 for the tax year 2004/05) will be subject to CGT at 40 per cent.

4.3.5 Taper relief was introduced by FA 1998, and replaced indexation allowance for individuals and trustees. The effect of the relief is to reduce the amount of the chargeable gain subject to CGT. (To say the relief reduces the rate of tax on the sale of shares to 10 per cent would be technically incorrect, since in fact it reduces the chargeable gain on which tax is charged at 40 per cent to one-quarter of what it otherwise would be.) Taper relief is applied to the gain after all other reliefs have been deducted. It applies to the sale of business assets, which includes:

■ all shareholdings in unquoted trading companies;

■ all shareholdings held by employees in quoted trading companies.

4.3.6   The reduction of the chargeable gain through taper relief depends on the period of ownership of the relevant business assets (in the case of share sale the period in which the shares have been held by the vendor). FA 2002 reduced the period for business assets to qualify for maximum relief to only two years. Thus, the chargeable gain will be reduced by 50 per cent after one year and 75 per cent after two years of ownership. This very wide relief therefore has a major impact on the tax payable on a share sale and increases the difference between the tax position on a sale of shares and a sale of assets, as noted in Chapter 3. A basic example of the application of CGT and taper relief on a sale of shares is shown below.

EXAMPLE 1: CGT ON SALE OF SHARES

Gavin acquired the share capital of WhiteCo in 1982 for £100,000. During his period of ownership, the company has carried on only trading activities. He now sells the company for £1 million.

	£
Proceeds	£1,000,000
Base cost	(£100,000)
Chargeable gain before indexation	£900,000
Indexation from 1982 to 1998 (1.047)	(£104,700)
Gain after indexation	£795,300
Taper relief at 75 per cent	(£596,475)
Net tapered gains	£198,825
CGT payable at 40 per cent	**£79,530**

4.3.7   As explained above, tax planning on a sale of shares will now be fairly restricted. The relatively benign regime of taper relief goes hand in hand with the more aggressive and determined stance taken by the IR against tax avoidance. Thus, any tax planning measures need to reflect commercial reality rather than being artificial. Subject to this, the following steps may be justified:

■ **Gifts to family members.** A transfer of shares before completion to the vendor's spouse or children should be tax effective. The charge to CGT arising on the gift would be held over. On disposal of the company, the gain realised on the shares is chargeable on the family member, allowing use of his or her annual exemption from CGT and lower rate tax band. Also, that family member may have capital losses that could be utilised to offset the capital gains.

■ **Termination payments.** Payments on the cessation of employment, by way of compensation for loss of office, are tax free up to £30,000. The IR takes a firm line on when these payments are properly made by way of compensation for loss of office. For example, if they are in fact contractual payments, they are taxable. This is therefore not a planning measure, but part of the structure for payment when an individual sells shares and ceases employment, where a termination payment is properly made.

- **Residence.** Ceasing to be resident or ordinarily resident in the UK remains a method of avoiding CGT. However, specialist advice is needed on the timing and duration of emigration and any taxes payable in other jurisdictions.

4.3.8   Pre-sale dividends were a common feature of share sale tax planning before the full effects of taper relief changed the tax environment. Perhaps a bigger issue now arises where a company has significant cash balances which are to be 'included' in the sale for extraction by the purchaser. The existence of these cash balances could affect taper relief, in that they may be regarded by the IR as a non-business asset. The argument would run that, where the cash represents undrawn and undistributed profit, it is not being used to carry on the trade. If this affected taper relief, the implications to the vendor's tax position could be quite dramatic. Therefore, specialist advice should be taken wherever a company has significant cash resources. The extraction of that cash through dividends well before a sale is completed could be an advance tax planning measure.

4.4   Structural planning

4.4.1   As noted previously, problems can arise where a vendor wishes to sell shares in the company that has assets the vendor wants to retain or the purchaser will not wish to acquire. Extracting those assets or businesses at a late stage may involve a reconstruction that could be costly and complicated. There may be no alternative but to sell the assets of the business rather than the shares in the company, which could adversely affect the vendor's tax position.

4.4.2   Advance planning to avoid these issues may involve a great deal of foresight, but also basic common sense. The rule of thumb is that a purchaser will want to own assets necessary to generate profits from the business. The purchaser may not be willing or able to pay full value for other assets. Note also that non-business assets may restrict taper relief.

4.4.3   It follows that assets designed for the vendor's personal use should not be owned by the company and should be extracted at an early stage. Less obviously, property occupied by the target may have a significant capital value but less value to a purchaser. It may even be the case that the purchaser cannot afford to fund the acquisition of the property. Conversely, if the property is held outside of the company but used in the business, it would not be difficult to include the property in the sale, should this be appropriate, and the vendor's tax position should not be any worse. It will therefore often be sensible for freehold or long leasehold properties to be owned by the vendor, a separate company or a pension fund established by the vendor. Note that, in any of those circumstances, an arm's length lease should be put in place between the owner and the target.

4.5   Grooming

4.5.1   Assuming that the company has maximised its financial performance and financial potential, the key area of grooming for sale will be to deal with any areas of the business that give rise to risk or uncertainty. Failure to address these areas at the planning stage could give rise to the following disadvantages:

- being highlighted in due diligence as a 'problem', resulting in delay or renegotiation;
- warranties and indemnities specifically on that issue, where the financial risk to the vendor could be far greater than the cost to the vendor of handling it before completion;
- reducing the value a purchaser would be prepared to pay for the target.

4.5.2   By definition, this area is about reviewing the actual business and finding out where its particular problems lie. Some common areas of concern are shown below.

PROBLEM AREAS

Assets	■ Held by the wrong person or by another company in the group ■ Lack of good title, due to claims by third parties
Liabilities	■ Outstanding litigation or disputes ■ Breaches of legislation, for example environmental matters ■ Tax investigations
IPR	■ Rights of employees or originators of the IPR ■ Incorporation of third party technology without clear licensing ■ Limits on the extent of the rights, which restrict development of the business
Employees	■ Poor records and failure to provide statutory particulars of employment ■ Unclear contractual rights, particularly where matters have been 'promised' in correspondence ■ Lack of restrictions on post-termination activities of key people
Pensions	■ Underfunding of final salary schemes ■ Sex discrimination, through failure to achieve equalisation of rights and benefits in the scheme rules ■ Lack of records and appropriate documentation (often causing delays)
Contracts	■ Major projects without proper contracts ■ Change of control clauses (often unavoidable) ■ Onerous obligations, particularly guarantees and warranty periods

4.5.3   One of those common problem areas relates to litigation and disputes. Naturally, these cannot always be avoided, and there may be a potential upside from litigation. However, a purchaser would not usually place too much reliance on the potential rewards of litigation and is more likely to concentrate on the potential liabilities including legal costs. Settling outstanding litigation before a sales process has begun would be the preferred route.

4.5.4   On the question of contracts, there are two types of clause in commercial contracts that could affect the ability of the vendor to pass the benefit of that contract to a purchaser:

- Restriction on assignment of the contract – this would mean that the other party's consent would be required on a sale of the business of the target, because each of the assets (including contracts) has to be transferred from the name of the vendor to the name of the purchaser, (but there is no assignment of contracts on a sale of shares).
- Change of control, which provides that the contract may be terminated by one party if the other party is a company whose ownership changes – usually the clause operates where a third party acquires more than 50 per cent of the shares or votes in the target and accordingly there is a change of the control, but certain clauses apply even on a change to the board of directors.

4.5.5   Change of control provisions are common in major contracts, particularly with large public sector bodies that wish to have some control over the persons with whom they deal. The best planning measure would be to avoid having any contract terminable on change of control. If this is not possible, the next best route is to limit the circumstances in which the clauses operate (for example only when control passes to a competing organisation or one that deals in unethical activities). It may also be possible to have change of control clauses that set out a pre-determined path for obtaining clearance, including a timescale for gaining approval. One of the problems in the sale process will be determining at what point an approach is made to the third party to ascertain that the change of control is not a reason to terminate the contract. Clearly, there is the possibility of disruption in the relationship with the other contracting party, particularly at a time when the sale is not necessarily going to proceed to completion.

4.6   Role of advisors

4.6.1   It is rarely possible for the parties to carry out a business sale, let alone a share sale, without professional advisors. The significant professional costs that arise on corporate acquisitions do sometimes deter the parties from involving the advisors throughout (let alone at the planning stage). It is however clear that early advice on accounting, tax and legal issues can save the vendor a lot of money in sorting out problems at a later stage and maximises the value of the business that is for sale.

4.6.2   This book is not intended to be an advert for professional services. Each vendor will decide how and when to source that help and whether to opt for a lead advisor who puts together a professional team or use a number of existing advisors. The key aspects of the roles typically provided by professional advisors are set out below.

KEY ROLES OF THE VENDOR'S ADVISORS

Accountant/ financial advisor
- Lead advisor and project management of the sale process
- Advice on grooming the target for sale
- Potentially, marketing the target for sale and sourcing the purchaser
- Advice on structure
- Advice on taxation implications for the vendor
- Dealing with the accounting and financial due diligence requirements of the purchaser
- Negotiation of the financial terms and the commercial deal

Lawyer
- Where no lead advisor has been appointed, project management of the sale process
- Assisting with grooming issues, by review of the target's assets, liabilities and contractual relationships
- Assisting with advice on structure and taxation implications
- Dealing with legal due diligence, including replies to questionnaire and disclosure
- Preparing and obtaining confidentiality undertakings
- Dealing with sale documentation, principally the sale agreement and disclosure letter
- Advice on employee issues, including requirements of TUPE, competition law, FSMA and other preliminary matters
- Negotiation of legal agreements and the terms of the sale
- Ensuring the consideration is duly received on completion and accounting to the vendor(s) for this correctly

Taxation advisor
- Usually, but not always, personnel from the vendor's accounting or legal advisors
- Advice on the tax implications of the sale and any tax planning measures
- Advice on residency issues, where the vendor is to leave the UK
- Advice on reliefs, including Enterprise Investment Scheme and reinvestment relief of the proceeds of sale

Pensions advisor
- May include personnel from the accounting and legal advisors, specialist advisory practices and actuaries
- Analysis of existing arrangements
- Advice on particular difficulties such as equalisation issues
- Where appropriate, preparation of transfer documentation
- Advice on funding and compliance issues

Property surveyor
- Valuation of existing properties and future marketability
- Advice on property and environmental issues

Insurance brokers
- Advice on existing insurance cover
- Providing purchaser with accurate and comprehensive details of current insurances
- Advising on any new insurance requirements, such as 'run off' indemnity policies
- Specialist insurance covers, such as insurance against warranty claims

CHAPTER 5

Marketing

5.1 Overview

5.1.1 In this context, marketing refers to the process of sourcing a potential purchaser of the target and then engaging in negotiation with that purchaser. It could be divided up into the following steps:
- putting together relevant information about the target;
- identifying potential purchasers;
- passing that information to those purchasers in a controlled manner;
- entering into initial negotiations with interested parties.

5.1.2 This chapter goes through that process. Obviously, the process differs greatly depending on the size of the undertaking and who might be interested in acquiring it. The chapter also deals with a specific issue relevant to share sales (and not asset sales) – the restriction on promoting investments under FSMA.

5.2 Information on the target

5.2.1 The target's business may, in certain cases, be well-known to the potential purchaser. The classic example of this would be a management buy-out (MBO), where management would be fully aware of the target's business opportunities and financial affairs. In such a case, there may be no need to put together information before the sale is negotiated. Equally, the intending purchaser may be a competitor, keen to proceed without a formal marketing process. The vendor may be happy to enter negotiations with such a purchaser before taking steps to market the business fully. However, it may be sensible to carry out a marketing exercise to ensure that the best deal is available to the vendors. Weighed against this are issues of confidentiality, as many vendors will be anxious that their customers are not aware that the sale is proceeding (particularly as it may never complete). Also, there will be a financial cost of marketing the business, which must be taken into consideration.

5.2.2 In such cases the process of marketing the business will start with a review of the target's business in order to put together a marketing document. This is usually referred to as an information memorandum. The document's length and complexity depends on the circumstances, but it should include the areas listed below.

CONTENTS OF INFORMATION MEMORANDUM

- An initial summary that concisely sets out the opportunity offered to the purchaser and the key reasons why it would want to acquire the target.
- Target's history and ownership.
- A description of the target's products and services.
- The market sectors in which the target operates.
- Details of its customer base (usually without naming customers).
- Key suppliers or supply arrangements.
- Details of management and management structure.
- Details of the workforce and any key employee issues.
- Details of IT systems and IPR the target owns or uses.
- The record of its financial performance for, say, the last three years.
- Current trading and prospects.

5.2.3   The information memorandum would usually also include or have attached a summary of the intended sales process and how purchasers should bid to acquire the target. This is dealt with in more detail in paragraph 5.5.

5.2.4   It usually contains statements to the effect that the information is not warranted as accurate, with the intention that any purchaser should verify the information and/or rely on warranties contained in the sale agreement. However, it is still essential for the contents of the information memorandum to be accurate and not misleading, for two reasons. Inaccuracies may give rise to claims for misrepresentation (even where exclusions of liability are included). Secondly, and in fact more importantly, misunderstandings at this early stage are likely to give rise to serious problems in the negotiation process.

5.3   Prospective purchasers

5.3.1   The major accountancy practices and specialist corporate finance firms maintain databases of potential purchasers for businesses in different sectors. In compiling these, they rely upon:
- other transactions in which they have themselves been involved;
- other reported transactions and publicly available information;
- proactive enquiries of companies.

Picking up on this last point, 'deal origination' has become a major feature of the corporate finance market. This refers to the process whereby advisors and venture capitalists (VCs) talk to companies about whether they will be interested in selling their companies or in making new acquisitions (either now or in the future). Not only does this increase their level of knowledge, it may also enable them to put forward opportunities, matching vendor and purchaser, so that the deal is well and truly originated by the advisor. With the advent of the institutional buy-out (IBO), where the VC originates and leads the transaction, it is increasingly common for VCs to approach companies direct for this purpose.

5.3.2   The vendor will often be the best source of information on potential purchasers of the target. These include the existing management team, direct competitors and persons known through the vendor's network of business contacts. The vendor may already have had contact with prospective purchasers and start the process with a clear idea of who will buy the target. It may still be legitimate to carry out the full marketing exercise to make sure that the prospective purchaser offers the best deal. Note also that provision of an information memorandum puts the process on a more organised footing and thus maximises the value obtained for the vendors.

5.3.3   Cross-border transactions are an established part of the corporate finance market. Selling the target to a competitor or supplier overseas may offer the best deal for the vendor since the purchaser may pay more for the strategic advantage of moving into a new territory. The key issue for the vendor will be to ensure that all prospective purchasers will have the opportunity to consider the information memorandum.

5.4   Confidentiality

5.4.1   The information memorandum is not 'published' and remains a private matter between the vendor and any person to whom the vendor decides to send it. The vendor will usually be very sensitive about the confidentiality of the information being provided, in order to prevent:

- the target's customers, suppliers and employees being aware that there is a potential sale;
- competitors becoming aware of the sale process and using it to disrupt the target's business;
- competitors, customers and suppliers becoming aware of unpublished information about the target.

5.4.2   In the absence of a contractual obligation, the law does not adequately protect the vendor from unwanted disclosure of information about the target and about the sales process. Breach of confidence exists as a legal right, but is very limited and would require the vendor to prove that a duty of confidence had arisen. For this reason, the vendor should always take steps to obtain a written undertaking from anyone who would receive information (including in particular the information memorandum) not to disclose or use its contents.

5.4.3   A confidentiality undertaking is an agreement between the party giving information and each recipient. It is a contract in a normal sense and the consideration provided is the agreement to make available information about the target. (The agreement may also recite other considerations, such as continued negotiations or a nominal £1 payment, or it may be in the form of a deed.) Another term commonly used for a confidentiality undertaking (particularly in the USA) is a non-disclosure agreement or NDA. Such an agreement can be in the form of a letter or contract, the key issue being that it clearly sets out enforceable obligations on the information recipient.

5.4.4   A sample confidentiality undertaking is included on page 150. It would be possible to create an obligation of confidentiality in just a few lines, in effect stating that all information provided in relation to the target is to be treated as confidential and may not be disclosed to any third party without consent. The advantages of a longer agreement include:

- clarifying particular categories of information that are confidential, particularly where these may be received from different sources;
- setting out particular obligations of confidentiality, for example use of the information as well as disclosure to third parties;
- setting out related restrictions, such as solicitation of staff;
- limiting the individuals who may have access to the information and imposing a requirement that such persons accept duties of confidentiality;
- specifying that the vendor will be entitled to enforce the undertaking by an injunction (which would assist with enforceability in the courts);
- clarifying that the fact that negotiations that are taking place, as well as the information about the target is confidential.

5.4.5   The summary below lists the issues a good confidentiality undertaking would address.

CONFIDENTIALITY UNDERTAKING – KEY ISSUES

- Clarify that all information regarding the target is confidential, however and from whom it is received.
- Specify that the negotiations themselves are also confidential.
- Spell out the obligations of confidentiality, which are basically not to disclose or use the information, which must be returned or destroyed if the sale does not proceed.
- Define exactly who may share the information, usually named individuals or classes of individuals such as directors or the purchaser, professional advisors and funders.
- List specific exclusions from the confidential information, such as the information lawfully known to the purchaser, to ensure the undertaking is enforceable.
- State ancillary obligations not to use the information to damage the vendor, for example by poaching staff.
- Specify particular remedies for breach of the undertaking, including an acknowledgement that the vendor may seek an injunction.

5.4.6   Even with a well drafted confidentiality undertaking, the vendor may in practice be exposed to difficulties. If information is leaked into the market place, it may be difficult to prove who has done this. It will be even more difficult to prove that confidential information has been used by a competitor in the competitor's own business. Also, a breach could be difficult and expensive to pursue in the courts. The normal remedy for breach of contract is damages. It would be difficult to assess the level of financial loss suffered via a breach of the undertaking. However aggrieved the vendor feels, damages are awarded by reference to financial loss and the vendor may not be able to prove any. Where damages are not an adequate remedy, the courts have discretion to award an injunction (and the confidentiality undertaking will usually specify that this is an available form of relief). To obtain an injunction, the vendor would have to act quickly and decisively (and, accordingly, at some cost) in order to persuade the court that this remedy should be granted. Even if the vendor were successful, it is likely that the injunction would only prevent future breaches. The damage may already have been done and it is not practical for it to be undone.

5.4.7   For this reason, the best way to preserve confidentiality would be to include only non-sensitive information in the information memorandum. It is unlikely that it will include information on key customers and contracts. It may be possible to provide information, right up until completion, without names or by using code names. The vendors will often refuse to give particularly sensitive information to the purchaser until the very point of completion.

5.4.8   In order to reduce the number of persons receiving information about the sale, it is usual for the initial information given to prospective purchasers to be a limited 'taster' document which does not name the target and describes the target in a way that does not give the game away. It is at this point, where a prospective purchaser shows interest, that the vendor's advisors would request a confidentiality undertaking. At the risk of stating the obvious, the undertaking should be obtained (and duly signed on behalf of the prospective purchaser) before any confidential information is obtained. It is of course a question of balance between generating the most interest in the sale and guarding from prying eyes the fact that the sale process is underway.

5.4.9   There may be regulatory reasons to break confidentiality of the deal. These include the duty to inform or consult employees about a proposed transfer of an undertaking under TUPE (which does not apply on share sales), and the obligations on public companies to make announcements regarding sales transactions, so that there is not a false market in publicly quoted shares. These issues are dealt with in later chapters.

5.4.10   Even when there is no legal duty to disclose the proposed transaction, vendors sometimes decide to tell customers or employees about their plans. This may be a 'pre-emptive' announcement, because the vendor feels that there is likely to be a leak of information at some stage during the process. Voluntarily informing customers or employees that a sale is being considered is likely to do less damage than a leak. Rumour and speculation can be damaging to the business and a voluntary statement about the process will allow the vendor to retain the initiative.

5.5 Data room

5.5.1 Having found a prospective purchaser, the next step for the vendor is to enter into negotiations on price and other terms. However, there may be a number of prospective purchasers willing to make offers for the target who have indicated that their offer would be within the expected range. In this case, the vendor may wish to obtain firm offers before discounting a prospective purchaser. Equally, the purchasers may not be willing to give any firm indication of price until they have carried out due diligence. This could result in an auction process.

5.5.2 A formal auction process involves a procedure whereby the vendor enters into a legally binding commitment with one of the purchasers after certain steps are followed. This may involve sealed bids being delivered by each of the prospective purchasers in a certain timescale. The sale of a business or the share capital of a company is very different from the sale of a piece of equipment or a work of art. In particular:

- the form of the sale contract will need to include those terms described in Chapters 11 and 12;
- the target will carry with it assets, liabilities, contracts and employees, making it necessary for the prospective purchaser to examine it through due diligence.

5.5.3 An auction process will therefore include the creation of a data room. This should contain the information the vendor and its advisors believe the bidders will need to see in order to finalise bids. If the auction process will result in a legally binding commitment, the data room also needs to include the form of contract upon which the vendor would sell the business. This means that the vendor and its advisors need to anticipate what will be acceptable and sufficient to satisfy the requirements of the bidders and their advisors.

5.5.4 As regards the form of contract, this mainly contains the vendor's obligations including warranties, a covenant regarding taxation liabilities of the target and restrictions on the future activities of the vendor. Thus, for the vendor, there is a delicate balance between offering an acceptable contract to the purchaser without leaving the vendor with onerous obligations. If the draft contract is too favourable to the vendor, often the purchasers will seek to amend it. It may become difficult to maintain consistent treatment for each of the respective purchasers as their advisors will have their own issues. Thus, the auction process may not of itself result in a binding contract. It may be that the data room is sufficient only to enable the purchasers to make their formal offers for consideration by the vendor. After that, the sales process, including any further due diligence and legal negotiation, would take the course described in the remaining chapters of this book.

5.5.5 In any event, the data room will contain a large quantity of information on the target. Compiling this is a significant task and making the right decisions about what to put in and what to take out will affect the ease of the process. The summary below sets out some issues to be addressed when compiling a data room. This includes reference to data room rules that govern the practical running of the process. For an example of data room rules see sample document 2, page 148.

DATA ROOM ISSUES

Q Who will manage the data room and where will it be located?

A *The vendor's accountants and/or lawyers will manage the process. The location will usually be their offices but this needs to be a sensible location for prospective purchasers to visit.*

Q How much information should be included?

A *The information provided should be enough to enable prospective purchasers to confirm their offer. Too much information is a costly waste of time, but an omission of important information could disrupt the process.*

Q What if inaccurate information is provided?

A *The purchaser may have a claim for misrepresentation. Also, the vendor may commit an offence under s.397 FSMA (see below) if misleading statements are made or material facts are dishonestly concealed in order to induce the purchaser to acquire shares in the target. This offence is thus only relevant to share sales.*

Q What practical steps can be taken to manage the data room properly?

A *Preparing a good index of the information available and creating a proper set of data room rules.*

5.6 FSMA

5.6.1 The Financial Services and Markets Act 2000 (FSMA) replaced the Financial Services Act 1986. It deals with two key areas relevant to the acquisition of shares in private companies:
- restrictions on financial promotions unless they have been approved by an authorised person;
- establishing the regime both to become an authorised person and to carry on investment business.

5.6.2 The regime for authorised persons is beyond the scope of this book, but suffice to say that anyone giving advice on investments or dealing in investments should be authorised under FSMA. Anyone dealing with such a person should be satisfied that they have authority. The regime is designed to ensure that such persons are properly qualified and trained and demonstrate high standards of honesty and integrity.

5.6.3 The restriction on financial promotions is contained in s.21 FSMA and is very wide. It prohibits any person communicating an invitation or inducement to engage in 'investment activity' in the course of business unless that person is an authorised person or an authorised person has approved the communication. Investment activity includes the purchase of shares and the requirement that the communication must be 'in the course of business' refers to any business, not just investment business. Thus, anyone offering to sell shares is likely to be caught by the restrictions.

5.6.4 On the face of it, this would mean that any contact regarding a share sale, from making a phone call to a prospective purchaser to sending a share purchase agreement to the purchaser's solicitor, would be unlawful unless approved by an authorised person. This in fact would be a very onerous position because:

- the authorised person would need to go through certain procedures to vet, control and record the communication;
- there would be a cost consequence for the vendor;
- certain methods of contact (such as cold call telephoning) would be unacceptable.

5.6.5 In fact, certain communications are exempt. There are a significant number of exemptions; the task is to ensure that particular communications fall within an exemption. Specialist advice should be sought on the issue, but a few key exemptions are highlighted below. The statutory instrument containing these exemptions is the Financial Promotions Order 2001 SI 2001/1335 ('the Order').

5.6.6 Paragraph 62 of the Order exempts communications on the 'sale of a body corporate' where:

- the shares being sold consist of 50 per cent or more of the voting shares in the company;
- the transaction is between parties, each of whom is a company, a partnership, a single individual or a group of connected individuals.

5.6.7 A 'group of connected individuals' includes vendors who are all directors or managers of the company, or their close relatives. Thus, this catches a large number of transactions. Furthermore, even if the conditions referred to above are not met, the exemption still applies where 'the objective of the transaction may nevertheless reasonably be regarded as being the acquisition of day to day control of the affairs of the company'. A commonly held view is therefore that most if not all acquisitions where the purchaser takes over control of management will be exempt.

5.6.8 On the takeover of a private company, paragraph 64 of the Order provides an exemption where an offer document is sent out satisfying certain requirements set out in Sch.4 to the Order. These basically entail a document similar to that used on public company transactions containing information about the transaction, the target and the purchaser. It also requires an independent authorised person to give advice on the financial implications of the offer. It is thus an expensive and cumbersome procedure compared with reliance upon paragraph 62.

5.6.9 There are a number of exemptions based on the financial worth and experience of the investor which apply even if a minority stake is acquired. However, it is not sufficient to rely upon the fact that the investor is wealthy or understands business matters to gain exemption. The facts must be certified.

5.6.10   A key example arises under paragraph 48 of the Order whereby a communication (excluding an unsolicited telephone call) made to a 'certified high net worth individual' will be exempt. This refers to an individual who has obtained a certificate signed by the investor's accountant or employer, to the effect that that investor either had:

■ an annual income of not less that £100,000 in the last financial year; or
■ net assets of not less than £250,000 (which excludes the value of the investor's home and any mortgage secured on it) throughout the last financial year.

Importantly, the certificate must be produced before any information is given to the relevant investor, even if it is known that the investor satisfies one or both of the above tests. The certificate relates to the individual and not the specific investment so it would be sufficient for high net worth individuals to obtain a certificate each year and produce it when requested.

5.6.11   A similar regime applies for certified sophisticated investors. Again there is a requirement for a certificate to be obtained in advance which, in this case, could be given by any authorised person. The certificate should state that the investor is sufficiently knowledgeable to understand the risks associated with a particular description of investment. This is, on the face of it, a very useful exemption for business people. However, it may not be so straightforward in practice to get an authorised person to commit to that certificate since it involves taking responsibility for a matter of opinion.

5.6.12   The consequences of breach of s.19 FSMA are quite severe. The investment is liable to be void. What this means in practice is that the investor could ask for return of the money or take action against the directors and other persons involved in promoting the investment. Those persons could also be guilty of a criminal offence.

Purchaser Preparations

6.1 Taking control

6.1.1 The last two chapters have looked at the preliminary stages of the transaction, from the vendor's perspective. They took the process to the stage where a prospective purchaser had been identified and was ready to make an offer for the target's shares or business. This and the next chapter look at the next steps up to the point where the purchase agreement is negotiated, from the purchaser's perspective.

6.1.2 It is appropriate to look at this stage from the purchaser's perspective, as the purchaser will now wish to take control (vendor permitting) of the process. The purchaser will be looking to protect its position in the following ways:

■ before committing further time and expense on the transaction, the purchaser will want to ensure that the vendor's marketing has ceased;

■ the purchaser will seek clarity of the terms of the transaction, so as to appraise properly what is involved and obtain necessary funding;

■ investigation of the target, through due diligence, will help to flush out any problems or misconceptions about the target.

6.2 Confidentiality

6.2.1 The previous chapter looked at confidentiality as a vendor requirement. From the purchaser's prospective, there are two issues:

■ the purchaser may itself require confidentiality about the fact that negotiations are taking place, for example if the target is a competitor;

■ the purchaser will want to ensure that any obligations of confidentiality it accepts are not unduly onerous.

6.2.2 Quite often the purchaser will sign a confidentiality undertaking in the form provided by the vendor. Failure to do this will slow the process down. However, even though most forms of undertaking are similar, it could include some onerous obligations. For example, the undertaking might seek to restrict information the purchaser has already obtained or which is generally known (usually referred to as being in the public domain). This exception should be included in the undertaking, but is sometimes not. Equally, the purchaser will be hampered in its efforts to raise funding if the under-taking does not permit it to pass information to the bank and/or venture capitalist (VC) with which it intends to deal. This is not always a straight-forward issue for the vendor. VCs have begun to initiate and lead institutional buy-outs (IBOs), and individuals within the VC may sit on the boards of competitor companies. Therefore the vendor may not wish the purchaser to have the ability to pass on the information. The compromise is sometimes reached whereby certain information can be passed on, perhaps later in the process. Also, the VCs may be required to sign a separate confidentiality undertaking.

6.3   Exclusivity

6.3.1   The process of investigating the target through due diligence and preparing draft purchase documentation is likely to involve the purchaser in substantial professional fees as well as considerable time and effort on the part of the purchaser and its directors and employees. Thus, the purchaser will want to restrict the vendor from negotiating with third parties at the same time. It is common for the purchaser to seek exclusivity, when for a period the vendor is not permitted to negotiate or provide the information about the target to any other prospective purchasers. This is also known as a 'lock-out', for obvious reasons.

6.3.2   One of the purchaser's objectives with an exclusivity agreement may be to lock the vendor into negotiations. For this reason, exclusivity agreements may contain obligations on the parties to continue negotiations. Under English law, an 'agreement to agree' is not enforceable and so there are limits on what an exclusivity agreement can achieve. Following a decision of the House of Lords, the legal position on exclusivity agreements appears to be as set out below.

EXCLUSIVITY AGREEMENTS – THE LEGAL POSITION ON 'AGREEMENTS TO AGREE'

- Because the parties cannot be 'forced' to reach an agreement, undertakings that oblige the vendor to negotiate or to continue negotiations with a purchaser will not be effective.
- Undertakings to pay damages or costs if the transaction does not proceed to completion will be unenforceable unless good consideration can be shown .
- An undertaking not to negotiate with or sell to third parties during a specific period will, however, be enforceable and it is possible for damages and/or costs to be recoverable for breach of such an undertaking and also for the parties to seek a remedy through an injunction.
- Where damages are expressed as a fixed sum, this will not be enforceable if it amounts to a 'penalty' as opposed to a genuine pre-estimate of the loss.

6.3.3 An exclusivity agreement may be in the form of a letter or may be a clause contained in heads of terms (in which case care should be taken to ensure that this part of the agreement is legally enforceable). A well-drafted exclusivity obligation should define:

- the restricted activities, principally negotiating with a third party or selling the target to a third party;
- a specific period during which the restrictions will apply which would cover the period required by the purchaser to complete the transaction, with an allowance made for possible delays;
- the consequences of breach.

6.3.4 Sample document 3 (page 152) is a form of lock-out agreement dealing with those areas. Note that the obligations comprise:

- termination of any existing negotiations;
- a prohibition on any further discussion or negotiation with prospective purchasers;
- a restriction on providing information to third parties – this is important, not just because it prevents the vendor from keeping its marketing exercise alive by continuing to pass that information, but also because breach of the other obligations may be more difficult to prove than the act of passing information;
- an obligation to co-operate with the purchaser, although note that there are doubts as to the enforceability of such a clause in the light of the principles set out above.

6.3.5 Damages for breach of an exclusivity agreement would be calculated as for any breach of contract. This would be to put the purchaser in the position it would have been in if the breach had not been committed. This is known as damages for 'loss of bargain'. It would be difficult to prove the amount of such damages, particularly where the final terms of the proposed purchase had not been finalised when the breach took place. For this reason, it is quite common for the exclusivity agreement to provide that the vendor is liable to indemnify the purchaser in respect of:

- legal, accountancy and other professional costs and expenses incurred by the purchaser in relation to the proposed transaction, usually subject to a maximum figure; and/or
- internal management costs and expenses suffered by the purchaser, potentially at an agreed daily rate or in a specific fixed sum.

This express right to compensation may be in addition to or instead of the right to claim damages on the usual basis. If not specified, the right will be in addition to the right to claim damages.

6.3.6 Where the agreement provides for payment of a fixed sum on breach, this might be construed as a 'penalty', which would be unenforceable under English law. Thus, if the sum is high and it is intended as deterrent to breach, there would be serious doubt as to whether this could be enforced. However, where the sum is calculated by reference to the purchaser's estimated losses (and this can include internal time, costs and lost opportunity in devoting time to the acquisition), it is possible for the compensation to be fixed in advance. This is known as 'liquidated damages' and is distinguished from a penalty by being a 'genuine pre-estimate of loss'.

6.3.7　It was mentioned above (6.3.2) that an undertaking to 'continue with negotiations in good faith' is likely to be unenforceable under English law. (This is in contrast to the laws of certain other European countries including France and Germany, which recognise a duty on the parties to negotiate in good faith and restrict the right to withdraw from a transaction without good reason, once terms have been agreed in principle.) The parties may still include such an obligation in the exclusivity agreement, on the basis that it might be enforceable and the parties are likely to give some recognition to it if it is included. It was also noted in the exclusivity agreements summary above that an undertaking to pay damages if the transaction does not proceed requires good consideration to be shown for that obligation. The consideration will usually be that the purchaser is incurring fees on due diligence. The exclusivity agreement should recite that this commitment is made at the request of the vendor and accordingly comprises consideration for the costs undertaking.

6.4　Heads of terms

6.4.1　This document sets out the key terms of the transaction and thus forms the basis on which the parties continue their negotiations. Other expressions used for the same document including 'heads of agreement' and 'term sheet'. The expression 'letter of intent' is also common, particularly in transactions with US parties, and refers to the parties' intention to transact business on the terms described in the letter. Heads of terms are usually (subject to the terms related to confidentiality and exclusivity, as noted below) intended to be subject to contract. In other words, they are not legally enforceable, on the basis that detailed terms are to be negotiated and concluded in a formal purchase agreement. This is often referred to (particularly in US transactions) as the 'definitive purchase agreement'.

6.4.2　The format of heads of terms can also vary significantly, from a single sheet of bullet points not going much beyond the shares or assets to be purchased and the consideration to be paid, right through to a detailed offer letter summarising the whole proposed transaction. The approach to be taken is largely a matter of style but also depends on:

- the complexity of the transaction;
- whether terms are adequately described elsewhere (for example in correspondence or a draft agreement);
- the timescale of the transaction and how quickly the parties will start to negotiate full agreements;
- whether there are a number of steps to be taken before a formal contract will be entered into, in which case it may be sensible to summarise all of these with a timetable in the heads.

6.4.3　In short, the approach depends on the circumstances. The overall purposes are, or at least include:

- a record of the outcome of initial negotiations;
- a briefing note for advisors and other people who will be involved in negotiating the final agreement;
- a document to be referred to, with moral force, if either party attempts to change its position and re-negotiate the deal at a later stage.
- Sample document 4 (page 155) gives a set of heads of terms. This antici-pates a management buy-out (MBO). It refers to the payment of deferred consideration to the vendor, merely by way of illustration of the style and level of detail. Like many sets of heads of terms, it contains confidentiality and exclusivity provisions that are legally enforceable (as opposed to the rest of the heads which are not). Clearly these provisions will not be nec-essary if there is an existing confidentiality undertaking and/or lock-out agreement. By definition, heads should set out the specifics of the given transaction and so there will be a standard form. The summary below gives an outline of typical heads and may help as a checklist for preparing them.

HEADS OF TERMS – OUTLINE/CHECKLIST

- **Heading** – used to identify the parties, describe the transaction generally and introduce key definitions.
- **Introductory paragraph** – clarifies the terms which are agreed 'subject to contract' and so are not legally binding except for specific terms such as confidentiality and exclusivity undertakings.
- **Timetable** – not necessary but can be a useful addition if it is not going to be expressed elsewhere.
- **Conditions precedent** – steps to be taken before the purchase can proceed to completion; can be included in the timetable.
- **Agreed terms** – the main substance of the heads; a précis of the terms of the transaction, roughly following the headings and order of the main purchase contract.
- **Warranties/restrictive covenants** – the basic choice is between setting out the expected key warranties in summary (usually providing that any list of warranties is not exhaustive) or using general words to describe the type of provisions to be included (such as 'the vendor will provide warranties appropriate to the transaction').
- **Exclusivity** – when there is no separate lock-out agreement.
- **Confidentiality** – where there is no separate confidentiality undertaking.
- **Signatures** – unless there are legally enforceable provisions, execution of the heads is not strictly necessary, although it indicates commitment and gives moral force to the terms.

6.4.5　It is essential that the document makes it clear that the terms are agreed sub-ject to contact. If not, the parties could find themselves legally bound by terms which are incomplete or possibly do not even reflect what they intend. The heads should also clarify any conditions that must be satisfied prior to legally binding agreements being entered into. These may include:

- board or shareholder approval (although it would be unusual for heads to be signed without already have been approved by the directors of both parties);
- the results of due diligence (and the heads would usually contain obligations relevant to completing that due diligence);
- agreement of the purchase contract, which is often expressed, even though that naturally follows from using the words 'subject to contract';
- funding arrangements;
- competition law approvals where relevant;
- any specific requirements such as planning permissions, transfer of licences or contracts.

6.5   Third party consents

6.5.1   The focus of the purchaser will now be on any matters that must be dealt with before acquisition of the target can be completed. Some are dealt with in the following chapters:
- due diligence;
- the impact of competition law on the transaction, whether because it is subject to merger regulation or the terms could have an anti competitive effect;
- in the case of publicly quoted companies, specific regulations that may necessitate shareholder approval and/or a Stock Exchange announcement;
- in the case of a business sale, the requirements to inform and consult with employees under TUPE;
- in the case of many share purchase transactions, the approval of financial assistance by a whitewash under s.155 CA.

6.5.2   Depending on the target's particular activities, there may be specific regulatory requirements for the sale. It could require approval from public bodies. It could also include the renewal of licences required under particular regulations. In the case of a business transfer, it has already been noted that these licences will need to be transferred or renewed. Some of the areas of regulation where licences or approvals are required are set out below.

LICENCES AND APPROVALS

Consumer credit licence	■ Required for providing consumer credit, consumer hire or ancillary credit business.
	■ Covers transactions with individuals, including sole traders and partnerships as well as private consumers.
Data protection	■ Licence required by many businesses that hold or use personal data.
	■ Many businesses that should have a licence, do not.

Investment business
- Most businesses involved in financial services need to obtain authorisation under FSMA.
- Application forms for authorisation are lengthy and complicated and just completing them requires significant resources.

Environmental matters
- Waste disposal and waste management activities may require the target to hold a licence.
- On a business transfer, the purchaser will need its own licence or approval from the Environment Agency of the transfer of the vendor's licence.
- Specific processes and the discharge of specified substances into the environment require licences from local authorities or statutory authorities.

Heavy goods vehicles
- The purchaser could require an HGV operator's licence from the Department of Transport.
- Licences may refer to specified, trained individuals so the purchaser should ensure that ongoing employees include such persons.

Due Diligence

7.1 Purpose

7.1.1 The expression 'due diligence' refers to the process by which the purchaser and its advisors gather and analyse information on the target. Overall, the purposes of due diligence could be summarised as being to:

- analyse assumptions made in valuing the target;
- discover problems early in the process that may justify a price reduction or even a decision not to proceed;
- identify areas that need to be covered by warranties and specific indemnities;
- avoid reliance on warranties;
- ascertain areas which may require third party consents, licences or approvals;
- arm the purchaser with the information necessary to manage the business of the target after completion.

7.1.2 The process of due diligence and the negotiation of warranties and indemnities go hand in hand. The drafting of the warranties should take into account the results of the due diligence exercise. In any event, making a warranty claim is not a straightforward legal process and the amount recoverable through a warranty claim is potentially uncertain. The process is also expensive and time consuming. It is far preferable to identify issues before completion and as early as possible in the process.

7.1.3 In certain cases, warranty cover may not be available. This applies, for example, where the vendor is in receivership or is at risk of financial failure at some time after completion. Here, the purchaser is relying almost entirely on the pre-contract investigation. Also, the vendor may be unwilling to give warranties, for example on a management buy-out (MBO) on the basis that existing management has full knowledge of the business of the target and the vendor requires a clean break. The same point applies, namely that investigation is vital (particularly by the funders, who do not have the same level of knowledge as the management).

7.1.4 The purchaser and its advisory team should consider at the outset the scope of due diligence to be carried out, in light of the circumstances of the particular target. Potential funders will also require input in this process.

Common areas of due diligence undertaken on acquisition of a private company are set out below.

KEY AREAS OF DUE DILIGENCE

Financial
- Carried out by accountants or accountancy personnel of the purchaser.
- Assesses the historic financial performance of the target.
- Attempts to project the future financial performance of the target.

Commercial
- Carried out by specialists in the target's field of business.
- Analyses the products or services, marketing and prospects of the target.
- Scope very much dependant on the particular target.

Legal
- Carried out by lawyers from all of the relevant disciplines.
- Identifies problem areas and legal issues in the target's affairs.
- Highlights areas for improvement to the business going forward and suggests safeguards against potential problems.

Customer referencing
- Often commissioned by venture capitalists (VCs) or other funders.
- Ascertains the current health and prospects of the relationship of the target with its key customers.
- Will require the co-operation and support of the vendor.

Insurance
- Carried out by insurance brokers or other specialist advisors.
- Analyses whether existing cover is adequate.
- Recommends extensions to the cover and/or new policies.

7.1.5 Due diligence is often supposed to be less important on the purchase of business assets than with a share purchase. It is correct to say that the purchaser is less concerned about liabilities, since it will only assume those provided for in the purchase documentation plus those that transfer by operation of law (for example under TUPE). However, the point remains that the purchaser is investing in an ongoing business and should take steps to investigate all aspects of that business before completion.

7.1.6 This book is mainly concerned with legal issues arising on acquisitions and this chapter concentrates on the process of legal due diligence. Other aspects are dealt with briefly.

7.2 Financial due diligence

7.2.1 Financial due diligence, at its most basic form, comprises the review of the historic financial performance of the target by reference to its accounting records. It will therefore usually involve a review of the following:

- statutory accounts for the last two or three financial years;
- auditors' working papers in respect of those accounts, to ascertain whether any particular issues were identified and the technical approach adopted on them;
- management accounts, to assess the up to date position and compare current periods with similar periods in previous years;
- the company's accounting records, to ascertain that they are adequate and that the statutory and management accounts properly reflect them;
- accounting systems and the personnel who manage them.

7.2.2   More sophisticated financial due diligence will apply on significant transactions, particularly where these are funded by VCs and the acquisition finance units of the clearing banks. This may involve the accounting advisors' opinions on the future prospects as well as historic performance.

7.2.3   Assessment of future prospects would usually begin with the target's business plan. This may be an existing plan prepared by the vendor or, particularly in the case of a buy-out transaction, one prepared by the proposed new management team. The business plan will project future performance by reference to certain assumptions. The projections would typically predict the target's cash flow and profit for the next two to three years. Such projections cannot, by their very nature, be guaranteed. The principal objective of financial due diligence will be to examine whether those projections and the assumptions on which they are based are reasonable in all the circumstances.

7.2.4   The results of financial due diligence should be set out in a written report from the accountants. This will usually be addressed to the purchaser and the proposed funders. Addressing the report to those funders establishes a duty of care on the part of the accountants, therefore it will invariably set out the scope of what is covered and clarify the accounting firm's limits of responsibility.

7.2.5   If the acquisition fails, it is likely that the purchaser and its funders will look critically at the terms of the report. Following high profile claims against major accounting practices on the financial failure of acquisition targets, accounting practices have become more defensive in their approach to reporting. This has had two key effects. First, the accountants will seek to limit their liability under the terms of the report, both by specifying a narrow scope of responsibility and by including exclusion/limitation clauses. Secondly, the text of the report will carefully comment on information provided and express opinions on that information in terms that might appear to be guarded and non-committal. Nevertheless, the report will be regarded as a key element in due diligence and will be a reference point for negotiations between the parties and the negotiation of warranties and indemnities.

7.3   Commercial due diligence

7.3.1   As the name suggests, commercial due diligence describes the purchaser's appraisal of the target's business. In deciding to proceed with the acquisition, the purchaser will have made certain assumptions about the products and services, trading relationships and organisation of the business. These should be tested, since the purchaser will not previously have been privy to much information about the target. The due diligence exercise gives the purchaser a unique level of access to the running of the target and the purchaser should take full advantage of this.

7.3.2   Often, the purchaser and its personnel will be best qualified to carry out commercial due diligence. The purchaser may be carrying on a directly competing business and thus be able to assess the target using its own specialist managers. This will be particularly appropriate where the target will be integrated into an existing business or group structure.

7.3.3   However, there is an increasing use of industry experts to carry out commercial due diligence. They would be able to analyse the systems and performance of the business by reference to other companies in the field (not just the purchaser) and be trained in business analysis and reporting. Use of industry experts may be a stipulation of a VC proposing to fund the transaction.

7.4   Legal due diligence

7.4.1   Legal due diligence describes the process whereby the lawyers acting for the purchaser and/or the funders will analyse legal issues and compliance of the target. This process often follows financial and commercial due diligence, which may attract more attention from the parties. Part of legal due diligence will be to pick up on points identified by the accountant's report. However, it can also reveal issues sufficient to stop a deal from going ahead that have not been highlighted by financial or commercial due diligence. More often, it reveals issues that affect the terms or structure of the deal, for example:
- requirements for third party consents, such as landlords;
- regulatory issues, such as competition law;
- change of control issues;
- other contractual issues, where for example a variation to a material contract may be a pre-completion condition;
- problems that should be addressed by holding back part of the consideration or making it dependent on a future event or obligation.

7.4.2   An important purpose of legal due diligence is to highlight areas for improvement to the target business. For example, where employee records are inadequate, the required action would be:
- extract any information held by the vendor that may be required post completion;
- ensure future compliance by setting up new systems;
- measure the risks to the purchaser from past defaults;
- protect against those through warranty cover.

7.4.3   It is important that legal due diligence is focused and does not merely involve sending out long questionnaires to the vendor on every legal aspect imaginable. A summary of the exercise is set out below. This will be managed by the corporate finance partner in the purchaser's law firm, who would project manage the activities of specialists from different departments and then oversee the submission of a report.

LEGAL DUE DILIGENCE PROCESS

- **Step 1** – ascertain the purchaser's objectives and concerns regarding the transaction as a whole. The purpose is to ensure that the legal team focuses on what is important rather than what it believes is important.
- **Step 2** – set the scope for the legal due diligence exercise, in light of Step 1. The purpose is to ensure the report is properly focused and does not consist of large and costly reports on less relevant issues.
- **Step 3** – briefing of specialist lawyers on Steps 1 and 2 and agreeing the extent and timescale for the individual tasks.
- **Step 4** – gathering initial information through enquiries of the vendor, searches of public registers and review of other sources (many internet-based).
- **Step 5** – initial reporting to the project manager and then to the purchaser and funders, particularly where significant issues arise or whether further action is needed.
- **Step 6** – further investigation based on feedback from interim reporting, to finalise the legal due diligence investigation.
- **Step 7** – issuing a formal report (in whatever format has been agreed with the purchaser and the funders), sufficiently in advance of completion to enable the parties to make maximum use of it.

7.4.4 It was suggested above that financial due diligence reports are sometimes criticised for their failure to give hard opinions and being bland. The same view is often held about legal due diligence reports, which are often criticised for being too long and uncommercial. Significant time and effort is put into preparing the reports and so they are relatively expensive to produce. It is therefore even more important that they are seen as providing value for money. The following attributes would assist to achieve this:
- focused – highlighting key issues;
- relevant – containing useful information;
- commercial – identifying where actual risks exist;
- readable and not too long;
- delivered on time, allowing the purchaser to do something about the issues raised;
- offering solutions to the problems identified.

7.4.5 An overview of the reporting system is set out below. The remainder of this chapter deals with particular areas of the investigation. Employment issues are dealt with in Chapter 10.

- **Why?** To record and distribute the findings of the lawyers' investigation into the affairs of the target.
- **Who?** Contributions by specialist lawyers but co-ordinated and managed by lead corporate finance lawyer.
- **What?** A written report that sets out its basis and scope, an executive summary highlighting the most significant areas, a list of action points to highlight what should be done about these areas, and the main body of the report which provides a more detailed analysis of the results of the investigation and the issues this has raised.
- **How?** Interim reporting of key issues, followed by drafts of the main report, which is 'signed off' when the purchaser and its funders are satisfied.
- **When?** Issues to be communicated as early as possible and the contents of the report to be available in good time to enable the purchaser to act on them, including re-negotiation with the vendor.

7.5 Questionnaire

7.5.1 Sample document 5 (page 160) is a standard questionnaire relating to a share acquisition. Sample document 25 (page 276) is a questionnaire relating to a business purchase. The questionnaires should be tailored to the particular circumstances of the target. In most cases further specialist enquiries would be needed. They would be prepared by the purchaser's lawyers and sent to the vendor's lawyers at an early stage in the transaction. There are three common failings in this approach:

- the purchaser's lawyer sends out the 'standard precedent' without any regard to the nature of the target, thus asking some irrelevant questions and needing to add further relevant questions at a later stage;
- the vendor's lawyer passes the questionnaire on to the vendor, expecting the vendor to compile the replies without assistance, often resulting in delay or even a refusal to deal with the request;
- the vendor may believe that all issues are adequately covered by financial due diligence and so be reluctant to part with any further information.

7.5.2 These problems can be avoided by better communication. The vendor needs to appreciate the importance of providing proper information. Even though information may have been available as part of the financial due diligence exercise, it is still vital for copies of relevant documents to be exchanged for legal review and for a record to be kept of the information provided. Since the replies to legal due diligence enquiries will usually form the backbone of the disclosures against the warranties, it is for the vendor's benefit to have those documents produced.

7.6 Title to shares

7.6.1 On a share purchase, the first issue to ascertain is that the vendor(s) has/have good title to the target's shares. As a matter of company law, the entries made in the target's register of members (being within the statutory books of the company) are the defining test of legal title to the shares. Review of the original statutory books will be a necessary part of legal due diligence. This should be done to ensure that the books are duly written up, adequately record the vendors as shareholders and do not contain indications of defects in the title to the shares (for example lack of pre-emption waivers or stock transfer forms which have not been duly stamped).

7.6.2 In practice, the company's statutory books may be reviewed later in the transaction process (although before completion). In such a case, the preliminary indications that the vendors own the shares in the company will come from enquiries of the vendors and by checking the last annual return filed by the company with the Registrar of Companies. Note that there may be transfers of the shares between the vendors or to family members, right up until the point of completion. This would be the case where, for example, the vendor transferred shares to spouse and children to utilise annual exemptions and lower rates of tax, as mentioned in Chapter 4. In such cases, care needs to be taken to ensure that the transfers are duly stamped or certified as exempt from stamp duty, that they are approved for registration by the target directors and that the names of the transferees are entered in the register of members.

7.6.3 Contrary to popular belief, share certificates do not represent a document of title to shares. They are secondary evidence of ownership, strictly subject to the correct entries being made in the register of members. It is still best practice, however, to check that share certificates match the vendors' identities. On completion of the purchase, vendors will be expected to hand over their share certificates or, if the share certificate cannot be found, an indemnity intended to cover losses arising from the missing certificate. This allows a replacement certificate to be issued.

7.6.4 The measures described above are only sufficient to ascertain legal ownership of the shares. They will not reveal beneficial ownership, where this is different. For example, the registered owners of the shares may have agreed to sell their shares to a third party or to grant an option over them. If the purchaser acquires the shares from the registered owners without the knowledge of the third party rights, the purchaser will acquire a good title. However, the purchaser will still want a right of recourse against the vendors in case it is deemed to have knowledge of the rights. This will be covered, not just by the warranties, but also by the covenants implied on the transfer of shares by statute. The share purchase agreement will usually state that the shares are sold 'with full title guarantee', which includes an implied warranty that the vendor is entitled to sell the shares free of any third party rights and will take all necessary steps to pass good title to the purchaser.

7.6.5 Where the purchaser has knowledge of a third party who has beneficial ownership or indeed any third party rights, the appropriate course would be to extinguish those rights by agreement with the third party or join the third party into the contract for sale so that the rights of that third party are acquired alongside legal title to the shares.

7.7 Title to assets

7.7.1   On a business purchase, the purchaser will want to be certain that the vendor has title to the assets being sold. The purchase agreement will (in a similar manner to a share sale) state that the vendor sells 'with full title guarantee' so as to incorporate implied covenants that the vendor is passing good title. On a share purchase, the purchaser will want to ascertain that the target company owns its principal assets. The purchaser will not have the benefit of implied covenants for title but will almost certainly want a warranty as to title contained in the purchase agreement.

7.7.2   Unlike a share purchase, there is no straightforward method of checking title to the assets of a business. The special cases of property and intellectual property rights (IPR) are dealt with below, but for other assets the purchaser will be relying on the representations given to the purchaser in replies to enquiries and warranties within the purchase agreement. It would be possible to check ownership of individual items by reference to original purchase records, but it would be unusual to do this, except for specific key assets. Particular enquiries flush out useful information such as:

- whether any of the individual vendors have any personal interest in assets used by the target;
- in the case of groups, whether another group company owns any assets used by the target;
- whether any third party has made a claim to have rights over the assets;
- whether there are any finance agreements with third parties;
- whether any items have been supplied on retention of title terms.

7.7.3   Ownership of vehicles by a finance company may be revealed by contacting HPI, which maintains a register (but not a conclusive record) of hire purchase agreements. In fact, most acquisitions proceed without such enquiries being made.

7.7.4   Specific issues arising on a receivership sale were dealt with in Chapter 2. Basically, the sale of assets by a receiver, administrator or liquidator will not carry any guarantee of good title. The ability to investigate title may be limited, by time if nothing else. The minimum requirement would be to ascertain that the receiver has the capacity to sell the assets so at least any title held by the company in receivership would pass to the purchaser. In the case of receivership, this involves checking the terms of the charge under which the receiver is appointed and the appointment documents.

7.8 Charges

7.8.1   In the case of a share purchase or a business purchase from a company, the purchaser must ascertain whether any charges have been registered with the Registrar of Companies. This will be revealed by a search of the Companies House records. These are public records and the information can be extracted using a company search agent or by professionals who hold a relevant account with Companies House for on-line searching. It would also be prudent to check the register of charges maintained by the company within its statutory books. However, if the charge is not registered within 21 days of creation at Companies House it will (except in very limited circumstances) be void, so the Companies House search is the primary information to be investigated. Where charges are revealed, unless the purchaser agrees that these charges should remain in force, steps should be taken to ensure their removal on or before completion.

7.8.2   It is quite common for charges registered at Companies House to relate to previous lenders of the target, where the indebtedness has long been satisfied. The target should have taken steps to remove those charges by lodging a memorandum of satisfaction under s.403 CA but often this is not the case. The process involves a director declaring that all the indebtedness has been cleared or (where appropriate) that there has been a release of the relevant assets from the charge. If no such memorandum of satisfaction has been lodged, the purchaser may want clear evidence that the charge no longer affects the target. If not satisfied with the directors making a declaration to this effect, the purchaser may want to see a deed of release executed by the chargee. This is a question of judgement in each case.

7.9   Property

7.9.1   The initial investigations into the property affairs of the target will be to ascertain the issues set out below.

INITIAL PROPERTY ISSUES

- Which properties are owned or occupied by the target.
- Does the target have a freehold or leasehold interest in such property or occupy under some form of licence or sharing arrangements?
- Any third party rights or encumbrances in respect of the property such as restrictions on use or rights of way, particularly in the case of freehold or long leasehold property.
- In the case of leasehold property, the duration and terms of the lease.
- 'Hot issues' in relation to leases, which include rent, rent review, repair obligations, current dilapidations, break clauses and security of tenure rights.
- Planning use and planning conditions, such as restrictions on working hours.
- Rights of access, preferably over publicly adopted highways.
- Other local matters such as compulsory purchase proposals.
- Liability for leasehold property previously occupied by the target.

7.9.2   Property investigations will follow similar lines to a 'normal' commercial property transaction. Accordingly, the purchaser's lawyers will raise enquiries specific to each property and submit the usual conveyancing searches including:

- a local search, to ascertain matters registered as local land charges and local authority departments' replies to standard questions;
- a search at HM Land Registry to obtain copies of the entries on the register for each property;
- for any property not registered at HM Land Registry, examination of title deeds and a search at HM Land Charges Registry;
- additional searches of the Commons Registry, British Rail or a coal mining search, as appropriate.

7.9.3   The system of proving title to registered land through production of a land certificate has recently been abolished. Details of the title to HM Land Registry are available by on-line searching. This should speed up the process of title investigation, although the purchaser will need to ascertain the title number for each property either from the vendor or by carrying out a search at HM Land Registry using a plan of the property.

7.9.4   Other aspects of due diligence are associated with property. These include ascertaining that the property carries a fire certificate, where necessary. This includes factory, office and shop premises where more than 20 people are at work at any one time or more than ten people are at work at any one time elsewhere than on the ground floor of the building. Planning and construction issues arising in the particular circumstances of the transaction may necessitate the involvement of specialists in those fields.

7.9.5   A certificate of title may be given as an alternative to investigation of the title to property. This would usually be provided by the vendor's lawyers or by the lawyers who acted for the vendor on acquiring the property. This certificate should clearly set out any issues relating to the property and confirm that the target has good title without any defects or material issues affecting the property, other than those set out in the certificate. In practice however, lawyers will spend considerable time and effort negotiating the form of the certificate, which takes away much of the point of the exercise.

7.10 Intellectual property rights

7.10.1 Intellectual property rights (IPR) will be the principal asset of many businesses, particularly in the field of technology. The investigation of these rights is a specialist topic beyond the scope of this book but a few key issues are set out below.

INTELLECTUAL PROPERTY RIGHTS – KEY ISSUES

Patents
- Registered rights for novel ideas.
- Patent rights are registered separately for different parts of the world and so multiple searches may be necessary and expensive.

- Specialist skills of a patent attorney may be necessary to review the patent specification and assess the patent's value and/or robustness.

Trademarks (TMs)
- Words and/or logos and/or 3D images applied to goods and services.
- As for patents, TMs are registered by reference to different parts of the world and so multiple searches may be needed.
- TMs are registered for specified classes of use and so registration in one class does not prevent use by a competitor in other fields.
- Specialist advice may be required on whether relevant products are adequately covered by registration and whether those registrations are subject to challenge.

Registered designs
- Registered rights so can be searched for.
- Relates to the novel appearance of a product.

Design right
- Unregistered right that applies to an original design of the shape or configuration of an item.

Copyright
- The most common right, applicable to the physical representation of an idea (but not the idea itself); includes documents and software.
- Is unregistered and so investigation will entail enquiries of the vendor and examination of agreements with third parties such as licences.

7.10.2   In the case of a business purchase, the other aspect to IPR investigation will be to ensure that all relevant IPR is properly transferred. In the case of unregistered rights, such as copyright, the main purchase agreement may be sufficient to transfer ownership to the purchaser. Note however that the assignment should adequately define the IPR being transferred and it may therefore be sensible to have a separate assignment. In the case of registered IPR, specific forms of transfer will be required, so these can be despatched for registration after completion.

7.11 Litigation and insolvency

7.11.1   The principal source of information on litigation, arbitration and other disputes will be enquiries of the vendors. Where there is significant litigation, the purchaser should review the prospects of success and the likely costs involved.

7.11.2   Warranties should flush out all disputes with customers, suppliers, distributors, agents, employees, statutory bodies and tax authorities. These should be investigated properly, not just because of potential liabilities (less of an issue on a business purchase) but because they may reveal ongoing problems with the target.

7.11.3   A telephone search of the Companies Court will enable the purchaser to check that no winding up or administration petitions have been presented against the vendor, the target or its subsidiaries. The existence of a petition is likely to frustrate the sale, since dispositions of property are more than likely to need court approval.

7.12   Environmental issues

7.12.1   Investigation into environmental issues will involve enquiries of the vendor specific to environmental legislation and licensing. However, it will also include review of information with an environmental aspect which is disclosed against enquiries relating to:
- properties owned or occupied by the target;
- trading activities, in particular processes using hazardous materials or involving the disposal of waste products;
- litigation or prosecutions, for example relating to discharge of waste.

It follows that some co-ordination is needed between members of the team examining all these aspects.

7.12.2   The Environmental Protection Act 1990 developed a wide ambit for environmental issues. The concept of pollution has been broadened to cover emissions into the air, ground and watercourses that are hazardous, toxic or could otherwise be harmful. This caused a significant concentration of effort by purchasers, funders and their advisors to ensure that there were no historic liabilities and no ongoing problems. The passing of the Environment Act 1995 created additional issues on share and business acquisitions. The Act established a framework under which owners of land could be liable for cleaning up 'contaminated land'. This liability could arise even if the owner had not caused the contamination.

7.12.3   Contaminated land is defined by the Environment Act 1995 as being 'land which appears to the local authority in whose area it is situated to be in such a condition, by reason of substances in, on or under the land, that:
(a) significant harm is being caused or there is a significant possibility of such harm being caused; or
(b) pollution of controlled waters is being or is likely to be caused.'

It is evident from this that not only is the definition wide but also that it is left in the discretion of local authorities. Local authorities are under a duty to take note of statutory guidance in assessing whether land is contaminated but otherwise will adopt their own approach. In addition, the Environment Agency has separate enforcement powers for particularly contaminated land, known as 'special sites'.

7.12.4   Once contaminated land has been identified, the local authority is obliged to consult with those persons who may be liable under the Act for cleaning it up. If no voluntary clean up takes place, the local authority can serve a 'remediation notice' which sets out the action to be taken to clean up the land. The remediation notice will usually be served on the person who caused or knowingly permitted the contamination in, on or under the land. Where the original polluter cannot be found (for example, a company that has been wound up), the current owner or occupier may be liable for the clean up. Any purchaser of land or purchaser of shares in a company owning land will therefore want to know about past contamination as well as current activity.

7.12.5 Furthermore, in certain circumstances, liability of the polluter may transfer to the next owner. This would arise, for example, where property is sold to a purchaser who receives information about the extent of contamination. In that case, the new owner is assuming a liability for the contamination. This means that enquiries of the vendor should deal with any known contamination at the time the target acquired the land.

7.12.6 The other key area of environmental investigation is to ascertain that the target has all appropriate environmental authorisations. The relevant legislation is Part I of the Environmental Protection Act 1990, as replaced by the Pollution Prevention and Control Act 1999. Where the company carries on a 'prescribed process', it will require authorisation from the relevant local authority or the Environment Agency. In addition, a waste management licence under the Environmental Protection Act 1990 will be required in order to treat, keep or dispose of controlled waste. As noted above, controlled waste is very widely defined. The purchaser should be provided with copies of these authorisations and should have them reviewed by a specialist who understands the legislation.

7.12.7 The target will very often deal with disposal of waste products arising from its activities by engaging a specialist waste contractor. The legislation obliges the target to ensure that waste is only transferred to a person who is duly authorised to transport or dispose of that waste and that the waste is properly described to that contractor. Thus, environmental investigation will include review of the contract with that waste carrier and the systems in place for dealing with it. Also note that businesses with a turnover of more than £2 million that handle more than 50 tonnes of packaging each year are required to provide certain information to the Environment Agency under the Producer Responsibility (Packaging Waste) Regulations 1997. These regulations require that set proportions of packing materials are recovered and recycled. This could apply to the target regardless of its manufacturing processes, in that most businesses will need to dispose of packaging materials.

7.12.8 The nature of the environmental investigation could involve a number of steps, depending on the property and the view taken by the purchaser and its funders. The key steps that could be taken on an acquisition are summarised below.

KEY ASPECTS OF ENVIRONMENTAL INVESTIGATIONS

- ▓ Enquiries of the vendor to obtain details of properties, processes, authorisations and past problems.
- ▓ Reviewing existing authorisations and activities, to judge whether these comply with environmental legislation.
- ▓ Enquiries of local authorities and (where appropriate) other regulatory bodies such as the Environment Agency.
- ▓ Consideration of where the property is or could be treated as contaminated land and, where appropriate, ascertaining the identity of the original polluter.
- ▓ Commissioning a 'phase one' survey with regard to each site owned or occupied by the target.
- ▓ Where appropriate, following up with a 'phase two' survey including soil sampling.
- ▓ Co-ordinating all information obtained and ensuring this is reflected in appropriate warranties and indemnities.

7.12.9   A phase one survey comprises a review by an environmental consultant of plans and historical information relating to the site. This could provide useful information on previous uses of the site, waste management sites within the vicinity and watercourses and groundwater sources that could be affected by the property. It is usually a 'desk top survey', meaning that the consultant reviews existing available information and then makes a report. However, a phase one survey can be supplemented by a walkover of the site by the consultant. Note that on certain types of acquisition a phase one survey may be a minimum requirement of VCs and banks.

7.12.10 A phase two survey takes the investigation further. This would usually mean taking soil samples for a laboratory analysis, which would involve drilling boreholes at various places over the site. A phase two survey is therefore much more involved, needs a greater level of co-operation from the vendor and may take some time to complete. It could take days or even weeks to obtain the results. It is therefore vital to identify environmental issues and any requirements of the funders to carry out phase one and phase two surveys early in the process to avoid last minute delays.

7.13 Taxation

7.13.1   On a share sale, the purchaser's primary protection against tax liabilities for which no provision has been included in the target's accounts will be a tax covenant and tax warranties given by the vendor. These are covered in Chapter 11. Nevertheless, the purchaser should carry out tax due diligence in order to:

- ■ understand the target's tax affairs, including any special arrangements with the Inland Revenue (IR);

- anticipate areas that may require negotiation of the structure of the acquisition or the consideration;
- identify problems in advance, in order to be sure these are adequately covered by the tax covenant, warranties and specific indemnities.

7.13.2 On a business sale, the purchaser will not inherit tax liabilities automatically, so tax due diligence will be less comprehensive. Even though responsibilities for employees transfer under TUPE, liability under PAYE will not pass to the purchaser. It would be unusual for the purchaser to assume tax liabilities under the contract, the main exception being that VAT and PAYE for the current periods may be assumed if the amount can be quantified. However, the purchaser will inherit the ongoing activities and so will be particularly interested in their tax treatment, in particular VAT and PAYE.

7.13.3 Tax due diligence should cover:
- latest corporation tax returns and any disputed items;
- history of compliance;
- available losses;
- group issues including transfers of assets between group members;
- VAT affairs including any VAT group and any exempt or zero-rated supplies;
- VAT implications of any property transactions;
- PAYE affairs and any sub-contracted or self-employed labour;
- investigations by any tax authority;
- any 'unusual' transactions.

7.14 Pensions

7.14.1 As with most areas of due diligence, the investigation into pension arrangements will involve:
- ascertaining from the vendor current arrangements and, in the case of a share purchase, previous arrangements;
- reviewing those arrangements and relating documentation, to ascertain whether the arrangements comply with pensions' legislation and regulation;
- investigating funding issues and gauging what, if any, potential liability the target and/or the purchaser will assume;
- assessing what needs to be done to hand over current arrangements following the acquisition.

7.14.2 The issues depend on the types of scheme set up for the target and its employees, which are briefly described below.

PENSION SCHEMES IN BRIEF

Money purchase or 'defined contribution' schemes
- The rate of employer and employee contributions are fixed (with no guaranteed level of benefit, as would apply on a final salary scheme).
- The benefits at retirement depend on what can be acquired in the market at that time, using the 'pot' of money accumulated from investment of the contributions made in respect of the relevant individual.
- Popular with employers, giving that liabilities are fixed and lesser compliance burden than final salary schemes.

Final salary or 'defined benefit' schemes
- Benefits at retirement are based on a multiple of a specified proportion of the final salary of the relevant employee and his or her years of pensionable service.
- Contributions will be open ended, depending on the existing state of funding of the scheme and actuarial calculations of what will be required to pay out benefits.
- Employees may contribute, but the employer will meet the balance of necessary contributions.
- Potential liabilities and increasing regulation make final salary schemes unpopular and problematic on acquisitions.

Occupational pension schemes
- A term defined by statute, basically meaning schemes set up by employers to provide pension contributions to employees.
- May be final salary or money purchase.

Group personal pension schemes
- A scheme 'arranged' by an employer with an insurance company to provide benefits to employees – not an occupational pension scheme.
- Comprises a series of individual personal pension policies, into which the employer may make contributions at a rate agreed with the employee in the terms of employment.

Self administered and funded unapproved schemes
- An occupational pension scheme, usually on a money purchase basis.
- Often set up by the business owners for their benefit only and often raises issues relating to investment of scheme funds into the target company.
- Subject to special IR rules of approval and compliance.

Stakeholder pensions
- Government-designed financial product to be provided by private sector financial institutions.
- Required by all employers unless they fall within specific exemptions.
- Where non-exempt, the employer must provide access to its scheme and a payroll deduction system by all relevant employees.

7.14.3 An issue for all pension schemes will be to review existing documentation to check the legal compliance issues. This will include:

- the latest trust deed and rules;
- a list of existing members (ie those persons entitled to benefit from the scheme) and those employees who are likely to become members in the foreseeable future;
- the rates of contributions paid or payable for those members;
- for a final salary scheme, the latest actuarial valuation;
- a copy of the latest scheme booklet and/or letters given to employees about benefits;
- deeds of appointment of trustees (and minutes of trustee meetings, if available);
- evidence of the scheme's exempt approved tax status;
- copy of the contracting out certificate for the employer, if appropriate;
- where the scheme covers a group of companies, any deed of adherence by which the company agreed to be bound to the scheme.

7.14.4 There are many issues of legal compliance relating to occupational pension schemes. The requirement of the Pensions Act 1995 and regulations made under that Act deal with requirements relating to:

- appointment of member nominated trustees, unless a valid opt out is in place;
- the need to involve appropriate professional advisors, such as auditors, actuaries and fund managers;
- the production of audited accounts within seven months after the end of each scheme year;
- basic disclosure requirements to provide members with information on the scheme.

7.14.5 Equal treatment of men and women in relation to benefits provided by pension schemes remains a common problem to be dealt with on acquisition. Unequal treatment would amount to unlawful sexual discrimination. Unequal treatment for part-timers (for example excluding them from membership of the scheme) may amount to indirect sex discrimination, particularly where the majority of part-timers are of one sex. The whole area of 'equalisation' is complex and has been the subject of debate since before May 1990 when the European Court of Justice established that pensions represent 'pay' for the purposes of the requirements that men and women should be entitled to equal pay. Since then, the pensions industry and advisors have struggled with the complex and costly exercise of equalising schemes where:

- men and women had different retirement ages;
- part-timers, mainly women, were excluded from pension scheme membership;
- transfers were made from 'unequalised schemes' into new schemes which might therefore need a recalculation of benefits.

7.14.6 In the case of a final salary scheme, a key issue will be whether the scheme is adequately funded, meaning that sufficient contributions have been and/or are being made to meet the prospective liabilities to pay benefits. The scheme may be 'unfunded', meaning that the vendor is simply allowing the liabilities to accrue without any assets being put aside to meet them. Depending on the number of members (perhaps just the founders of the business), this could have serious implications for the solvency of the target, which will be liable to meet those liabilities.

7.14.7   If a final salary scheme is 'funded', the principal task of due diligence will be to establish whether the latest funding position is adequate to meet the liabilities on an ongoing basis. The regulations upon which adequate funding is to be judged are complex and subject to change, so professional guidance on this aspect should always be obtained when the target has established or adhered to an occupational final salary scheme.

7.14.8   In the case of a money purchase scheme, the purchaser will mainly be concerned to see that all the documentation is in order and that contributions payable into the scheme have in fact been paid. The purchaser will want full disclosure from the vendor of the rates of contribution, evidence that these contributions have been paid and confirmation that there are no outstanding scheme expenses. There may occasionally be 'guarantees' of a certain level of benefits to be provided to an individual member of the money purchase scheme. (In this way, the scheme has some of the attributes of a final salary scheme.) If so, the purchaser will be concerned to see whether that guarantee will require the target to make additional contributions into the scheme.

7.14.9   The requirements of due diligence into group personal pension schemes are more straightforward. The documentation establishing the arrangement should not impose obligations on the target, although this should be checked. The remaining points would include checking:
- contributions by the employer under terms of employment are up to date;
- deductions from pay in respect of contributions have been paid over to the insurance company within 19 days of the end of each month, as relevant regulations require;
- any unpaid or ongoing administration costs of the scheme to be borne by the target.

7.14.10 In relation to stakeholder pensions, the principal issues to be examined in due diligence are:
- is the target exempt from the requirement to offer access to a stakeholder pension scheme?
- in the case of a business purchase where an exempt target will be incorporated into an existing business, will this trigger the requirement to establish a stakeholder pension scheme?
- does any stakeholder pension scheme comply with the requirements, including a satisfactory payroll deduction facility and access to the scheme for all relevant employees?

7.14.11 To enjoy exemption from the requirements to establish stakeholder pensions, the employer must:
- offer an occupational pension scheme that allows employees to join within 12 months of commencing employment; or

- contribute at least 3 per cent of pay to a personal pension scheme (to which the employee may also be liable to contribute up to 3 per cent of pay); or
- employ fewer than five people (although this exception is subject to change).

7.14.12 On a share purchase, the emphasis of pensions due diligence will be to establish historic compliance and any existing liabilities (on the basis that all those liabilities will remain with the target). On a business purchase, obligations under existing occupational pension schemes will not transfer to the purchaser under TUPE. However, the purchaser will be concerned about the validity of existing arrangements, since the purchaser will need to continue these or offer satisfactory new arrangements.

Competition Issues

8.1 Introduction

8.1.1   When buying or selling any business (whether through acquiring shares or acquiring a business and assets), it is important to consider not only the commercial terms of the acquisition/disposal but also whether the arrangement will have any competition implications that may need to be considered either pre- or post-completion of the transaction.

8.1.2   There are two main issues that parties will need to consider from a competition perspective in any business sale or purchase:

   ■ will the transaction need to be considered under either the UK or European merger regime?

   ■ does the transaction documentation include any potentially anti-competitive restrictions?

8.1.3   The resolution of any competition issues is both a buyer's and a vendor's problem. For example, if the merger would affect competition, the parties could be ordered not to go ahead with the transaction or to unwind the transaction.

8.2 Merger control

8.2.1   If the transaction involves a 'relevant merger', the parties may refer the merger to the relevant competition authorities for them to assess whether the merger will create a 'substantial lessening of competition' in the market and, if so, the steps the parties will need to take to find an agreeable solution. Depending on the geographical areas in which the parties to the merger operate, the relevant competition authority may be either the Office of Fair Trading (OFT) in the UK, the European Commission if the merger has a European dimension or, if there is no European Community dimension to the merger but it affects competition in individual EC member states, the competition authorities in the affected member states.

8.2.2   The definition of a 'relevant merger' will catch not only share purchases but also transactions that involve a transfer of assets and the creation of joint ventures.

8.2.3   In most cases, if the parties to the transaction supply the same goods and/or services, ie are competitors, consideration should be given as to whether the proposed transaction may be a relevant merger.

8.3   UK merger control

8.3.1   If the transaction involves a relevant merger situation in the UK, it will be governed by the terms of the Enterprise Act 2002, which came into force in June 2003.

8.3.2   The OFT will make the initial assessment as to whether the merger will affect competition in the UK. Whilst parties can voluntarily notify the OFT of a relevant merger, the OFT has four months after it becomes aware of the transaction in which to decide whether to refer the matter for further consideration by the Competition Commission (CC). It may therefore be beneficial for the parties to a potential relevant merger to announce the merger soon after completion, in order to start the four month clock running.

8.3.3   In order to be classified as a 'relevant merger' and one that may be of interest to the competition authorities, the merger must meet the following three criteria:

- Two or more enterprises cease to be distinct or arrangements are in place or being considered by the parties that the enterprises will cease to be distinct. This will cover both the merging of business activities and where two or more enterprises are taken over by a third, for example a joint venture (JV) arrangement where the business activities of two or more companies are taken over by the JVco.

- The merger must not have taken place and the reference to the CC by the OFT must happen within four months of the merger either being made public or being referred to the OFT for consideration. Outside the four month period, no reference can be made to the CC.

- Either:
    - the UK turnover of the enterprise being acquired exceeds £70 million in the year preceding the transaction; or
    - as a merged entity, the enterprises will acquire and/or supply more than 25 per cent of the goods and/or services supplied by both enterprises within the UK. The merger must result in an increase in the enterprises' share of the market.

8.3.4   *Two or more enterprises ceasing to be distinct*: This will usually occur where the enterprises are brought under common ownership and/or control. This could be achieved by acquiring voting control, the ability materially to influence the policy of one of the enterprises and/or the ability to control the policy of one of the enterprises. The assessment as to whether one of the enterprises acquires material control/the ability to control policy decisions will be assessed by the OFT on a case-by-case basis.

8.3.5   *Turnover exceeding £70 million*: This will usually be assessed using the acquired enterprise's last published accounts. If it is a joint venture situation where two or more enterprises are being acquired by a new JVco, the turnover test is the sum of the turnovers of the enterprises ceasing to be distinct, less the turnover of the enterprise with the highest turnover.

8.3.6 *Supply exceeding 25 per cent:* This test is met if the merged enterprises supply and/or acquire the same goods and/or services in the UK and, after the merger, will supply and/or acquire more than 25 per cent of those goods and/or services in the UK or a substantial part of it. If one of the enterprises supplies or acquires more than 25 per cent of the goods and/or services pre-merger, the test is satisfied as long as the market share is increased due to the merger. The OFT will define the market as narrowly as possible, for example if the enterprises produce more than one product, the OFT will assess the market as being in relation to the goods and/or services where there is an overlap between the business activities of the parties to the merger.

8.3.7 If the transaction is a relevant merger, the OFT has a duty to refer the merger to the CC if it reasonably believes there is a significant chance that the merger will lead to a 'substantial lessening of competition' in the UK. This could be because the merger means that there will be fewer players in the market, giving customers less choice and/or the merged entity will have the market power to act independently of its competitors. It is more likely that mergers between enterprises acting at the same level of the supply chain will affect competition ie horizontal mergers.

8.3.8 Just because a merger can be defined as a relevant merger does not mean that it will result in a substantial lessening of competition. Factors the OFT will look at include the geographical market affected, the nature of the market pre- and post-merger, how easy it is for new businesses to enter the market and operate as competition to the merged entity, existing competition in the marketplace with which the merged entity will compete, how easy it would be for customers to switch to a new supplier in response to increased prices by the merged entity and whether there are any efficiency gains as a result of the merger that will be passed on to customers. In order to make this assessment, the OFT can ask for information from other organisations operating in the same market, customers and suppliers.

8.3.9 The OFT can decide not to refer the merger to the CC if:
- the merger is not sufficiently far advanced to merit a reference;
- the markets are not of sufficient importance to justify a reference to the CC;
- the customer benefits flowing from the merger outweigh any adverse effects.

8.3.10 The OFT can also accept undertakings from the enterprises instead of referring the matter to the CC. These undertakings are aimed at remedying/preventing any potential competition issues identified as arising as a result of the merger. These are only usually appropriate where there are clear, identifiable remedies available. Parties may propose undertakings to the OFT which they consider suitable to remedy any identified competition issues. These could include covenants as to the future conduct of the parties or divestiture of part of the merged entity. In most cases, the OFT prefers structural solutions to the problem as they do not require policing to ensure compliance.

8.4 Guidance as to whether a merger is a relevant merger

8.4.1   The OFT will provide guidance to parties as to whether it considers the merger is/will be a relevant merger that may be referred to the CC for consideration.

8.4.2   The OFT provides guidance at a number of levels, from informal oral advice to statutory voluntary notification.

8.4.3   In order to provide advice and guidance, the parties to the merger/prospective merger must provide information to the OFT about the merger, including information on the parties and details of the affected markets both pre- and post-merger.

8.4.4   The guidance provided by the OFT is not binding and the OFT could still refer a transaction to the CC even if that decision runs contrary to the advice previously given to the parties. This is particularly the case if the advice is provided by the OFT before the merger has been made public as the OFT will have been unable to consider representations from potentially affected third parties, which may have a bearing on its decision.

8.4.5   The benefit of approaching the OFT for guidance pre-merger is that any problem can be identified at an early stage and dealt with at the start rather than the parties incurring costs and facing an order by the CC to undo the transaction and/or for one of the merged entities to divest part of its business.

8.4.6   If the matter is referred to the CC, the CC has 24 weeks (subject to a limited right of extension) from the date of the reference in which to give its report. If it identifies that there is a relevant merger that will substantially lessen competition in the UK, it will state its proposed remedies and may either accept undertakings from the parties or make an order setting the remedies. These can include:
- prohibiting the merger taking place;
- recommending disposing of the assets and/or acquired interests;
- controlling the conduct of the new company and keeping conduct under review, eg imposing a cap on price increases;
- allowing the merger but subject to conditions.

8.4.7   It may be preferable to the parties to a transaction that may be a relevant merger to make the transaction conditional upon approval of the CC, thereby ensuring that the parties do not incur the costs of unwinding a transaction if ordered to do so by the CC.

8.5 EC merger regime

8.5.1   Depending on the size of the merger, the transaction may be judged under the EC merger regime rather than the UK regime. See below.

EC MERGER REGIME

Typically, the EC merger regime will apply where:
- the combined worldwide turnover of the merging parties exceeds €5 billion; and
- the combined EU turnover of at least two of the merging parties exceeds €250 million;

unless
- each of the merging parties achieves two-thirds or more of its EC turnover in the same member state; or
- the combined turnover of the merging parties exceeds €2.5 billion;

and in each of at least three member states:
- the combined turnover of the merging parties is €100 million; and
- at least two of the merging parties has a turnover of more than €25 million;

and within the EU as a whole:
- at least two of the merging parties each has a combined turnover of more than €100 million;

unless
- each of the merging parties achieves more than two-thirds of the aggregate community turnover within one and the same member state.

8.5.2 If the above thresholds are achieved, the merger should be referred to the European Commission by the OFT and/or may be of interest to and investigated further by the European Commission.

8.5.3 Furthermore, if the merger has a community dimension the parties are under an obligation to notify the European Commission of the merger within one week of the agreement being concluded or the merger being announced, whichever is earlier.

8.5.4 As with the OFT, guidance can be sought from the European Commission pre-merger.

8.5.5 Even if the transaction does not meet the above thresholds and is therefore not classed as a merger with a community dimension, the merger may affect competition in individual member states. If so, the parties may have to deal with the competition authorities in each member state affected, which could be time consuming and costly, particularly as each member state will have its own tests as to what will affect competition and the effects of the transaction may be different in each state.

8.6 Ancillary restrictions

8.6.1 Transaction documentation often involves imposing restrictions on the parties' future conduct. Typically, the restrictions will include a non-compete clause imposed on the seller that prevents the seller from acting in the same field as the business being sold for a set period after completion. The purpose of such a restriction is to allow the purchaser to take full advantage of the business assets and/or goodwill it has purchased and allow it a period to establish itself in the market without facing competition from the seller, who could exploit existing trading relationships.

8.6.2 It will be more difficult to argue that restrictions imposed on the buyer are ancillary and necessary to the transaction.

8.6.3 If the restrictions are 'directly related to and necessary' for the implementation of the merger, these are generally excluded from consideration under the competition legislation. If they are not directly related to the merger and are not necessary in order to implement the merger, they will be judged under the normal competition legislation. In the UK, this will be the Competition Act 1998.

8.6.4 Restrictions are generally regarded as being ancillary if, without them, the transaction would not go ahead or would go ahead but at a higher cost. The scope of restrictions (geographic, product range and duration) must be proportionate to the achievement of the overall aim.

8.6.5 The European Commission has published guidance on what will be regarded as an ancillary restriction to a transaction, which is also followed by the OFT. These are listed below.

TYPES OF RESTRICTIONS ALLOWABLE AS ANCILLARY

- **Non-compete clauses imposed on the seller:** This is to ensure that the purchaser obtains the full benefit of the business and goodwill it has purchased. It will also catch non-solicitation of employees/customer clauses. As a rough guide, a three year duration is acceptable if there is a purchase of goodwill and know how, and a period of two years if only goodwill is involved.

- **Licence of intellectual property:** Where the seller is retaining IPR and/or know how which the purchaser may need in order to operate the purchased business, the seller will sometimes need to grant the purchaser a licence of the required intellectual property. This licence will normally contain restrictions on duration, scope and use.

- **Purchase and supply agreements:** These may be acceptable if purchases were previously made intra group and the agreements are intended to last until the purchaser has established the business. Exclusivity will rarely fall within an ancillary restriction, as it is unlikely to be necessary to implement the transaction.

8.6.6 The OFT can be consulted about whether a restriction is likely to be regarded as ancillary.

8.6.7 Any restriction that is not an ancillary restriction will be considered under the competition legislation.

CHAPTER	**Funding Issues**

9

9.1   Sources

9.1.1   Assuming that the purchaser cannot fund the consideration for the acquisition out of existing resources, it will need to obtain funding by one or more of the following methods:
- borrowing from a bank or other financial institution;
- equity funding, by the issue of shares in itself or in the new limited company (Newco);
- asset finance – using the assets of the purchaser and/or target to raise funding;
- offering deferred consideration to the vendor, which is then repaid out of the target's own cash generation or new funding obtained after completion;
- use of cash within the target.

9.1.2   This chapter will comment only briefly on these methods of funding, as each is a subject in its own right. Deferred consideration is dealt with in more detail in Chapter 11. The remainder of the chapter will concentrate on a particular issue encountered on most share purchases – financial assistance. Each funding method described above could give rise to approving and giving financial assistance.

9.2   Bank funding

9.2.1   Borrowings from a bank to fund an acquisition would typically comprise:
- a commercial mortgage over freehold or long leasehold property of the purchaser or the target, which simply means a term loan secured on that property;
- other term loan facilities, either repayable by instalments over a period of, say, two to five years or incorporating a 'bullet repayment' after a given time or on specified events;
- an overdraft facility, repayable on demand, often referred to as a 'working capital facility';
- other facilities which are geared to the needs of the purchaser and/or the target, such as a foreign exchange facility, a facility for the issue of letters

of credit to support import purchasing and a performance bond facility to support contracts with customers.

9.2.2 The bank would typically require security by one or more of the following methods:

- a debenture containing fixed and floating charges over all the purchaser's assets;

- in the case of a share purchase, or where the purchaser is a member of an existing group, a corporate guarantee from each group company in respect of the purchaser's obligations, supported by a debenture over each group company;

- a legal charge over freehold and leasehold properties, or the bank could rely upon a legal charge contained in the debenture;

- personal guarantees from individuals, principally the directors/shareholders of the purchaser, although this may be contentious and many acquisition finance transactions proceed without any personal guarantees;

- where personal guarantees are taken, potentially a charge over the home of the guarantor(s), although this will be even more contentious and would give require independent legal advice to be given to any person who is a joint owner of that home;

- insurance policies on the lives of key managers of the purchaser/target ('keyman policies'), assigned to the bank by way of security.

9.2.3 It was noted in Chapter 2 that acquisition finance is often 'cash flow lending', meaning that the bank is not fully secured on assets and relies upon cash generation from the target. The bank will nevertheless take security. The additional risk is reflected in interest rates and other terms of the funding. It will also be reflected in the bank's attention to due diligence issues; its need to see satisfactory financial commercial and legal due diligence reports are mentioned in Chapter 7. Given that the debt assumed by the purchaser on an acquisition can be very high, servicing costs (principally the interest payable) may pose quite a serious burden. Interest will usually be at a floating rate (a percentage margin over base rate or LIBOR – the London Inter Bank Offered Rate for deposits) and so the purchaser should consider protection against interest rate fluctuation. Often, the bank will offer hedging facilities: contracts taken out by the purchaser which have the effect of balancing out interest rate fluctuations. Some banks offer an interest management agreement. Under this arrangement, the bank's customer can 'purchase' a cap, which is the maximum interest rate payable. Likewise, the purchaser can 'sell' a collar, which sets a minimum rate of interest payable on a given loan.

9.2.4 An overdraft will always be repayable on demand, meaning that the bank can request repayment at any time. A term loan will usually provide for fixed instalments and/or a final repayment date. However, the bank will want the right to demand repayment earlier in certain circumstances. Under a typical acquisition finance loan agreement, the bank will have the right to demand immediate repayment in the following circumstances:

- breach of financial covenants, which are a set of ratios negotiated for each loan that must be satisfied at given times throughout the term of the loan;
- breach of other covenants, such as requirements to provide financial information to the bank or comply with laws;
- events of default, such as insolvency or failure to pay any amount of capital or interest on the loan (or, subject to limits, other indebtedness of the purchaser);
- other circumstances where the bank feels it would be at risk, such as a key manager of the purchaser leaving the company without suitable arrangements being in place to replace that manager.

The key elements of a typical set of financial covenants are set out below.

TYPICAL FINANCIAL COVENANTS

- **Test dates:** Specified dates during the term of the loan, when the covenants are tested and certified by the borrower to be satisfied. May be monthly, quarterly or yearly. Periods between test dates are referred to as test periods.
- **Net assets**: The value of share capital and reserves (which includes the profit and loss account and share premium account but would usually exclude revaluation reserves and any value attributable to intangible assets such as goodwill) not to fall below a stated figure at any time during the term of the loan. The test may provide for increasing figures for net assets, effectively meaning that the purchaser must continue to generate profits.
- **Gearing:** The ratio of the purchaser's borrowings (from all parties, not just the bank) to net assets, not to exceed set levels at each test date.
- **Asset cover:** The ratio of the purchaser's total asset value (or potentially just current assets) to the purchaser's borrowings, not to fall below set levels at each test date.
- **Senior interest cover:** The ratio of the purchaser's profits before interest and taxation (and usually before depreciation and amortisation of goodwill) for each test period as compared with interest on the bank's lending in that period, not to fall below certain levels for each test date. This ensures interest is being matched by profit generation.
- **Debt cover:** The ratio of the purchaser's borrowings (as above) to its profits (as above) not to exceed certain levels for each test date.
- **Cash flow cover:** This is quite complex but attempts to compare cash generation with interest payable for each test period. Cash generation may be defined as profits before interest and tax plus or minus movements in working capital, less tax paid and capital expenditure incurred and then adjusted to take into account exceptional or extraordinary items.

9.2.5   The term loan agreement will also include warranties. These will relate to the affairs of the purchaser and the target and may include a warranty that the purchaser is satisfied with the due diligence reports and the warranties given by the vendor. Since these warranties are given by the company (and not usually by any of its managers) the only effective remedy for the bank is to treat the breach of warranty as an event of default and demand repayment of the loan.

9.2.6 Given the many rights to accelerate loan repayment (particularly for breach of the financial covenants, which are quite commonly broken at some point in the loan period), a term loan may effectively be an on demand facility. Indeed, where the bank also provides an overdraft facility and the loan contains a 'cross default' clause allowing it to demand repayment if any obligation of the bank remains outstanding, the bank could simply demand the overdraft and then immediately call this a cross default and demand repayment of the term loan. Assuming the purchaser is not able to repay the loan in full, the bank's choice would be to appoint a receiver under its security. The real protection for the purchaser is that the bank is unlikely to follow this course unless it has totally lost faith in the management of the business or its prospects of survival. On a cash flow lending transaction, the bank is unlikely to recoup the target's borrowings through its security and so appointment of a receiver is very much a last resort.

9.3 Equity funding

9.3.1 A trade buyer will usually fund acquisitions by using existing cash resources or borrowings from a bank or other group members. The issue of shares will usually only be a major part of the acquisition funding in the following cases:
- acquisitions by publicly quoted companies, referred to in Chapter 13;
- management buy-outs (MBOs) and other buy-outs funded by venture capitalists (VCs);
- subsequent acquisitions by a VC – backed buy-out (known as a follow-on investment).

9.3.2 The majority of funding provided by a VC is likely to be in the form of a loan with only a small amount being subscribed for shares. However, the loan from the VC, often called an institutional loan, will be on very different terms from bank borrowings in that:
- repayment usually starts after two to three years;
- the loan will often be unsecured;
- even if secured, it would be subordinated (see below) to the bank;
- interest may be 'rolled up' until final payment or may commence only after a given period.

9.3.3 The concept is that this loan is 'quasi-equity', which carries a far greater risk than the 'senior debt' provided by the bank.

9.3.4 In return for providing this beneficial lending, the VC will expect preferential rights attaching to its shares in Newco. These share rights may include:
- a fixed annual dividend payable before any dividends are payable on other shares;
- a participating dividend, which means that the amount of the dividend is based on the profitability of Newco and its subsidiaries (for example, 5 per cent of annual profits to be declared as a dividend just on the VC shares);

- the right to appoint directors and potentially a chairman with a casting vote;
- swamping rights, which give voting control at board level and shareholder level in certain events such as failure to pay dividends or failure to repay the loan provided by the VC, when due.

9.3.5   These share rights will be included in Newco's articles. The VC will also stipulate a form of subscription agreement, under which the VC investment is made. This is in effect a shareholders' agreement and many of the points made in Chapter 2 apply equally to it. Some of the characteristics typically found in a VC subscription agreement and VC articles are set out below.

OVERVIEW OF VC SUBSCRIPTION AGREEMENT

Conditions precedent	■ Matters to be dealt with before the subscription is completed. ■ Includes completion of the acquisition and availability of the bank facilities, in each case on terms satisfactory to the VC. ■ Requires delivery of appropriate due diligence reports.
Subscription	■ VC and managers agree to subscribe for shares on the agreed basis. ■ VC agrees to make loan to Newco (the terms of which are likely to be in a separate loan note instrument). ■ Arrangements for subscription of those shares, including passing of shareholder resolutions to authorise the allotment.
Warranties	■ Given by Newco and the managers to the VC. ■ Relate to the proper establishment of Newco as an 'untraded' company and acquisition of the target. ■ Managers will also give warranties about their personal affairs. ■ Subject to specific limitations.
Investor consents	■ As for any shareholders' agreement, there will be a list of reserved matters that require special approval by a specified majority of the shareholders. ■ The VC will want a veto on all of such matters. ■ These will cover a wide range of decisions, including changes to the share capital, unbudgeted expenditure and increases to managers' remuneration.
Covenants	■ Restrictions on the managers being involved in any other business activities whilst a director of Newco. ■ Restrictive covenants on the managers after they cease to be directors or employees (also included in employment agreements).
Appointment of directors	■ VC would have rights to appoint at least one director and possibly also a chairman or chairwoman. ■ Set frequency of meetings to ensure VC remains involved in management decisions.

Fees	■ VC will usually levy an arrangement fee and obtain reimbursement from Newco of all legal costs, due diligence costs and expenses of the investment.
	■ VC will usually charge an ongoing monitoring fee.
Exit	■ The agreement may state an intention to seek sale or flotation after a given period.
	■ Agreement may clarify that VCs will not give warranties on a sale of shares (other than as to title to their shares).
General	■ Both parties to agree any announcements (although the VC will usually want to publicise the investment).
	■ Both parties agree confidentiality.
	■ VC will want the right to assign the benefit of the agreement (including warranties) to another member of its group or another VC.
VC articles	■ Articles may require shareholder approval for reserved matters in order to 'back up' the subscription agreement.
Ratchets	■ Balance the respective interests of the VC and the managers according to performance.
	■ Change the percentage split of consideration, depending on valuation on exit.
Quorum	■ VC-appointed director to be present at each board meeting for it to be valid.
Swamping rights	■ Where there is default (for example, on loan payments) or poor financial performance, VC shares can 'outvote' managers' shares.

9.3.6   The above list refers to warranties being given by individual managers. These are addressed both to Newco and to the VC. A claim against the company in which the VC has invested or even against the managers and co-shareholders would indicate a very serious breakdown in the relationship. The VCs will usually state that they intend these warranties as a 'last resort' and that they are really designed to cover very serious situations, such as where the VC has been intentionally misled or fraud has occurred. The warranties are intended to concentrate the minds of management on key issues in the acquisition and to ensure that they have responsibility for key information on which the VC relies. That key information is reflected in the subject matter of the warranties; some key areas that differ from normal acquisition warranties are set out below.

VC WARRANTIES

| Personal interests | ■ No other business activities. |
| | ■ No contracts or arrangements with Newco or the target that have not been disclosed and approved. |

Business plan	■ Factual statements in the business plan are true and accurate.
	■ As far as the managers are aware, the business plan does not omit any factual matters that make it misleading.
	■ Business plan has been carefully prepared.
	■ The forecasts and projections are based on reasonable assumptions.
	■ The opinions in the business plan are reasonably and honestly held by the managers.
Due diligence reports	■ All factual statements in the due diligence reports are true and accurate.
	■ Opinions included in those reports are reasonable and, where they are attributed to the managers, are honestly held by the managers.
Venture capital trust (VCT) provisions (where the VC is a VCT)	■ Newco and its group will carry on 'qualifying trades' and will have no other significant activities.
	■ There are no companies controlled by Newco which are not 'qualifying subsidiaries'.
	■ Newco and its subsidiaries will comply with relevant provisions of the tax legislation to ensure the investment remains VCT qualified.
Target	■ The managers are not aware of any breach of the warranties given by the vendor.
Newco	■ Newco has never traded and has only issued the shares and entered into the obligations referred to in the subscription agreement.

9.3.7 Managers will take these personal warranties very seriously and will seek to negotiate limitations on them. These limitations are similar to those requested by a vendor on a share sale. Sample document 11 (page 234) gives an example of warranty limitations. The key difference will be that the maximum liability of each manager to the VC will usually be set at a much lower level, often based on one or two years' salary payable to the manager by Newco. The concept (albeit not very scientific, given that that salary will have borne tax and reflected executive responsibilities) is that the manager should not benefit from the company if the VC has been deprived of any benefit through breach of warranty.

9.3.8 As an alternative or perhaps in addition to an institutional loan, the VC may invest in preference shares in Newco. The rights attaching to preference shares are not standard and need to be negotiated for each situation; they have some of the attributes of a loan and some attributes of shares. For example:

- preference shares usually carry a fixed rate of return (equivalent to inter- est) but this is payable as a dividend and therefore depends on the com- pany having available distributable profits;
- preference shares will often be redeemable in fixed amounts (equivalent to repayment of a loan), but redemption will similarly be subject to the company having available distributable profits, and the holder of prefer- ence shares cannot sue for failure to redeem if those profits do not exist;
- preference shares do not usually have any voting rights, but they may acquire rights to vote when there is a failure to pay dividends or redeem shares and this may even give the preference shareholders control of the company (which is equivalent to a secured lender appointing a receiver).

9.3.9   The investment in shares of Newco by the managers (and any subscription for shares by a proposed director or employee) will be subject to a potential charge to income tax under Sch.22 FA 2003. This charge relates to any ben- efit from shares acquired 'by reason of employment' and is dealt with in more detail in paragraph 2.7. This applies in particular where the articles of Newco contain ratchet provisions to balance the interests of the VC and management on an exit. This has been addressed by the memorandum agreed between the IR and the British Venture Capital Association, as referred to in paragraph 2.7.13.

9.3.10   A tax issue will also arise for the VC if it is investing through a VCT. Investments by VCTs must predominately be in non-controlling invest- ments in unquoted companies. Newco must carry on qualifying trades and thus these conditions will be the subject of warranties and other obligations in the subscription agreement.

9.4   Asset funding

9.4.1   During the last few years, using asset funding to finance acquisitions has greatly increased, both in terms of profile and the size of transactions dealt with. This has to a certain extent been caused by:
- court decisions that clearing banks can only take a fixed charge on book debts in very limited circumstances, which has meant that the banks are far less likely to make loans on the strength of book debts;
- VCs' reluctance to invest in smaller MBOs.

9.4.2   Book debt finance provided by asset funders basically comprises invoice dis- counting or invoice factoring. Under these arrangements debts and their proceeds belong to the funder rather than the company and the funder is therefore relying upon ownership rather than a charge over the debts. This enables the asset funder to lend effectively against debts. Since the dis- counter/factor will have greater control over the collection of debts (even though in the case of confidential invoice discounting, the debtor ledger remains managed by the company itself), there is also a better chance of the asset funder recovering a higher proportion of the debts it has purchased. This enables significant funding lines to be available.

9.4.3 Asset funders will provide facilities against stock, plant and equipment and commercial mortgages over property. The terms of these facilities are beyond the scope of this book, but it should be noted that they are a common source of finance for acquisitions.

9.5 Deferred consideration

9.5.1 Issues surrounding deferred consideration or 'earn-outs' are dealt with in Chapter 11. Often, the purpose is to ensure that the payment of consideration is dependent on future financial performance but the effect is nevertheless to defer payment of part of the price to the vendor until a later stage. It can thus be looked at as part of the funding of the transaction.

9.5.2 Where venture capital funding is not available (for example on smaller buy-outs) and bank and asset funding would not be sufficient to match the vendor's price expectation, the vendor often stands in the place of a VC by allowing part of the consideration to remain outstanding without security or with security ranking behind the senior debt. In the case of an MBO, this gives rise to the expression 'vendor-assisted buy-out'.

9.5.3 Following the analogy, the vendor may require similar rights to those a VC would want, including:
- a commercial rate of interest for an unsecured loan;
- a veto on certain management decisions, including increases to managers' remuneration;
- possibly, equity participation in Newco in the form of 'consideration shares', which give the vendors a potential equity return;
- in some cases, the right to take back control of the target in the case of default, which is similar to a VC's swamping rights.

9.5.4 For tax reasons, a vendor will usually require deferred consideration to be payable under the terms of a loan note in a format that will qualify as a corporate bond. In broad terms, this permits deferment of the payment of capital gains tax (CGT) on that element of the consideration unless and until the loan note is redeemed.

9.6 Intercreditor agreement

9.6.1 This document regulates the rights of Newco's main creditors, which, as stated above, can include a bank, a VC providing an institutional loan, asset funders and the vendor. It has been noted that asset funders rely principally on ownership of assets rather than security, but they would be brought in as a party to an intercreditor agreement. They would in any event require a waiver of the bank's charge over book debts.

9.6.2 An intercreditor agreement deals separately with the various rights which the creditors have against Newco. Those rights are summarised below.

CREDITORS' RIGHTS

Priority
- Each lender with security may have charges over the same assets.
- The ranking of priorities deals with the order of priority of those charges in the case of an insolvent winding up.
- This ranking sets the order in which those secured creditors would be paid out of the assets covered by their security.

Enforcement
- Secured creditors will have the right to enforce their security, principally by the appointment of a receiver.
- If one secured creditor appoints a receiver, effectively the other secured creditors would also be obliged to take action, which may be disadvantageous to them (for example because they have a better prospect of full return of indebtedness if the company carries on trading).
- One secured creditor may wish to impose restrictions on the others enforcing their security.

Subordination
- All creditors have the prima facie right to sue for indebtedness that has become due and payable.
- A creditor with no security or security ranking behind the senior lender may be able to recover its indebtedness before the senior debt has been repaid, for example by the borrower making a voluntary repayment or being subject to a set-off.
- Subordination represents the senior lendor restricting recovery of other indebtedness before the senior debt.

9.6.3   An intercreditor agreement may deal with some or all of these rights, and may therefore be called a deed of priorities or a subordination deed. Each transaction is different but an MBO with multiple funders would typically include the following provisions:
- Only the bank and the asset funder are permitted to take any security over the assets of Newco and its group.
- The asset funder security has priority over the bank in respect of debts.
- The bank's security has priority over all other assets.
- The bank regards itself as the senior lender and thus imposes limited restrictions on enforcement on the asset funder, to the effect that the asset funder cannot appoint a receiver without the bank's consent or until a given period of notice is given (known as a standstill), except for the limited purpose of collecting the debts.
- The VC is subject to subordination in favour of the bank and the asset funder, in that no repayments of its institutional loan can be made before the due dates for payment of that loan or at any time when there is an outstanding event in default under the bank's loan agreement.
- The vendor is subject to similar subordination rights, in respect of the deferred consideration.

9.7 Financial assistance

9.7.1 It will be seen from the above that funding of share acquisitions, particularly MBOs, involves using the target's assets to assist with funding the transaction. To do this will usually involve the target and/or the target's subsidiaries giving financial assistance for the purposes of the acquisition of its own shares, which is unlawful under the Companies Act 1985 (CA). Giving unlawful financial assistance carries serious consequences for all parties and their advisors, which could be summarised as follows:

- the target and any subsidiary of the target that gives assistance has committed a criminal offence punishable by a fine;
- each of their officers who is in default has committed a criminal offence punishable by imprisonment, a fine or both;
- transactions created through the unlawful assistance will be void, so that security granted to a bank may be unenforceable and monies paid out to the vendor through an unlawful loan may be repayable;
- advisors involved in the transaction may be found to have been negligent and may even be involved in a criminal conspiracy, which would make them criminally liable and potentially void their professional indemnity insurance cover.

Thus, the importance of the issue cannot be overstated. In corporate transactions, the consideration of whether financial assistance exists will receive careful consideration, as will the procedures to approve it.

9.7.2 In any given transaction, there are a number of ways in which unlawful financial assistance can arise. The following methods by which financial assistance can be given for the purposes of the acquisition are set out in s.152 CA:

- gift (includes the transfer of an asset at less than its market value);
- guarantee, security or indemnity (includes any form of security a funder is likely to require) or a release or waiver (includes the target forgiving a debt to the vendor);
- loan or the assignment of rights arising under a loan (includes 'extraction' of cash in the target by a loan to the purchaser);
- an agreement under which the obligations of the target are to be fulfilled at a time when the other parties' obligations remain unfulfilled (for example, the provision of credit);
- any other financial assistance given by a company which has no net assets or whereby the net assets of that company are thereby reduced to a material extent (for example, payment of expenses of the transaction by the target).

9.7.3 Financial assistance can also be given post-acquisition where it would reduce or discharge an obligation incurred in relation to the purchase of shares. An example would be a post-completion transfer of the target's business to the purchaser (known as a 'hive-up'), where the profits of that business are then available to the purchaser to repay acquisition funding.

9.7.4 The general prohibition on a company giving financial assistance for the purpose of the acquisition of its own shares is contained in s.151 CA, but it is also a longstanding principle of company law. The rationale for that principle is creditor protection. If a company assists a third party to buy its shares, that may be for the benefit of the shareholders, but whatever is given away by the company is not then available to creditors. It would be unfair if the shareholders, who enjoy limited liability status, could benefit from that assistance without ensuring that creditors will be paid.

9.7.5 Thus, the exceptions to the general prohibition on financial assistance are concerned with ensuring creditors' interests are met. Examination of all the exemptions is beyond the scope of this book but two are highlighted below:

- the payment of a dividend which is lawfully made in accordance with CA and the general law;
- financial assistance given by a private company as approved under s.155 CA, known as a 'whitewash' (see 9.9).

9.8 Dividends

9.8.1 It is logical that dividends are not caught by the prohibition on financial assistance as they can only lawfully be made out of distributable profits. Thus, the shareholders would in any event be entitled to extract the cash as dividends. Distributable profits are defined in s.263 CA and basically mean a company's accumulated realised profits (less its realised losses) so far as these have not been previously distributed. These profits must be justified by reference to accounts satisfying s.270 CA. This primarily means the last annual accounts, prepared in accordance with CA and presented to the shareholders in a general meeting (although not necessarily filed at Companies House). If the company has not yet prepared those accounts or if they show insufficient distributable profits, the company can justify the dividend by reference to 'interim accounts'. This can mean unaudited management accounts, but must be sufficient to 'enable a reasonable judgement to be made' by the directors as to the company's profits, losses, assets and liabilities, any provisions to be made in those accounts and the amount of its share capital and reserves.

9.8.2 Therefore, under statute a company can pay a dividend if its last statutory accounts show sufficient profits, even if it has made losses since the date of those accounts. If however the last statutory accounts show insufficient profits, it can rely on management accounts if these are to a satisfactory standard.

9.8.3 In addition to these statutory tests, there is also a test under the general law (as developed by the courts) to say that the directors should not declare a dividend imprudently. What this means in practice is that sufficient distributable profits on paper should not entitle the directors to pay out a dividend if it would harm the company's ability to meet its commitments to creditors or where it is insolvent.

9.8.4   If these tests are satisfied, dividends could be a very useful tool in providing unlawful financial assistance by the extraction of cash from the target. If the company holds cash at completion, the vendors may choose to sell their shares with the cash retained by the company rather than by distributing the cash to themselves, for the simple reason that the consideration for their shares will be subject to CGT, usually with the benefit of taper relief, reducing the effective rate of tax to 10 per cent. Thus the effective rate of tax is lower than if they had received the cash as a dividend. Note however that taper relief may be denied if the company has undistributed cash that the Inland Revenue claims to be in excess of its requirements to continue trade so as to constitute a non-trade asset (see paragraph 4.3.6). Where the purchaser 'inherits' cash, it can be utilised to fund part of the purchase price, by a tax neutral intra group dividend paid from the target company to Newco.

9.9   Whitewash

9.9.1   The procedure for approving financial assistance, referred to as a 'whitewash', will form a major part of the arrangements to complete the acquisition. The basic conditions for applying this procedure are:

- the company to be acquired and the company giving the assistance (for example its subsidiary and any intermediate holding company) must be private rather than public companies;
- each company giving assistance must have net assets, in other words it must not have an insolvent balance sheet at the point when the assistance is given;
- the net assets of that company must not be reduced by the assistance or, to the extent they are reduced, the assistance must be provided out of distributable profits.

One of the effects of the above conditions is that any bank taking security over the target will invariably require a report from the target's auditors to the effect that the company has net assets. This report will rely in part on confirmation from the target's directors that this is the case. The form of the report is standard, set by the Institute of Chartered Accountants in England and Wales – see sample document 21 (page 266).

9.9.2   The basic steps for approving the financial assistance are set out in the table below. As regards the special resolutions required, these may be passed by written resolution. Since there is a time delay of four weeks (see next page) if not all the shareholders pass the special resolution, the written resolution procedure would appear to be best. Even though the share capital of the target may be acquired by the purchaser immediately prior to the giving of assistance, the share transfers will not usually have been stamped so the purchaser will not be registered as the sole shareholder of the target. For this reason, the view is usually taken that the target is not a wholly owned subsidiary, and therefore special resolutions are required.

WHITEWASH STEPS

■ Assistance must be approved by special resolution of the company giving the assistance, unless that company is a wholly owned subsidiary.

■ Assistance given by a subsidiary of the target must be approved by special resolution of the target.

■ The directors of each company giving the assistance and each holding company of that company must make a statutory declaration in a prescribed form including their opinion that the company is solvent and will remain so for the next 12 months.

■ The company's auditors must give a statutory form of report in support of the directors' statutory declaration.

■ The statutory declaration and auditors' report must be delivered to the Registrar of Companies with the special resolutions referred to within 15 days of making the declaration.

■ The assistance must be given within eight weeks following the above steps (and unless the special resolutions were passed by all shareholders must not be given until four weeks after the special resolution is passed).

9.9.3   The statutory declaration is in a prescribed form (see sample document 22, page 268) containing details of the assistance being given and certain other particulars relating to the target company. Only those with experience in this field should prepare or advise about this declaration. However, the crux of the declaration is a statement from the directors that they have formed the reasonable opinion that:

■ there is no ground on which the company could then be found to be unable to pay its debts immediately following the giving of the assistance; and

■ if it is intended to wind up the company within 12 months, the company will be able to pay its debts in full within 12 months of the winding up; or

■ if it is not intended to wind up the company within 12 months, the company will be able to pay its debts as they fall due during the year immediately following the giving of assistance.

9.9.4   In making this declaration, the directors must take into account all actual, contingent and prospective liabilities of the company.

9.9.5   The opinion of the directors expressed in a declaration must be made on reasonable grounds. This will require them to take steps to ensure that the opinion is correct, which will usually involve:

■ acquainting themselves with the target's financial affairs, for which purpose the due diligence exercise will be vital;

■ preparing profit and cash flow projections for at least the following year (and usually for a longer period) to satisfy themselves that the company will be able to service its obligations, including the additional interest and capital costs of the acquisition funding;

■ giving proper consideration to the assumptions underlying their projections and any factors that might affect those assumptions.

9.9.6   The auditors' statutory report states that:
- they have enquired into the state of affairs of the company giving assistance;
- they are not aware of anything to indicate the opinion expressed by the directors in the declaration is unreasonable in all the circumstances.

The report therefore backs up the directors' declaration. To give this report, the auditors will carry out certain tests, with particular regard to cash recourses and creditors and a review of the directors' projections and assumptions.

9.9.7   The whitewash procedure obviously involves the directors in serious responsibilities. It is the duty of the advisors to explain those and put them into context.

CHAPTER 10

Employees

10.1 Overview

10.1.1 This chapter deals with the following employee issues arising on acquisitions:
- due diligence;
- transfer of obligations under TUPE;
- the duties to inform and consult with employees;
- warranties and indemnities.

10.1.2 The provisions of TUPE do not apply on a share sale (because the employees will simply remain employed by the target). Accordingly, there is no duty to inform and consult with employees prior to a share sale. However, if there are planned redundancies, this could give rise to separate duties to inform and consult. In particular where 20 or more employees are to be made redundant, known as a 'collective redundancy' situation, statutory duties to consult arise. The basic duties in this case would be:
- consultation to begin at least 30 days before the redundancies take effect, where 20 or more employees are affected;
- consultation to begin at lease 90 days before the redundancies take effect, where 100 or more employees are affected.

10.1.3 The table below sets out a basic description of key concepts of employment law, as referred to in this chapter.

EMPLOYMENT LAW CONCEPTS	
Unfair dismissal	■ A statutory right to compensation (or reinstatement), under the Employment Rights Act 1996.
	■ Arises where dismissal is not for a fair reason or where the procedure was unreasonable.
	■ Compensation made up of a basic award, plus a compensatory award of up to £55,000.
	■ Employee must have one year's continuity of employment.
Fair reasons	■ Misconduct (not necessarily gross misconduct).
	■ Incapability (to carry out the employment duties).

- Redundancy (although unfair selection or unreasonable implementation could make the redundancy unfair).
- Inability to comply with legal requirements (for example, a driver losing his or her licence).
- Some other substantial reason justifying dismissal.

Basic award
- Number of years' service x weekly pay.
- 1$\frac{1}{2}$ weeks' pay is used in the calculation for periods where the employee is aged 41 to 64 and only $\frac{1}{2}$ a week's pay is used where the employee is aged 18 to 21.
- Maximum 20 years' service used in calculation.
- Maximum weekly pay used in the calculation is currently £270.

Continuity of employment
- The employee's length of service, as preserved by TUPE.
- This includes employment with the current employer and any previous owner of the business.

Redundancy
- Exists where the employer has ceased to carry on business (whether altogether or in that particular place) or where the employer's requirements for employees to carry out work of a particular kind have ceased or diminished.
- Gives rise to the right to a statutory redundancy payment where the employee has at least two years' continuity of employment.
- Statutory compensation is calculated on the same basis as the basic award for unfair dismissal.
- Rights under the employment contract or collective agreements may enhance this right.

Collective agreement
- An agreement reached with a representative body (such as a trade union) that relates to a particular group of employees.

Wrongful dismissal
- Contractual right to damages for termination of employment with insufficient notice.
- Damages will relate to the notice entitlement or 'reasonable notice' where no express notice period has been agreed.
- No claim can be made where summary dismissal was justified.

10.2 Due diligence

10.2.1 On a share purchase or a business purchase, the first concern of the purchaser will be to obtain accurate and up to date information on the employees, covering:
- names and job functions;
- commencement dates (to include any prior related employment so that the purchaser can calculate continuity of employment);
- dates of birth (which enables the purchaser to calculate redundancy entitlements, see 'Employment law concepts', above);

- hours of work;
- wages/salaries together with any bonus, commission etc;
- benefits in kind, including pension rights.

10.2.2 The vendor should be aware of the obligations to employees under the Data Protection Act 1998 not to disclose information to the purchaser which is classified as 'personal data': for example information that may lead to the individual being identified, such as name, address and telephone number and/or 'sensitive data', for example information that may reveal their membership of a trade union, religion or sexual orientation. It is therefore recommended that vendors do not disclose the names of employees, and provide 'sanitised' data.

10.2.3 The schedule of employees needs to be kept up to date as the transaction progresses. The final schedule should be warranted as accurate and would usually be appended to the business purchase agreement or the disclosure letter. Care should be taken to identify and include all employees who work in the target business, some of whom, for example, may be employed by other group companies.

10.2.4 The purchaser will also seek details of other persons who could or should be regarded as employees. These will include self-employed consultants who are engaged wholly or predominantly in the target business. Also, casual workers or homeworkers may have the right to be treated as employees.

10.2.5 Due diligence should also investigate claims made by present or former employees, such as:
- applications to the Employment Tribunal in respect of unfair dismissal;
- claims for wrongful dismissal or other contractual matters;
- claims for injuries suffered at work;
- disputes with employees, strikes and other threats of industrial action.

10.2.6 In the case of a share purchase, liability for these claims will remain with the target. Thus the purchaser is concerned with all claims and disputes whether relating to present or former employees. On a business sale, the purchaser will assume responsibility for all current employees at completion, so historic claims by former employees are of relevance only to the extent that they indicate ongoing problems. For this purpose however, current employees include any person who would have been employed in the business if they had not been unfairly dismissed for a reason connected with the transfer. In other words, the purchaser could be liable under TUPE for an industrial injury suffered by an employee who is not on the schedule of transferring employees but is dismissed by the vendor for a reason connected with the business sale.

10.3 TUPE

10.3.1 The TUPE regulations preserve employees' terms and conditions on a 'relevant transfer' to a new employer. Any provision of any agreement is void if it would exclude or limit the rights granted under the regulations. This brings into question the enforceability of the compromise agreements in some situations.

10.3.2 Employees employed by the vendor when the business changes hands will automatically become employees of the purchaser on the same terms and conditions. Continuity of employment is preserved, as are the terms and conditions of employment under their contract of employment (except for certain occupational pension rights).

10.3.3 The representatives of employees who are affected have a right to be informed about the transfer. They must also be consulted about any measures which the old or new employer envisages taking concerning affected employees.

10.3.4 The table below summarises the key provisions of the regulations and provides further commentary.

KEY TUPE REGULATIONS

Regulation 3	▪ Definition of relevant transfer: Article 1 of the Acquired Rights Directive (due to be implemented in the UK in 2004) provides a definition based on 'transfer of an economic entity which retains its identity'.
Regulation 5	▪ The rights, powers, duties and liabilities of the transferor employer pass to the transferee on a relevant transfer. ▪ No variation to terms and conditions is allowed which is to the detriment of the employee for a reason connected with the transfer.
Regulation 7	▪ Rights under occupational pension schemes are excluded from the transfer (but not that the 'pensions promise' may bind the transferee employer).
Regulation 8	▪ An employee is unfairly dismissed if the transfer, or a reason connected with it, is the reason or principal reason for the dismissal. This is subject to the ETO defence.
Regulation 10	▪ The duty to inform and consult with all classes of affected employees (which may include retained employees of the vendor or existing employees of the purchaser) prior to the transfer.
Regulation 11	▪ Failure to inform and consult gives the affected employees the right to make a claim to the Employment Tribunal within three months of the transfer. The maximum award is 13 weeks' pay.
Regulation 12	▪ Attempts to contract out of TUPE are void.

10.4 Relevant transfer

10.4.1 TUPE applies to the sale or transfer of a business, including transfer of part of a business, sales by receivers or administrators and transfers between group companies. The regulations are also capable of applying to a number of other transactions such as certain 'outsourcing' arrangements, but these are beyond the scope of this book. As noted above, TUPE does not currently apply on the sale of shares in a company.

10.4.2 A simplified explanation of a relevant transfer is the transfer of an economic entity from one person to another. The Acquired Rights Directive adopted by the EC member states in June 1998 defines a transfer as:

'a transfer of an economic entity which retains its identity, meaning an organised grouping of resources which have the object of pursuing an economic activity, whether or not that activity is central or ancillary.'

10.4.3 There has been a significant amount of litigation concerning this within both the UK and other EC member states. It has been found, for example, that the sale of equipment only would not be covered, but where there will in fact be a continuation of the activities of a business using that equipment (whether or not the contract reflects this), TUPE is likely to apply. It will also apply where the transaction is framed as a transfer of assets only with an intention to avoid the regulations. In short, this is a difficult area, where the particular circumstances of the transaction need to be looked at by employment law specialists. Suffice to say that business sales of the type covered by this book will almost certainly be covered by the TUPE regulations.

10.5 Effect of TUPE

10.5.1 When a relevant transfer takes place, the purchaser is deemed to replace the vendor for most legal purposes. The employee and the contract of employment for that employee pass from the vendor to the purchaser by operation of law and not by virtue of any agreements between them.

10.5.2 The contract of employment passes from the vendor to the purchaser as though the employee was always employed by the purchaser. In other words, continuity of employment is preserved. Rights under collective agreements are also liable to transfer, since they are effectively part of the contract of employment.

10.5.3 Occupational pensions do not transfer to the purchaser, because the regulations specifically exclude them. However, this exclusion has been the subject of significant debate and litigation and can be confusing. Certainly, the structure of an occupational pension scheme (for example the rights and obligations under a trust deed) does not automatically transfer to the purchaser. However, where the right to be a member of a scheme or the legitimate expectation to a certain level of benefit have become part of the contract of employment, these rights will become binding on the purchaser in the usual way. This is sometimes referred to as the 'pensions promise'. Whether that has become part of the contract of employment needs to be determined by reference to any written contract and any communication with the employee about pension rights.

10.5.4 Note that arrangements for personal pensions, permanent health insurance (PHI) schemes and stakeholder pensions are liable to transfer to the purchaser.

10.5.5 If a contractual term transfers under TUPE, it effectively becomes a fixed feature between the employee and the purchaser, except where the terms cannot easily be duplicated, such as car parking spaces, canteen facilities or share option rights. In that case, it will be a matter of reasonably reflecting changes to terms of employment in accordance with the usual employment law principles.

10.5.6 The purchaser takes over contracts of employment of all employees who were employed in the business immediately before the transfer or who would have been so employed if they had not been unfairly dismissed for a reason connected with the transfer. Thus, employees who are dismissed in contemplation of the sale may actually become employees of the purchaser.

10.5.7 If the business maintains an identity distinct from any existing business of the purchaser, the purchaser would be considered to recognise any independent trade union in respect of employees transferred to the same extent that it was recognised by the vendors. If the business does not keep its separate identity, the previous trade union recognition lapses; it will then be up to the union and the purchaser to renegotiate recognition.

10.6 Dismissals

10.6.1 Neither the purchaser nor the vendor can dismiss an employee because of the transfer or for a reason connected with the transfer, unless the reason for the dismissal is an economic, technical or organisational (ETO) reason entailing changes in the workforce. The ETO defence is described below. If there is an ETO reason and it is the cause or main cause of the dismissal, the dismissal will be fair provided an Employment Tribunal decides the employer acted reasonably in the circumstances in treating that reason as sufficient to justify dismissal. The classic example would be a redundancy situation, as long as this is a true redundancy. Accordingly, swapping new employees for the existing employees will not enable the purchaser to rely on the ETO defence. If there is a redundancy situation, the usual redundancy principles and procedures will apply.

ETO DEFENCE

- Any dismissal for a reason connected with the transfer will be automatically unfair unless it is for an 'economic, technical or organisational reason involving changes in the workforce'.
- Dismissal in connection with the reorganisation carried out prior to completion with a view to obtaining a better price will not be for an ETO reason, so will be automatically unfair.
- Redundancy, for example reducing the number of employees to save costs, can be an ETO reason.

- Reducing salaries or making other changes to terms of employment in order to reduce costs will not be an ETO reason because it does not involve 'changes in the workforce' and so an employee who refuses to accept those changes may be unfairly dismissed.
- Where an employee is properly and fairly dismissed for an ETO reason by the vendor and then re-employed by the purchaser on new terms, this can be perfectly acceptable (the key issue being a genuine dismissal for an ETO reason which is not connected to the transfer).
- To rely on the ETO defence, the employer must have acted reasonably in the circumstances in treating that reason as sufficient to justify dismissal.
- If there is a redundancy situation, the usual redundancy procedures will apply.

10.6.2 Where a reorganisation is planned, the most reliable solution in practice will be for all employees to be transferred to the purchaser who then carries out any reorganisation following the transfer. Dismissals after completion will need to be within the ETO defence if they are for a reason connected with the transfer, and planned redundancies will give rise to the duty to consult referred to below. The purchaser may however have no fixed intention to make dismissals and may decide to 'wait and see' what, if any, reorganisation is needed after a period of consolidation. In that case, the reorganisation may fall within the usual employment law rules.

10.6.3 It has been noted that genuine redundancies or the need to reduce the number of employees can constitute an ETO reason. Lack of appropriate skills or inability to adapt to new methods of working can constitute a technical reason for an ETO. A reduced combined workforce may give rise to an organisational reason for an ETO.

10.6.4 If an affected employee is dismissed for an ETO reason or accepts voluntary redundancy, there should be a compromise agreement wherever possible. This will help to reduce the risk of claims although it may be argued that this is an attempt to contract out of TUPE, which is prohibited under Regulation 12. This is an agreement between the employer and the employee confirming any terms of settlement. Because the agreement acts to exclude the rights of the employee to make a claim to an Employment Tribunal, the employee must receive independent legal advice on the agreement and the employee's lawyer would provide written confirmation that this advice has been given. Where the compromise agreement is entered into at, or shortly before or after completion it needs to be appropriately drafted to ensure the vendor and the purchaser have the benefit of it.

10.6.5 In considering whether an ETO reason exists (and also for the purposes of the duties to inform and consult referred to below) the parties should consider the purchaser's existing employees as well as the transferring employees. They are included in the employees affected by the transfer.

10.6.6 It will be clear from the above that changes to the contractual terms of transferred employees cannot be made unless there are ETO reasons. Harmonisation of the two workforces is not an ETO reason unless it is in connection with non-financial changes such as hours of work and places of work. The vendor can only make financial changes if they are for reasons not connected with the transfer. This will be difficult for the vendor to show if a sale is being negotiated or is contemplated. A causal link between the transfer and any change will remain unless there is an intervening act that breaks the link such as market forces or loss of a major customer.

10.6.7 Insolvency litigation has provided the greatest case law in this area. Redundancies made by the receiver before a transfer are likely to receive scrutiny, particularly from the Department of Work and Pensions where redundant employees make claims. The key is whether, at the time of the dismissal, the transfer was reasonably foreseeable and the dismissal was to make the business more attractive to the purchaser rather than for a genuine ETO reason of the vendor.

10.7 Duties to inform and consult

10.7.1 The vendor and the purchaser must inform and consult employee representatives. Failure to do so carries penalties, which are being used more and more. Employees can claim for up to 13 weeks' pay where there is failure to inform and consult, in addition to any claim for unfair dismissal. Trade unions and employee representatives are increasingly making class action claims on behalf of affected employees. As noted above, affected employees include existing employees of the purchaser and retained employees of the vendor.

10.7.2 Where affected employees are represented by an independent trade union recognised for collective bargaining purposes, the vendor as employer must inform and consult an authorised official of that union. This may be a shop steward or a district union official or, if appropriate, a national or regional official. The employer is not required to inform and consult any other employee representatives in such circumstances but may do so voluntarily if desired. A trade union may be recognised for one group of employees but not for another, in which case that other group will be subject to the following paragraphs.

10.7.3 Where employees are not represented by a trade union, the employer must inform and consult other appropriate representatives of those employees. These can be existing representatives or new ones especially elected for the purpose. If there are existing representatives, their remit and method of election or appointment must give them suitable authority for the employees concerned otherwise it will not be a valid consultation. For example, it would not be appropriate to inform and consult a committee established to consider the operation of a works canteen about a transfer affecting other staff, but it may well be appropriate to inform and consult a fairly elected committee of employees, such as a works council, that is regularly informed or consulted more generally about the business and personnel matters.

10.7.4 If the representatives are to be specially elected, certain election conditions must be met. The rules on elections and a guide to how these should be operated are set out below.

EMPLOYEE REPRESENTATIVES – ELECTION RULES

- The burden is on the employer to make arrangements for a fair election.
- The employer can choose the number of representatives to be elected provided there will be enough for the number and classes of affected employees.
- The employer can choose whether representatives can speak for all employees or just a particular class of employee.
- The term of office must be chosen by the employer before the election and must be long enough to enable the information and consultation to take place.
- Only 'affected employees' can stand as candidates for election.
- No affected employee can be unreasonably excluded for standing for election.
- All affected employees are entitled to vote, so proper arrangements must be in place for shift workers, night workers and absent employees.
- Employees are entitled to vote for as many candidates as there are representatives (either the total number of representatives or the total number in their particular class).
- The employer's obligation is to allow votes to be cast in secret wherever possible and to be accurately counted.
- If an elected person ceases to act as an employee representative (for example by leaving the business) another election must be held if this would leave the affected employees without a representative.

GUIDE TO HOLDING ELECTIONS

- Decide the number of representatives to be elected.
- Decide which employees the representatives will speak for.
- Decide the representatives' term of office.
- Decide how you will communicate the arrangements to affected employees, for example by letter at home and/or by putting a notice on the staff notice board.
- Inform all affected employees that an election is to take place for a specified number of representatives, inform them that they may nominate candidates and describe the nomination process.
- Once the period for nominations has closed, inform all affected employees of the date, time and place of the election (not forgetting employees who are absent from work).
- Provide each affected employee with an anonymous ballot form.
- At the close of the election the votes should be counted at least twice to ensure accuracy.

10.7.5   In each case, the employer (the vendor in the case of the target's employees) must tell the representatives:
- that the transfer is going to take place, approximately when and why;
- the legal, economic and social implications of the transfer for the affected employees;
- whether the employer envisages taking any action (for example a reorganisation) in connection with the transfer which will affect the employees and, if so, what action is envisaged.

10.7.6   The purchaser must give the vendor the necessary information so that the vendor is able to meet the above requirements. The information must be provided long enough before the transfer to give adequate time for consultation. The vendor will seek confirmation that there are no measures or action to be taken that will affect the employees or ask for sufficient detail of those measures or action to permit consultation to take place.

10.7.7   The duties to inform and consult are separate. In broad terms, the duty to inform will occur in every situation and the duty to consult will occur where measures or action is to be taken.

10.7.8   If action is envisaged that will affect the employees, the employer (the vendor in the case of the target's employees) must consult the representatives of the employees affected about that proposed action. The consultation must be undertaken with a view to seeking agreement. During these consultations, the employer must consider and respond to any representations made by the representatives. If the employer rejects these representations then it must state the reason. There is no mechanism for dispute resolution. Thus, at present, the consultation rules lack teeth.

10.7.9   There are no set time periods for advance consultation. The regulations envisage it will take place as early as reasonably possible. The risk for the parties in informing and consulting very late in the process (for example to preserve confidentiality) is that they will not have discharged their duties. If there are special circumstances that make it not reasonably practicable for an employer for fulfil any of the information or consultation requirements, it must take such steps to meet the requirements as are reasonably practicable.

10.7.10 In deciding whether the employer has given information on the transfer sufficiently before completion:
   ■ the primary test is whether the information is given long enough before completion to allow affected employees to be properly informed and for any consultation to take place;
   ■ the genuineness of the approach of the employer to the information process will be crucial;
   ■ each case will turn on its own merits, but an Employment Tribunal has held that three days before a relevant transfer is insufficient.

10.7.11 In exceptional circumstances, it will be possible to claim that confidentiality would constitute a special circumstance that renders it impractical for an employer to perform its duty to inform or consult. This is likely to require the employer to show that the transfer would not have taken place in the absence of complete confidentiality. The Employment Tribunal will be reluctant to accept that confidentiality constitutes a special circumstance and in one case the Employment Tribunal took the view that any commercially sensitive information could have been omitted from the information and consultation process, but the duty to inform and consult could still have been complied with.

10.7.12 A representative or candidate for election who is dismissed or has suffered detriment short of dismissal may complain to an Employment Tribunal. A representative who has been unreasonably refused time off by the employer or whose employer has refused to make an appropriate payment for time off may also complain to an Employment Tribunal. Those complaints must be made within three months of the date on which it is alleged time off should have been allowed but the Tribunal can extend the time limit if it considers that it was not reasonably practicable for the complaint to be made within three months.

10.7.13 Sample document 24 (page 274) sets out sample consultation letters to be given to employee representatives.

10.8 Warranties and indemnities

10.8.1   As noted in paragraph 10.2, the purchaser of shares or a business will want to ensure that it has accurate and up to date information about the employees. On a share purchase, the purchaser is concerned with claims and disputes with former employees as well as present employees as liability will remain with the target. On a business sale, for the reasons described in paragraphs 10.3 onwards, the purchaser will be particularly concerned with current employees' rights, plus existing collective agreements and trade union recognition.

10.8.2   Warranties in either case will centre on:
- accuracy of that information;
- compliance with employment legislation;
- adequacy of written records relating to employees;
- expectations of the employees, for example upcoming pay increases or pension benefits;
- any benefits that may not be contractual but are expected, such as discretionary bonuses or seasonal gifts.

10.8.3   Warranties relating to employment issues are included in the sample share acquisition agreement (see page 190).

10.8.4   Indemnities on a share purchase are only likely to arise to deal with problems or employment related issues identified through due diligence. If those issues have been disclosed against the warranties, an indemnity would be the only effective right of recourse for the purchaser.

10.8.5   On a business purchase, the purchaser will almost certainly want indemnities from the vendor for liabilities that are assumed under TUPE and relate to the period prior to completion. Typically indemnities are contained in the business acquisition agreement, sample document 26 (see page 288). For example, the purchaser will wish to be indemnified against:
- arrears of salary or benefits;
- accruals of holiday pay;
- any claim by an employee who transfers to the purchaser that he or she has been dismissed by the vendor, where this would amount to wrongful or unfair dismissal;
- sex, race or disability discrimination;

- any other claim the employee may have against the employer, for example for industrial injuries, which will pass to the purchaser under TUPE.

10.8.6　The indemnities required by the purchaser may also include liability for failure to inform and consult with the employees in accordance with the duties described in paragraph 10.7. Note that those duties are to be complied with by the vendor as employer, but liability will pass to the purchaser on completion since it is an employment right. The vendor will want to exclude from that indemnity any liability that results from the failure of the purchaser to notify measures to be taken post completion. Indeed, the vendor will often seek its own indemnity against the purchaser for that failure, although there is a good argument that this is not necessary because liability for the failure will have passed to the purchaser.

10.8.7　It would be usual (certainly on a business purchase) for a list of employees attached to the agreement or the disclosure letter to be warranted as accurate. These are the persons of whom the purchaser has knowledge and hopefully full details of employment. It follows that the purchaser will want an indemnity from the vendor as regards any person not on the list who may be treated as an employee for the purposes of TUPE.

CHAPTER

11

Purchase Documents

11.1 Overview

11.1.1 Having completed the preparatory steps, the legal documentation for the acquisition needs to be prepared and negotiated between the parties. This should in theory commence once the due diligence exercise has been substantially completed. In practice, the parties may want to circulate the share acquisition agreement at an earlier stage. As noted in paragraph 5.5, a draft acquisition agreement would usually be prepared in advance where due diligence is being carried out via a data room.

11.1.2 In limited circumstances, the vendor's lawyer would prepare the acquisition agreement. Prime examples are where the agreement is included in the data room and on a sale by receivers. Usually however, since these documents are primarily for the protection of the purchaser, the purchaser's lawyer will prepare the following:

- acquisition agreement;
- ancillary documents to transfer the shares or assets of the target;
- in the case of a share purchase, the tax deed (which may form part of the share acquisition agreement) and financial assistance 'whitewash' papers;
- any service agreements or consultancy agreements with individual vendors or key managers of the target, regarding their activities post completion.

11.1.3 The vendor's lawyer would usually have responsibility for the following:

- the disclosure letter;
- warranty limitations (to the extent these are not already incorporated in the acquisition agreement);
- loan note or loan stock instrument, where necessary to reflect deferred consideration terms.

11.1.4 Funding documents are invariably prepared by the funders or their lawyers, for example:

- facility agreements would usually be generated by the bank or its lawyers;
- security documents would usually be generated by the bank and will often be in a standard 'non-negotiable' form;
- lawyers acting for a venture capitalist (VC) would draft the subscription agreements and articles of Newco;

- any intercreditor agreement (see paragraph 9.6) will be drafted by the bank's lawyers.
- Sample key acquisition documents are included in the second part of the book. This and the following chapter briefly review key issues arising on the drafting and negotiation of those documents.

11.2 Share acquisition agreement

11.2.1   In order to pass legal title to shares in a company, it is only necessary for the vendor to execute a share transfer form (see sample document 7, page 207) in favour of the purchaser. As noted in paragraph 7.6, this will (subject to stamping and registration) be sufficient to pass legal title to the shares, but may not be sufficient to deal with their beneficial ownership. Also, the purchaser will invariably require other terms relating to the purchase to be documented, principally warranties and restrictive covenants. Accordingly, a share acquisition agreement would usually be prepared to set out all the terms on which the shares in the target are sold.

11.2.2   A sample share acquisition agreement (sample document 6) can be found at page 166. These agreements vary in length, although most are considered to be lengthy by vendors and purchasers. The 'front end' of the agreement usually contains the following key provisions:

- the agreement to sell, including the words 'with full title guarantee' (which imply covenants as to title of the shares as referred to in paragraph 7.6.4);
- the consideration in cash or otherwise, dealt with in paragraphs 11.4 to 11.6;
- the timing of completion of the sale, usually immediately following execution of the agreement, but (where necessary) after an interval, which is dealt with in paragraph 11.7;
- the mechanics of completion, including delivery of share transfers and certificates, passing of resolutions and retirement of officers;
- warranty provisions, dealt with in Chapter 12;
- restrictions on future activities of the vendors, dealt with in paragraph 11.9;
- other clauses dealing with issues such as costs, assignability of the share acquisition agreement, assignment of the contract, announcements and choice of law.

11.2.3   The 'back end' of the agreement will comprise the schedules referred in the front end, and typically comprise:

- details of the vendors and their respective entitlements to the consideration;
- information on the target company and its subsidiaries;
- the actual warranties themselves;
- the form of the tax deed, dealt with below.

11.3 Business acquisition agreement

11.3.1   Sample document 26 (page 280) is a sample business acquisition agreement. As with share acquisition agreements, these agreements can vary considerably in length. This will depend to a large extent on the range and complexity of the assets to be sold and whether any liabilities or contracts are to be discharged by the purchasers.

11.3.2 The contents of the business acquisition agreement will in some respects be similar to the contents of the share acquisition agreement as described in paragraphs 11.2.2 and 11.2.3. In particular, they would deal with the consideration, the timing of completion, warranties and restrictions on future activities.

11.3.3 The key difference will be that the business acquisition agreement must adequately describe the assets to be sold and any obligations to be assumed and so would include the following key provisions:

- definitions of the assets to be sold, where appropriate by reference to schedules listing out the items;
- the agreement to sell those assets, 'with full title guarantee' (which implies obligations on the vendor as per paragraph 11.2.2);
- specific provisions for transfer of freehold and leasehold property, usually incorporating the standard conditions which would apply on a stand-alone property transaction;
- any special arrangements for transferring other assets, such as registered intellectual property rights (IPR);
- provision for assignment of contracts, some of which may not be assignable, hence the provisions for obtaining consent contained in the sample agreement;
- recognition of the transfer of employees under TUPE and appropriate indemnities, which are dealt with in Chapter 10;
- assumptions of defined liabilities (where appropriate) and clarification that other liabilities remain the responsibility of the vendor.

11.3.4 As noted above, the agreement should specify which assets are included. Often however, the agreement will go on to say that all assets owned by the vendor or used in the business are included in the sale. This protects the purchaser, in case items are missed off any list or fall outside definitions. The purchaser's argument would be that it is for the vendor to exclude specific assets since the business is being sold as a going concern. From the vendor's perspective, this 'catch-all' provision may be dangerous as it gives rise to argument that third party assets are used in the business and so the vendor is warranting ownership of them. Accordingly, the vendor may reject this clause or reach a compromise by:

- excluding specified items and/or specified classes of assets; and/or
- allowing the 'catch all' provision to apply to certain categories of assets, such as plant and equipment, but not generally to other assets.

11.3.5 The book debts for the business may be included in the sale, in which case it will give rise to an assignment of those debts to the purchaser. This could be achieved within the business acquisition agreement itself or by a separate assignment. Since the abolition of stamp duty on the transfer of debts, there is less reason to exclude them, although it would be quite common for the vendor to retain existing debts in order to discharge creditors. This avoids the purchaser having any exposure to credit risk on those debts. On the other hand, the purchaser may wish to take over collection of the debt to preserve continuity of the business and prevent possible damage to its goodwill by allowing the vendor to pursue those debts. In this case, the alternatives are for:

- the debts to be assigned, in which case the purchaser will want warranty coverage for any bad debts, to the extent the purchaser has paid for them in the purchase price; or
- the purchaser may collect the debts as agent on behalf of the vendor, perhaps deducting a percentage of the debt value collected as a collection fee.

11.3.6   In either case, it is unlikely that the purchaser will want to pursue the debtor into the courts. There is therefore likely to be a provision that the debt will be 'handed back' to the vendor for collection after certain steps have been taken to collect the debt. It would be usual for the purchaser to have the right to retain the debt, having paid face value for it, if it believes this is necessary to preserve the goodwill of the target business.

11.3.7   An assignment of the debt between the vendor and the purchaser will be sufficient to transfer the beneficial ownership of that debt. However, assignment of legal title to the debt (which brings with it the right to pursue the debtor in the courts) would require notice of assignment to be given to the actual debtor. Accordingly, each debtor would usually be sent a letter post completion, informing them that payments should be made to the purchaser. This letter need not be worded in a formal legal manner, as long as it is sufficient to let the debtor know to whom payment should be made. Most debtors would want to see that letter coming from the vendor before making any payment to the purchaser, so as to be sure that the debtor was discharged from its obligations by making payment to the purchaser. Assuming the purchaser will take over the vendor's trading premises and perhaps the same or a similar corporate/trading name, the letter is actually a means of preserving the continuity of the business.

11.3.8   Specific assets may require a particular document of transfer to be executed in addition to the business acquisition agreement. The classic example would be freehold or leasehold property registered at HM Land Registry. In this case, the appropriate land registry transfer form (TR1) would be required.

11.3.9   In the case of leasehold property, an assignment of the lease would be required (again in the form of a land registry transfer if the leasehold interest is registered at HM Land Registry). The purchaser would execute this assignment in order to give appropriate indemnities to the vendor for any retained liability under the terms of the lease. Perhaps more importantly, the assignment is likely to require the consent of the landlord (and any superior landlord) under the terms of the lease. The requirements for a consent and the process to be followed will depend on the terms of the lease and, generally speaking, the length of the term of the lease. A longer-term lease reserving only a ground rent is less likely to require the consent of the landlord and may only require notice of the assignment to be given to the landlord after completion. Where the lease is for a term of 25 years or less, at a market rent, the landlord's consent will usually be required. The lease may provide that this 'cannot be unreasonably withheld' but this still involves satisfying the landlord that the financial covenant offered by the purchaser is equivalent or better than the vendor's financial covenant and there may be requirements for guarantees, rent bonds or other security. The detail of this is beyond the scope of this book but the issue of landlord's consent can delay a business sale transaction if not requested in good time.

11.3.10 A business purchase will often be concluded without landlord's consent being obtained in advance, particularly where there are a large number of leasehold properties involved. This carries with it the risk that the vendor is in breach of the terms of the lease, which could entitle the landlord to forfeit the lease. The business acquisition agreement may provide that the leasehold properties are not assigned on completion, but rather the vendor allows the purchaser to occupy them as licensee until landlord's consent is obtained. This may still give rise to a breach of the terms of the lease, if it includes the covenant on the part of the tenant not to part with possession of the leasehold premises. The vendor may look to the purchaser to indemnify the vendor against any liability for this breach (assuming it is the purchaser who wishes to proceed before consent is obtained). There is also the considerable commercial risk for the purchaser if landlord's consent has not been obtained, as it would have no right to occupy the trading premises of the business. Completing without landlord's consent is therefore an unsatisfactory situation, only justified where commercial issues relating to timing outweigh these risks. A middle course (which mitigates some of the problems but is still unsatisfactory) is for the parties to have applied for consent to assignment before completion but then to proceed to complete on the basis that it would be unreasonable (and thus unlawful) for the landlord to refuse permission.

11.3.11 Separate forms of assignment of registered IPR will also be required, meeting the requirements of the relevant registration authority (which may be different in different jurisdictions of the world). In any event, there may be a separate assignment of IPR, to include terms subject to that IPR. A sample form of assignment of IPR is included as sample document 27, page 294. Such documentation should however only be prepared and negotiated by specialists in this field.

11.4 Consideration

11.4.1 Where the consideration represents a sum payable in cash on completion, drafting should be fairly straightforward. The task is to reflect the following:
- the correct amount to be paid and the respective entitlements of each vendor (if more than one);
- the method of payment, which would usually be by telegraphic transfer to a specified account;

■ agreement that this payment will discharge the purchaser from its obligation to the vendors to pay the price (assuming the payment is being made to the vendors' lawyer).

11.4.2 The consideration may be or include the issue of new shares in the purchaser. In this case, the vendors should have ascertained the worth of the shares (by carrying out due diligence on the purchaser) and should negotiate the form of a shareholders' agreement and possibly new articles to be adopted by the purchaser. The acquisition agreement should deal with:

■ the amount of shares to be issued to the vendor, which should be a number of shares rather than just a percentage;

■ the mechanics of the share issue, including issue of share certificates and entry of the names of the vendors in the register of members;

■ any new shareholders' agreement and new articles to be entered into/ adopted;

■ in the case of quoted shares, the arrangements for the consideration shares to be admitted to dealings on the relevant stock exchange, and any special requirements of the stock exchange that might affect the vendors (for example restrictions on dealings).

11.4.3 Sample provisions relating to the issue of consideration shares are included in section B of sample document 8 (see page 212). Those provisions deal very simply with a situation where quoted shares are being issued as consideration. Section A of the sample document (page 210) deals with an interval between exchange and completion, as the quoted company will often need shareholder approval for the transaction and/or the issue of shares.

11.4.4 Where a quoted company is offering consideration shares, it may be agreed that those shares will immediately be 'placed' or sold to other investors or in the market in which these shares are dealt. This is known as a vendor placing. The effect is that the vendors would realise cash on the sale of the consideration shares almost immediately. There would be a vendor placing agreement between the vendor, the purchaser and the stockbroker (and usually also the purchaser's directors, to accept obligations to assist the process). The vendors would need to be satisfied that the arrangements were such that they were adequately protected by the obligation to sell the shares at an acceptable price. The share acquisition agreement itself, however, will still specify that the consideration is satisfied by shares.

11.4.5 Part or all of the consideration may be deferred, in other words payable on a set date or dates following completion. Where the amount of that deferred consideration is fixed, the principal issues will be:

■ specifying the time(s) payment is due;

■ setting out the effects of default, for example providing that the whole amount will become due and payable if any instalment is not paid on the due date or, say, within three working days of the due date;

■ providing for interest to be payable on the deferred consideration;

■ providing for grant of security for that deferred consideration (issues relating to this, including intercreditor agreements, were dealt with in Chapter 9);

- acceleration of payment in certain events, such as a sale of the target or a substantial part of its assets;
- any other restrictions on the purchaser, for example limits on the purchaser's directors' remuneration so that the vendors' position as creditors is not unduly affected.

11.4.6 Chapter 9 referred to 'vendor-assisted buy-outs' and the role of deferred consideration as a source of funding for the acquisition. It is very important in this situation to protect the vendor(s). Many vendors would not be prepared to accept deferred consideration unless this was guaranteed by a clearing bank. Where this is agreed, the vendor's lawyer should be entirely satisfied with the terms of the bank guarantee (particularly as these documents often have limitations and quite specific procedures for any claims). However, for the purchaser to procure a bank guarantee for the whole amount of the deferred consideration would partly defeat the object. If the purchaser cannot borrow the relevant amount, it is unlikely to be able to procure a guarantee from the bank, which will regard the maximum exposure under the guarantee as being part of its funding facilities.

11.4.7 It is thus far more likely on a vendor-assisted buy-out that the deferred consideration will either be unsecured or will be secured by a debenture over the assets of the purchaser and the target, ranking behind the bank. Occasionally, the vendor may be the primary or sole source of funding for the transaction. In effect, the vendor is allowing the purchaser (often, in effect, meaning a management buy-out (MBO) team) to pay for the target company out of its own future performance. In such a case the vendor is quite seriously exposed to the future fortunes of the target and will probably want restrictions on the MBO team similar to those required by a VC. At first sight it appears that the vendor is losing control of the target in exchange for mere debt. However, the vendor may gain a significant tax advantage from this arrangement in that the deferred consideration would be subject to capital gains tax (CGT), with the benefit of taper relief, which is likely to result in a significant tax saving compared with the extraction of profits from the target by dividends.

11.5 Earn-outs

11.5.1 This is the expression used to describe deferred consideration that is contingent, in other words dependent on a future event. That will usually mean future financial performance of the target in terms of either the profits or revenues of the purchaser and the target. Alternatively, part of the consideration could be contingent on some other event such as obtaining planning permission or the renewal of the material contract.

11.5.2 A typical set of earn-out provisions can be found in sample document 12, page 238. This would form a schedule to the acquisition agreement. The principal issues dealt with are:
- determination of the profits to be used for the purposes of the earn-out;

- calculation and payment of the earn-out consideration based on the above;
- protection of the vendors, often referred to as 'ring fencing'.

11.5.3 The need to protect the vendors' interests under earn-out provisions arises because the affairs of the target will be under the control of the purchaser from completion. Where the contingency relates to the target's financial performance, the earn-out would be affected if the purchaser changed the basis on which the business of the target was run, or worse still, manipulated the manner in which profits or revenues were calculated. Weighed against this, the purchaser will expect to manage the target business as it sees fit from completion and will therefore be reluctant to accept any 'ring fencing' that would inhibit this. To an extent, the vendors can assume that the purchaser would want to maximise post-completion profits and revenues for its own benefit. However, where the earn-out is based on a multiple of post-completion profits, the purchaser's motivation to maximise those profits is in question. Also, the purchaser might, for quite commercial reasons, want to change the shape of the target business so as to get rid of loss making activities and/or invest for the longer term. In contrast, the vendor is only interested in the earn-out period, which would usually be relatively short.

11.5.4 Where the earn-out is based on future revenues (for this purpose meaning the value of gross sales) there is in theory less scope for manipulation. However, the value of those gross sales could be affected by:

- a change to accounting treatment with regard to calculation of revenue in a given period (in other words, timing issues);
- in light of the previous point, changing the basis of contracting with customers, for example to render invoices at an earlier or later stage;
- reducing prices, particularly where the purchaser is selling other products to the same customers;
- discontinuing the sale of certain products or services, because these are less profitable;
- increasing prices significantly, perhaps for strategic reasons to reduce turnover but increase profit margins.

11.5.5 Where the amount is based on profits, there are many additional matters to consider concerned with the calculation of those profits. This is likely to result in provisions similar to those in paragraph 4 of sample document 12 (page 238), which adjust profits to take into account changes to the business or to the methods of account for profits. Some are simply to ensure a 'like for like' comparison, where for example there are changes to the accounting methods in calculating profits. Others are to ensure a 'level playing field', for example to add back management charges the purchaser or other member of the purchaser group may levy on the target business which reduce profits over and above the value of the services provided.

11.5.6 The other key aspect of ring fencing would be to prohibit certain actions which change the target business during the earn-out period. For example, the purchaser may be restricted from removing key directors or managers from their positions and/or involvement in the business. As noted above, the purchaser will not want to be restricted in management of the business, because there could be very good reasons for changing the target business, including for example removing managers who were holding it back. The purchaser might quite justifiably refuse to allow the vendors to have a veto on such a decision. One method of dealing with this conflict of interest is to provide that those acts may be carried out by the purchaser, if it agrees to pay the full amount of the earn-out to the vendor. This allows the purchaser to retain control but preserves the interest of the vendors under the earn-out. This will only be acceptable to the purchaser in very limited circumstances because it effectively allows the vendors to recover the earn-out regardless of the actual performance of the target business.

11.5.7 Where the contingency relates to a non-financial matter, it may be possible for the vendors to have control of that contingency or at least be consulted about the process. For example, if the contingency relates to sale of a property owned by the target company, it will be perfectly feasible for the vendors to manage the sales process on behalf of the target company. In that case, it would be the purchaser who would require protection, for example from a poorly managed sale. Where the contingency relates to obtaining a planning permission, it will be a matter of negotiation who would make and pursue the application. Where the contingency relates to renegotiation of a contract, it is likely that the purchaser will want control of the entire process because it affects the business going forward. Often, the appointment of some of the vendors as consultants of the business to assist with handover will enable the vendors to participate in achieving the earn-out. However, it is important to remember that a consultant is under the control of the directors of the purchaser/target and that any consultancy agreement could be terminated.

11.6 Completion accounts

11.6.1 Completion accounts refer to financial statements to be prepared as at the date of completion (or an appropriate date close to completion) that will show, typically:
- on a share sale, the net asset value or shareholders' funds of the target company; or
- on a business sale, the value of assets transferred less liabilities to be assumed of the target business; or
- in either case, some variation of this according to the commercial deal.

11.6.2 The need for completion accounts will arise out of an agreed term of the acquisition whereby:
- the deal is dependent on a minimum value of net assets; or
- the price varies upwards or downwards (or both) depending on the value of net assets at completion; or
- a combination of the two.

11.6.3 It may be possible to ascertain and agree the value prior to entry into the sale agreement, in which case the agreement will specify a fixed amount of consideration. However, this will not usually be possible, because of the need to collate and analyse financial information. In that case, the parties may include a warranty to the effect that net assets are above a certain level. This has dangers for both parties in that:

- the definition of net assets and calculation method need to be clear for this warranty to be acceptable to either party;
- the purchaser is exposed to the risks of enforcing a warranty and to warranty limitations (see Chapter 12);
- the vendor is exposed to an uncertain and perhaps lengthy process, plus there is no scope for the consideration to increase according to the level of net assets.

11.6.4 The sample share acquisition agreement and the sample business acquisition agreement (sample documents 6 and 26, pages 166 and 280) include provision for completion accounts. These attempt to bring certainty to the process and would have the following key features:

- defining what is being calculated and the basis of calculation;
- setting a process for this to be agreed by the parties or determined by an independent third party if not agreed;
- setting out the process for the consideration to be adjusted by reference to these accounts.

11.7 Loan notes

11.7.1 Deferred consideration would usually be satisfied by the issue of loan notes or loan stock by the purchaser on completion. The principal exception would be where the deferred consideration was payable over a fairly short period after completion. The differences between loan notes and loan stock are technical, and for the purpose of this book they can be assumed to be synonymous. The following paragraphs refer to loan notes on this basis.

11.7.2 The principal reason for the use of loan notes would be to achieve deferral of CGT payable on the sale of shares. In broad terms, the 'exchange' of shares in the target or loan notes of the purchaser will not give rise to an immediate liability to pay tax. Tax is payable upon repayment or redemption of the loan notes. This is a non-technical explanation, in that the tax treatment of loan notes depends on whether they are qualifying corporate bonds (QCBs) or non-qualifying corporate bonds (non-QCBs). There may be reasons, based on the vendor's personal circumstances, for wishing to express the loan notes in either way, and it is important to take specialist advice.

11.7.3 Sample document 13 (page 242) shows a sample form of loan note instrument. The legal mechanics of loan notes usually involve creation of an instrument which is a deed poll (a document with only one party) by which the purchaser creates a certain amount of loan notes. Available loan capital governed by the terms of the instrument is therefore created, in a similar way to which share capital is governed by the articles. Thus the instrument would set out terms as to:

- repayment;
- interest;
- security;
- transferability.

11.7.4   All those issues are important to ensure appropriate tax treatment for the loan notes. In particular, to qualify as a QCB or a non-QCB, the loan notes must:

- not be repayable earlier than six months from issue (and a longer period may be advisable);
- carry a commercial rate of interest (and this should have regard to whether the loan notes are secured and the commercial risk assumed by the holders);
- be freely transferable so that they are treated as a marketable security for tax purposes.

11.7.5   If a non-QCB is required, the loan note will need to include provisions to take it outside of the definition of a QCB. Methods to achieve this through drafting include:

- the right of the purchaser to redeem the loan note in another currency (for example US dollars);
- including a right of the vendors to receive additional loan notes;
- the right to convert the loan note into shares.

11.7.6   From a vendor's perspective, the right to additional loan notes or shares is the preferred clause, given that the currency clause on its own may appear less commercial and more open to challenge by the Inland Revenue. However, the purchaser is likely to have commercial and tax reasons for resisting any obligation to issue further loan notes or shares, even in very limited amounts. Thus, in practice, the currency conversion clause is most commonly seen. A limit on the scope for increase in the sterling value of the repayments in another currency is designed to ensure that the loan notes would not comprise 'relevant discounted securities' since, if they do, they will be classified as QCBs. In any event, for commercial reasons, there will usually be a lower and upper limit on the sterling value of the payment in a foreign currency.

11.7.7   It has already been noted that the vendors may require additional rights to protect the value of the loan notes where these are not guaranteed or adequately secured. These could restrict expenditure and other decisions by the purchaser and its subsidiaries or even give the vendors rights to participate in business decisions. These provisions can be included in the loan note instrument and/or the acquisition agreement. Care needs to be taken in the document to see that these do not affect the tax status of the loan notes. The key issue is to make sure that the loan notes represent marketable securities rather than being personal to the vendors themselves.

11.8 Interval between exchange and completion

11.8.1   Wherever possible, the parties will wish completion to take place immediately following signature of the agreement. This is preferable because:

- the purchaser is not exposed to the risk of changes to the target in the period between exchange of contracts and completion;
- the parties do not need to negotiate provisions to deal with the period between exchange and completion, which can be contentious;
- the vendor is not subject to the risk that the contract may be rescinded under those provisions, if a material event occurs;
- all the completion documents can be tabled, agreed and executed at the same time;
- arrangements with funders and the approval of financial assistance in relation to the acquisition are simplified.

11.8.2 Sometimes an interval is unavoidable, for example:

- where one of the parties is a quoted company and the transaction (and/or issue of consideration shares) requires shareholder approval – see Chapter 13;
- where the transaction requires third party approval, for example sale of a company or business involved in financial services where the Financial Services Authority (FSA)'s approval may be required;
- where the parties decide for commercial reasons that they want to have a commercially binding agreement in advance of a pre-completion condition being satisfied, for example, obtaining a planning permission on the property.

11.8.3 Part A of sample document 8 (page 210) sets out typical provisions to be incorporated in the share acquisition agreement where there is a gap between exchange and completion to deal with conditions. Naturally, each agreement needs to reflect the particular circumstances. The table below sets out some of the key considerations.

CONDITIONAL CONTRACTS

Fulfilment of conditions	■ Are the conditions adequately defined, so that fulfilment can be determined clearly and objectively?
	■ Are the conditions adequately defined, so that fulfilment can be within the control (or subject to the influence) of either or both parties? If so, does the agreement effectively amount to an 'option' in favour of the party controlling the condition?
	■ Do the provisions adequately oblige the parties to take necessary steps to achieve fulfilment? This is likely to include taking steps within their power and using 'all reasonable endeavours' to achieve the conditions.
Time limits	■ Does the agreement set sensible and achievable time limits for fulfilment of the conditions?
	■ Does this allow an adequate period (or a secondary period) during which the parties will take further steps (for example, planning appeal or arbitration of a disputed matter)?

Non-fulfilment
- Will the contract be void or does one party have the choice between rescinding the contract or continuing to complete? (The answer depends on whether the condition is purely for the benefit of one party.)
- In the case of rescission, should one party be responsible for costs and should any provisions remain in force? (For example, the parties may intend that confidentiality and restrictions on announcements should continue to oblige.)

Warranties
- Are these given as at exchange, as at completion or at both dates?
- If given at completion, the vendors are exposed to liability for matters outside their control that arise in the gap before completion.
- If given only at exchange, the purchaser is exposed to those matters and is thus reliant on its right to rescind the contract.
- The compromise is often for warranties to be repeated at completion, but allowing the vendor to choose between the contract being rescinded or the contract being completed with a claim for damages.

11.8.4 With these points in mind, the parties need to think carefully before exchanging conditional contracts for the sale and purchase of a company. There are lower risks on a business purchase, because the purchaser is unlikely to be assuming liabilities (with the clear exception of employee liabilities under TUPE). Quite often the parties will consider exchange of contracts on a conditional basis, simply because they are keen to enter into a binding agreement rather than wait for third parties. The classic examples would be contracts conditional upon:
- tax clearances being obtained;
- funding arrangements being in place;
- a third party consent, such as a landlord, being obtained.

It will often be prudent to avoid the risks associated with an interval between exchange and completion by waiting for these conditions to be fulfilled, perhaps having agreed the form of the acquisition documents and agreeing (with moral force only) that the parties will not seek to renegotiate the documents.

11.8.5 Finally, it will often be the case that parties are ready to complete except for a single event such as arrival of purchase proceeds or admission of consideration shares to dealings on a stock exchange. In these cases, there is technically no interval between exchange and completion, as the following paragraphs explain.

11.8.6 In the case of proceeds to be paid to the vendor's lawyer by the purchaser, the parties would usually complete the transaction on the strength of a professional undertaking from the purchaser's lawyers (or perhaps from the bank's lawyers if the monies are held by them) to arrange for monies to be transferred from their client account to the vendor's lawyers' client account. This professional undertaking will bind the purchaser's lawyers both contractually and as a matter of professional conduct. This being the case, the purchaser's lawyer will be extremely careful to ensure that the obligations in the undertaking are under the control of that lawyer and/or law firm. It stands to reason that such an undertaking can only be given when monies are held in the client account of that law firm in cleared funds. (An arrangement whereby the lawyer undertakes to forward monies as and when these are received from a third party would be unacceptable to the vendor unless backed by corresponding obligations from the third party's lawyers.) Note also that the purchaser's lawyers may be reluctant to undertake 'to transfer' the relevant sums to the vendor's lawyers, since they are reliant upon their own bank complying with those instructions and the money not being lost or delayed in the telegraphic transfer system. Accordingly, they may limit their undertaking 'to giving instructions to their bank to transfer' the money.

11.8.7   Where undertakings cannot be relied upon, the parties may agree to complete in escrow. This has a technical, if rather archaic, meaning. In crude terms, it means that the parties have entered into the documents but they are not 'delivered' and thus not legally effective until a certain event takes place. The expression 'in escrow' is often misused, simply to refer to the fact that the parties have executed the documents but left them with their solicitors to agree completion when a final event has occurred. This is not an escrow unless the parties have agreed that the documents are binding upon that event and that the parties are not entitled to withdraw in the meantime. It follows that, to effect a proper escrow arrangement, the parties should have a written record of the terms of the escrow detailing the condition to be fulfilled and a time period after which the escrow will lapse.

11.9 Restrictive covenants

11.9.1   Justification for restricting the business activities of the vendor(s) after completion includes:
- in the case of a business purchase, the purchaser is acquiring goodwill of an existing business and thus the vendor should not be entitled to diminish the value of that goodwill;
- in a case of a share purchase, part of the goodwill of the target may be reflected in the relationships between the vendors and principal customers/suppliers;
- in either case, the vendors are likely to have confidential information concerning the target which would put them at a competitive advantage.

11.9.2   In this context, goodwill has its everyday meaning of business reputation and customer connections (rather than a strict legal or accounting meaning). The point applies whether or not the agreement refers to a sale of goodwill.

11.9.3   The well-known legal doctrine of 'restraint of trade' prevents restrictions of business activities, unless these are reasonable, in order to protect the legitimate business interests of the party seeking to enforce them. Most business people will be familiar with the application of this doctrine to restrictive covenants contained in employment contracts. Those restrictions need to be limited in extent and time and there is often serious doubt as to whether they will be enforceable in the courts. The same doctrine applies to covenants contained in share purchase or business acquisition agreements, but the assessment of what is reasonable will be different:

- it should be possible to show that the purchaser has legitimate business interests to be protected when it has purchased the target as a going concern;
- where the vendors have been involved in management of the target, it may reasonably be supposed that they have information that may need to be protected, not just by restrictions on disclosure but by restrictions on use in other competing business activities;
- in the case of employment, it may be supposed that the employee has less bargaining power in negotiating the employment contract than the employer, whereas the vendor and purchaser on an acquisition can usually be said to have equal bargaining power (particularly where both have independent legal advice).

11.9.4 Thus, it can be said with more certainty that restrictions in an acquisition agreement may be enforceable. They still need to be limited in extent and time but the time periods are likely to be significantly longer than under employment contracts. The test as to how long the restrictions should continue depends on:

- the useful life of any confidential information;
- the extent to which the purchaser is 'paying' for goodwill (whether expressed in the agreement or not);
- generally, the reasonableness of protecting the purchaser from the activities of the vendors.

11.9.5 In the case of the agreements included as sample documents 6 and 26, the clauses would restrict those activities briefly described below.

RESTRICTIONS ON VENDORS

Solicitation of customers
- Prevents active steps to entice customers away from the target.
- Will include direct contact by the vendors or through third parties but will not, for example, preclude generally advertising a competing business.
- The definition of customers should be limited (to increase enforceability) to current or recent customers and those prospective customers who are already in communication with the target.
- Where appropriate, the restriction should also be limited to persons with whom the vendors had material contact.

Dealing with customers
- This is wider than solicitation as it attempts to restrict any contractual relationship with the target's customer in relation to a competing business.

- Enforceability may therefore be more difficult in certain cases.
- The advantage to the purchaser is that it does not require proof that the vendors took active steps to conduct business.

Competition

- It may be reasonable (and therefore enforceable) for the vendors to be prevented from carrying on any business activity in a competing field.
- The restriction needs to be more closely limited as to scope and period in order to be enforceable.
- There should also be a geographical limit on the restriction, based on the appropriate 'market' serviced by the target (which may mean the whole world).

11.9.6   There are other ways of protecting the target business from unfair competition which can be used instead of or alongside restrictions on the vendors. These include:

- in the case of individuals, entering into fixed-term employment contracts (with garden leave provisions) or consultancy agreements which control their activities for a period after completion;
- in the case of corporate vendors, entering into supply contracts which effectively commit supply of goods or services to the target rather than direct to third parties;
- creating an earn-out structure which motivates the vendors not to compete.

11.9.7   Restrictions in the acquisition agreement or in any ancillary agreement entered into with the vendors will be subject to competition law considerations. These are briefly looked at in Chapter 8. However, the restrictions referred to in sample documents 6 and 26 (pages 166 and 280), binding only upon the vendors, are unlikely to infringe existing competition law. Greater care is required in the case of reciprocal obligations accepted by both the vendor and the purchaser, for example in an ongoing supply agreement.

11.10 Pensions

11.10.1 As noted in paragraph 7.14, the target may have established or administered various types of pension schemes which benefit its employees. The 'handover' of these arrangements to the purchaser will mainly depend on the type of scheme and the details of individual schemes. This is a complex and involved area, which requires involvement from legal and pension specialists.

11.10.2 The required arrangements are likely to be more complex on a business purchase, particularly where there are occupational pension schemes. On a share purchase, the purchaser will have the benefit of existing arrangements entered into with the target. However, where the target is a subsidiary, the holding company or other subsidiaries may be involved in the scheme, requiring changes to those arrangements.

11.10.3 In the case of a group personal pension scheme, as explained in paragraph 7.14 these are actually individual pension plans for each participating employee. The arrangements on completion will thus relate only to varying or renewing the contract with the pension scheme provider, usually an insurance company.

11.10.4 Arrangements with regard to an occupational pension scheme are likely to be more involved, particularly where this is a final salary scheme (see paragraph 7.14). The arrangements are likely to include one or more of the following:

- changes to the trustees;
- on a business sale where the whole scheme will be 'taken over' by the purchaser, a deed by which the purchaser adheres to the scheme and becomes the employer for the purposes of the trust deed;
- on a share sale where the scheme involves other group companies or on a business sale where the purchaser will not take over the whole scheme, arrangements for a bulk transfer of the employee entitlements into a new scheme.

11.10.5 Adhering to an existing scheme will impose potential liabilities on the purchaser/target with regard to legal compliance and, on a final salary scheme, underfunding issues. The purchaser will want to avoid this, even as an interim measure before a new scheme is set up. Thus, it should be ready with its own arrangements to be implemented at or shortly following completion.

11.10.6 Where part of the fund is to be transferred from one scheme to another, the 'transfer value' needs to be determined. The acquisition agreement would set out (usually in the schedule) the basis of a calculation in the transfer value and the arrangements for the transfer. The table below sets out different bases of valuation.

BASES FOR CALCULATING A TRANSFER PAYMENT

Cash equivalent	■ The value of members' accrued rights in the vendor's scheme based on their salaries and pensionable service up to the agreed transfer date.
	■ No allowance for any future salary increases nor for discretionary pension increases above those guaranteed by the scheme.
	■ This is the minimum transfer value to which members would be entitled on leaving the vendor's scheme.
	■ This basis may be described in the agreement as 'the value of the accrued benefits of the transferring members'.
Past service reserve	■ Calculated by reference to anticipated salaries at retirement and may include some allowance for discretionary pension increases.
	■ In other words, it assumes that the scheme has been properly funded so provision should have been made for likely salary increases.

- A set of actuarial assumptions is needed (set out either in the agreement or in a letter from the actuaries) to expand and explain what this basis means in a particular case.
- The transfer provisions in the agreement would refer to 'the past service reserve applicable to the employees at completion calculated in accordance with the actuarial assumptions' (being those set out).

Share of fund

- Involves partitioning the whole of the pension scheme fund between those employees transferring to a new scheme and those remaining in the existing scheme.
- The fund would be partitioned in proportion to the value of their respective benefits.
- This basis would produce the highest transfer payment if the scheme was in surplus but a smaller transfer payment than past service reserve or even cash equivalent methods if the scheme was in deficit.
- The wording in the agreement would refer to 'such proportion of the scheme assets as the actuarial interests of the employees of the target bears to the actuarial interests of all members of the scheme at completion'.

11.10.7 Under the Pensions Act 1995, members of an occupational pension scheme would be entitled to a transfer value calculated on the cash equivalent basis. However, the parties may negotiate a more generous basis such as a past service reserve basis. They may be entitled to agree and implement this transfer to another approved occupational pension scheme without the consent of the members, although it is normally advisable to obtain the consent of relevant members before the transfer. Each member may wish the cash equivalent value to be paid into the purchaser's new scheme or in one of the other statutory approved ways.

11.10.8 Given the problems relating to legal compliance and funding (briefly referred to in Chapter 7), purchasers are increasingly reluctant to establish any new final salary scheme. Also, the bulk transfer of values from an existing scheme to a new scheme is less common. The purchaser will usually be keen to start afresh with new arrangements and leave it to the scheme trustees and advisors to inform the members of their rights and to deal with their entitlements under the old scheme.

11.10.9 As well as the arrangements for transfer of rights and payments (including any 'on account' payment from one scheme to another pending final calculation), the purchaser is also likely to require warranties and indemnities, as referred to Chapter 12.

CHAPTER 12 Warranties

12.1 Purpose

12.1.1 The purposes of warranties are:
- to uncover any information about the target that has not been revealed by due diligence;
- to give the purchaser a means of redress from the vendor if the target turns out to have liabilities that were not disclosed to the purchaser.

12.1.2 Warranties may be given by persons other than the vendor, particularly on a management buy-out (MBO) transaction. Thus, warranties may be given:
- by Newco and members of the MBO team, in favour of a venture capitalist (VC) or other investor, as noted in paragraph 9.3;
- by Newco (and potentially by members of the MBO team) in favour of a bank providing funding for the acquisition, as noted in paragraph 9.2.5.

The purpose of these warranties is to protect the investment made by the funders, particularly as the vendor on an MBO is likely to want to restrict the warranties given to the purchaser. Another purpose is to ensure that members of the MBO team, whose investment in Newco may be relatively small, have taken adequate care to examine and understand the affairs of the target and its business plan.

12.1.3 Where the consideration includes the issue of consideration shares, the vendor should think about obtaining warranties from the purchaser (or other third parties) in relation to the information provided on the purchaser, its good standing and financial affairs. Care should be taken in this case to ensure those warranties do not amount to unlawful financial assistance. The purchaser, particularly if it is a quoted company, will usually be reluctant to give such warranties.

12.1.4 The vendor may also seek a warranty from the purchaser to the effect that the purchaser is not aware of any matters likely to give rise to a claim under the warranties given by the vendor. This is known as a 'reverse warranty'. Its purpose is to guard against the purchaser waiting until after completion to make a claim against the vendor under the warranties in respect of a matter already identified through due diligence. The due diligence process may have involved a more thorough investigation of the target business than has previously been carried out by the vendor itself, so it is possible that financial and legal due diligence will reveal problems. It would arguably be unfair for the purchaser to be entitled to claim for these by not sharing the information with the vendor. From the purchaser's perspective, a reverse warranty will be contentious, because any statement based on the purchaser's knowledge could negate the warranties. It allows the vendor to defend any claim made on the basis that the purchaser knew or ought to have known about the matter. This problem can be mitigated somewhat by clearly limiting the words of the reserve warranty to refer to actual knowledge or the contents of specific reports.

12.2 Documentation

12.2.1 Warranties are factual statements given by the vendor in favour of the purchaser about the state of the target company or the target business, covering the whole range of its assets and liabilities. These warranties are included in the purchase agreement, and usually consist of:

- a clause in the 'front-end' of the agreement, setting out the actual warranty obligation;
- a schedule setting out the statements themselves;
- a schedule setting out limitations on the warranties.

12.2.2 The vendor will not be liable under the warranties to the extent that matters are fairly disclosed in the disclosure letter – a document prepared by the vendor and its lawyers.

12.2.3 The purpose of this chapter is to highlight key issues in the drafting and negotiation of the warranties and the disclosure letter and the legal effect of each. It also considers the related issues of the tax covenant and specific indemnities.

12.3 Legal background

12.3.1 Without contractual warranties, the protection of the purchaser under the general law is very limited. This follows from the well-known legal principle of *caveat emptor*, meaning 'let the buyer beware'. As noted in Chapter 11, the use of the words 'full title guarantee' in the sale clause of the purchase agreement will imply covenants that the vendor gives good title to the shares or assets being sold, free from third party rights. Also, where the purchaser buys assets, the statutory implied warranties on a sale of goods will apply. These are, in brief, to the effect that the vendor has good title, that the goods are of satisfactory quality and that they are fit for their intended purpose. However, how these warranties would apply in the context of a business acquisition is unclear and this is unlikely to be satisfactory to the purchaser.

12.3.2 The law of misrepresentation will give the purchaser a right to claim damages and/or rescind the contract if the vendor makes a wrong or misleading statement to the purchaser about the target, which induces the purchaser to complete the acquisition. Some basic points on the law of misrepresentation are set out below. This protection is unlikely to be sufficient and it is quite likely that the vendor will exclude all liability for misrepresentation (other than fraudulent misrepresentation, which cannot be excluded) under the purchase agreement. The vendor will invariably exclude any right to rescind the agreement and it would in any event be quite difficult to put the parties back into the position they were before the contract in the case of share of business acquisition.

LAW OF MISREPRESENTATION

Basic requirements
- A statement of fact (not a statement of opinion or law):
  - made by one of the contracting parties to the other (or by their representatives)
  - which induces the other party to enter into the contract.

Omissions
- In general there is no misrepresentation by silence.
- Even when one party is aware that the other misunderstands the fact, there is no liability in general.
- However, giving half a story may be sufficiently misleading to amount to a misrepresentation.
- A change of circumstances causing a true statement to become false may amount of misrepresentation if the party does not disclose the change.

Remedies
- The principal remedy is rescission, meaning the parties are restored to their original positions.
- This is impractical on most acquisitions and the right will usually be excluded.
- Damages are only available for fraudulent misrepresentations or negligent misrepresentations.

Exclusion
- Liability for fraudulent misrepresentation cannot be excluded.
- Exclusion of negligent misrepresentation requires clear words.
- Liability will also in effect be excluded where one party makes it clear that the representation cannot be relied upon.

12.3.3 Warranties are therefore intended to provide a contractual right to damages should the statements made in the warranties be found to be untrue, inaccurate or misleading. The extent of the liability and the right to damages will depend on the terms of the purchase agreement.

12.3.4 The basis of calculating damages for breach of warranty is usually regulated by the clause in the 'front end' of the agreement. If the vendor 'warrants' to the purchaser certain facts without further embellishment, the purchaser will be entitled to contractual damages. These would be based on the difference between the market value of the shares or business assets (as the case may be) as they actually are and their value as they would have been if the warranty had been true. This may limit the value of the warranties on a share acquisition, since the measure of damages will be calculated according to the value of the shares, and a breach of a warranty, such as an undisclosed liability or a shortfall in assets, may have no or only a small effect on the value of those shares. Where the consideration for the target was based on profit earning capacity and thus the value of the shares is by reference to profits, a shortfall of assets will affect the value of the shares only if the profit earning capacity of the target is reduced. Thus the purchaser may wish to insert provisions to extend or clarify the basis of damages.

12.3.5   The purchaser will usually want the clause in the front end of the agreement to read that the vendor 'represents and warrants' the matters set out in the warranty schedule. To the extent that those warranties are factual statements, the purchaser could then be entitled to damages based on misrepresentation, in crude terms being the difference between the market value of the shares or business assets (as they are) and the amount of the consideration. If the purchaser could show that the breach of warranty amounted to a negligent misrepresentation which induced the contract, the purchaser might be able to claim damages to reflect the loss suffered by acquiring the target (not just the loss by reason of the breach of warranty) if, for example, there were serious problems that were not otherwise caught by the warranties. This could give rise to the more advantageous measure of damages for the purchaser, although more often it will not, on the basis that the purchaser is not entitled to any 'loss of bargain' if the shares or assets are still worth what the purchaser paid. The purchaser will wish to choose either basis for claiming damages, but the vendor will usually resist this.

12.3.6   The draft purchase agreement prepared by the purchaser will often contain provisions which give the purchaser the right to claim damages for breach of warranty on an indemnity basis or 'pound for pound' basis. This would usually be expressed as a choice for the purchaser to claim loss of bargain under the normal contractual test or the right to be reimbursed for the amount of any undisclosed liability or shortfall in assets, regardless of whether this affects the value of the shares. This is the best position for the purchaser because, in crude terms:

■ where the consideration is based on profits, a breach of warranty relating to a reduction of those profits could result in recovery of a multiple of that reduction; and

■ regardless of whether the breach affects those profits or the value of the company, the purchaser will be entitled to recover pound for pound any undisclosed liability.

12.3.7   Not surprisingly, the vendor will seek to resist or at least limit the right to claim damages on an indemnity basis. Alternatively, it might prefer a pound for pound claim over a potential 'loss of bargain' claim, which could give rise to a very large claim and a prolonged dispute. The most sophisticated clause would set out circumstances where the indemnity measure would be applied and, in the case of matters that reduce profitability, a specified multiple of that figure which reflects the calculation of the price.

12.3.8 The warranty clause will also oblige the vendor to reimburse costs and expenses incurred by the purchaser in pursuing a claim under the warranties. This clause needs to be negotiated carefully, as it may include an attempt to obtain an indemnity measure of damages by an indirect means and also permit professional costs to mount up at the vendor's expense. At the very least, those costs should be limited to those 'reasonably and properly incurred'. It would be more advantageous to the vendor if no costs indemnity was given and the purchaser had to rely on the contractual right to recover expenses as part of its recoverable loss and/or to recover costs through the courts if a claim was successful.

12.4 Disclosure

12.4.1 The disclosure letter qualifying the warranties will typically be comprised of the following elements:
- preamble to identify the letter and its purpose – any attempts in this section to vary the warranty provisions contained in the share purchase agreement should be strongly resisted by the purchaser;
- general disclosures (examples are given in clause 2 of sample document 10, page 231, and further comment is set out below);
- specific disclosures against the warranties, usually by reference to paragraphs of the warranty schedule;
- the disclosure bundle, containing documents relevant to the disclosures and/or warranties.

12.4.2 The agreement would usually provide that matters 'fully and fairly disclosed in the disclosure letter' will preclude claims under the warranties. The vendor would prefer to delete the reference to disclosing matters 'fully'. The concept of fair disclosure requires that the purchaser is given enough information to make an assessment of the issue. It is not necessary for the vendor to quantify that risk in money terms, although the purchaser will often require a specific disclosure to do so.

12.4.3 The general disclosures may sometimes be contentious. These should refer to the information the purchaser has or could have obtained from searches in public registers and enquiries of statutory authorities. Even then, the purchaser may not be willing to accept disclosure of all public registers (for example the Trade Mark Registry, where searching would be very expensive) if it would be more reasonable for the vendor to disclose specific matters. The vendor may also seek to disclose a physical inspection of the company's properties and other assets. Whether this is reasonable depends on what level of due diligence the purchaser has been able to do, whether it would be feasible to inspect each item of machinery and whether it would be fairer for the vendor to take responsibility for checking the physical state of the assets. This general disclosure is however usually accepted in respect of properties where the vendor would not expect to warrant the physical condition of its land and buildings.

12.4.4 More contentious general disclosures relate to reports prepared for the purchaser in relation to financial, commercial and/or legal due diligence. There are arguments on both sides on whether such disclosure is fair. On the vendor's side, the content of those reports is available to the purchaser before completion and the vendor will usually have assisted in some way in providing relevant information. On the purchaser's side, the purpose of those reports was not to limit the obligation of the vendor to go through the warranties and make its own disclosures. In many cases, the due diligence reports will not be shown to the vendor, although the vendor should ask to see them. Lastly, the request to disclose 'all matters in the public domain' sounds quite fair, but should be resisted by the purchaser on the basis that it is too open-ended and uncertain.

12.4.5 The specific disclosures should be set out as clearly and succinctly as possible. Although they will invariably be listed by reference to specific warranties, the disclosure letter will state that each disclosure qualifies all warranties. The purchaser will usually accept this, but perhaps subject to limitations. For example, it may not accept that any disclosures will qualify the warranties as to title to the shares/assets. As noted above, the purchaser will usually want any disclosure of a problem to include an estimate or a cap in respect of the financial liability involved. This will particularly be the case where the disclosure relates to potential liabilities or claims by third parties.

12.4.6 The disclosure bundle can vary from one or two lever arch folders containing copy documents through to many boxes of papers. The vendor may be tempted to disclose too much, in effect giving the purchaser vast quantities of irrelevant information. It is the job of the purchaser's lawyer to control this process and ensure that the disclosure bundle contains only information pertinent to disclosures in the disclosure letter or information requested in the warranties.

12.4.7 It is very important that the disclosure bundle is properly indexed with cross-referencing to the warranties/disclosure letter. On completion, there should (where feasible) be two copies of the disclosure bundle prepared, to be retained by the purchaser's lawyers and the vendor's lawyers. It will often be impractical to initial every page of the disclosure bundle but the parties should certainly agree and exchange a detailed index.

12.5 Particular warranties

12.5.1 The schedule in sample document 6 (page 166) sets out typical warranties on a share purchase. Warranties on a business purchase would be similar in nature, although need to be tailored to the individual circumstances of the deal. The purpose of these should be fairly self-explanatory and it is not intended to go though all sections in detail. Comments have been made in previous chapters on issues such as employees and pensions.

12.5.2   On a share purchase or on a business purchase where debts are included in the sale, the purchaser will want some assurance that the full value of the debts will be collected. Usually, the purchaser will want claims under the debt warranty to be on a 'pound for pound' basis, for the reasons described in paragraph 12.3. This is likely to be onerous for the vendor, who will seek limits in one or more of the following ways:

- excluding claims to the extent that the bad debt has been provided for in the vendor's accounts (being the accounts on which the purchaser has relied);
- excluding claims to the extent that all bad debts are within any general provision in those accounts;
- allowing for a proportion of the debts to be bad, by rewording the warranty to say that, for example, 'not less than 95 per cent of the debts will be collected within 90 days of completion';
- limiting the obligation by reference to the vendor's knowledge, although note this seriously weakens the warranty in that the purchaser would have to show the vendor knew the debt would not be collected.

12.5.3   The accounts warranties will be a fundamental part of any warranty schedule, particularly in the case of a share purchase. There will usually be a warranty on a share purchase that the last annual audited accounts of the target comply with the Companies Act 1985 (CA), show a true and fair view of the state of affairs of the target as at the accounts date and make provision for all liabilities. Individual vendors in an owner managed company will often claim that they have relied wholly upon the company's auditors, but it is unlikely that the purchaser will have an adequate remedy against the auditors and will thus insist upon this warranty. The purchaser will usually also seek warranties on up to date management accounts, which is more contentious because such accounts have not been audited, may not be as precise and will have been prepared to provide management information rather than to a statutory standard. There will usually therefore be some relaxation of the words regarding management accounts, perhaps even limiting them to the awareness of the vendors.

12.5.4   With regard to property, the attitude of many lawyers (based on their experience of commercial property transactions) is that the purchaser should rely on its own investigations. Therefore, warranties relating to the property, at least as regards its physical state and condition, should not be given. In place of warranties, the purchaser may rely upon investigation by the purchaser's lawyer of the title, usual searches and perhaps a certificate of title provided by the vendor's lawyers. These issues were dealt with in paragraph 7.9.

12.6 Tax

12.6.1   On a share purchase, the purchaser will want protection in the form of:

- a tax covenant;
- tax warranties.

12.6.2 These provisions are usually contained in a separate schedule to the main agreement, as shown in sample document 9 (page 215). Alternatively, the tax covenant may be contained in a separate deed. These provisions are relatively complicated and the following paragraphs merely give an overview of the issues involved.

12.6.3 The tax covenant requires the vendor to pay to the purchaser an amount equal to any liability of the target to pay tax in respect of events occurring on or before completion. In other words, it draws a line as to the respective responsibilities of the vendor and/or the purchaser for the tax liabilities, with the act of completion being on the vendor's side of the line to ensure that charges triggered by completion (perhaps combined with earlier events) are caught by the covenants. An important exclusion is any tax for which provision has been made in the vendor's accounts (the accounts on which the parties have relied in agreeing the consideration). Where there are completion accounts, it follows that there should be no liability under the tax covenant to the extent that provision is made in the completion accounts.

12.6.4 The covenant will also usually cover loss of certain tax reliefs. The classic example would be a relief that had been taken into account in determining the tax provision in the accounts. If that relief is not available due to any act for which the vendor was responsible, the provision for tax will not be sufficient and the liability for the target will have increased.

12.6.5 The tax covenant will protect the purchaser on a 'pound for pound' basis from these unprovided tax liabilities. The covenant will also provide that costs and expenses in disputing the matters with the tax authority and the vendor are recoverable in full.

12.6.6 The tax covenant should deal with the conduct of claims, here meaning any action taken by the Inland Revenue or another tax authority to recover tax or dispute a relief. The purchaser will want to control the affairs of the target, but the vendor will want to participate in conducting the matter (on the basis that it is bearing the cost of any tax arising from the claim).

12.6.7 Tax warranties would also be requested from the vendor covering:
- compliance with tax legislation, including correct and timely submission of returns;
- due payment of tax;
- special arrangements made with tax authorities;
- specific activities that have a particular tax effect;
- activities which are or might be treated as tax avoidance.

12.6.8 The vendor may question why warranties are required in addition to a tax covenant. There are two reasons:
- the warranties flush out information concerning the affairs of the target which may be necessary or useful for the purchaser to know in order to manage the affairs of the target in the future;
- the measure of damages under warranties may on occasion be greater than that under the tax covenant, where for example the liability has the effect of reducing profitability of the target (see paragraph 12.3).

12.7 Warranty limitations

12.7.1 Provisions are invariably included in the main warranty clause and/or a separate schedule limiting and excluding claims under the warranties in certain circumstances. This aspect of the acquisition often causes more negotiation than any other aspect and specific issues on it are often the last to be agreed, just before completion.

12.7.2 A typical set of limitations is included as sample document 11 (page 234). Also, clause 7 in the share purchase agreement (sample document 6, page 166) sets out some basic limitations. Whether the purchaser includes limitations on the warranties in the first draft of the agreement is a matter of style. However, it will usually be appropriate to include at least basic provisions, because:

- it is inevitable that these limits will be incorporated into the agreement;
- including the provisions in the first draft means that the purchaser has retained the initiative.

12.7.3 The most basic provisions will limit:

- the period during which claims can be made;
- the aggregate maximum amount which can be claimed under the warranties, referred to as the 'total cap';
- the thresholds before any warranty claim can be made, known as the 'de minimus'.

12.7.4 The time limit for warranty claims will typically be two or three years from completion. It is often calculated by reference to the period in which the purchaser will have completed one or two statutory audits of the target. The vendor will obviously want as short a period as possible and will look for it to be as short as one year after completion. The negotiated deal usually lies somewhere in between these figures.

12.7.5 The total cap for claims is usually based around the total consideration payable for the target. Where the target has existing debt to be refinanced by the purchaser or where the purchaser is making a significant new investment into the target there may be arguments to increase the maximum beyond the level of the consideration. This would certainly be the case where the consideration was a nominal figure. Conversely, where part of the consideration is to be satisfied by existing cash in the target, the vendor may argue that the effective purchase cost for the purchaser is reduced by that amount and seek a total cap based on the net amount.

12.7.6 The de minimus provision is intended to prevent the purchaser from making claims for small amounts or amassing a number of small claims into one larger amount. The concept behind this is that the parties should not be bothered with 'trifles', but quite often the thresholds will be quite significant sums. In fact, the de minimus provision has become a way for the vendors to feel more comfortable about giving warranties.

12.7.7 The de minimus provision will usually comprise a combination of the following:

- a low threshold for each individual matter giving rise to a breach of the warranties, below which the claim can neither be made nor counted towards the next threshold;
- a higher threshold for the value of all or any claims under the warranties;
- potentially, a separate threshold that is specific to any individual warranty or an individual matter.

12.7.8 It is usual when the aggregate threshold has been reached for the purchaser to be entitled to recover the whole amount of the loss, not just the excess.

12.7.9 Other limitations of the warranties protect the vendor from changes to the business occurring after completion, changes to accounting methods and legal issues relating to mitigation of loss. The schedule will usually also deal with conduct of claims to enable the vendor to participate in, if not conduct, disputes with, third parties that could give rise to liability under the warranties.

12.8 Warranty insurance

12.8.1 If a vendor is concerned about exposure under the warranties the vendor and its advisors should consider obtaining insurance against claims. This is available from specialist insurers in appropriate cases.

12.8.2 The premium will reflect a number of factors, including the complexity of the transactions, limits of liability and the scope of the warranties given. The insurers will become quite involved in assessing the business as well as the purchase documentation.

12.8.3 Alternatively, the insurance may be taken out to cover specific risks. An example would be where a potential environmental liability has been identified through due diligence and the purchaser requires a specific warranty or indemnity to cover this. This may be the subject of a bespoke policy for that risk.

12.8.4 Directors' and officers' insurance policies cover individual directors from liability incurred in their capacity as officers. This would not include insurance against warranty claims on sale of the target. A separate policy would be required.

12.8.5 As noted above, VCs would not expect to give any warranties on a sale of a buy-out vehicle, other than as to their title to the shares being sold. Warranty insurance may therefore be taken out to fill the liability gap.

12.9 Specific indemnities

12.9.1 A matter may be disclosed, in due diligence or in the disclosure letter, concerning a risk the purchaser is not willing to accept. Simple deletion of the disclosure from the disclosure letter would not be sufficient to preserve the purchaser's rights to claim against the vendors. This is because the purchaser must prove that it has suffered loss as a result of breach of warranty under the normal principles of assessing damages for breach of contract. If the matter has become known to the purchaser, there will be difficulty in making a claim. For this reason, such matters will be dealt with by specific indemnities, if the vendor accepts that the risk should be borne by the vendor.

12.9.2   On a business purchase, there will usually be indemnities covering particular areas such as employee liability. On a share purchase, indemnities will usually only be included for very specific topics and so their wording depends on the particular circumstances.

12.9.3   A common example would relate to pensions, where there is an occupational pension scheme in which the purchaser will participate and the purchaser is concerned about issues such as equalisation and the other potential liabilities referred to in paragraph 7.14. A simple form of indemnity in this case is set out below.

PENSIONS INDEMNITY

In consideration of the Purchaser agreeing to purchase the Target, the Vendor covenants with the Purchaser that the Vendor will indemnify the Purchaser against any liabilities which the Purchaser may incur as a result of participating in the Pension Scheme up to the date on which the Pension Scheme is transferred to the Purchaser's control, including (without limitation) liabilities under article 119 of the Treaty of Rome.

Public company issues on acquisitions

13.1 Overview

13.1.1 The UK Listing Authority (UKLA) is part of the Financial Services Authority (FSA). Since transfer of this role from the London Stock Exchange to the FSA in 2000 there have been two levels of control and regulation for companies with listed securities:

- the UKLA, which has legal responsibility for the admission of securities to the Official List and EC and UK legislation;
- the London Stock Exchange plc (LSE), which regulates the admission of those securities to trading on its markets as a recognised investment exchange. The LSE retains responsibility for supervision and monitoring of its secondary markets, which is primarily the AIM Market.

The UKLA is responsible for the issue of the Listing Rules and the LSE is responsible for issuing the rules of the markets it regulates, such as the AIM Rules.

13.2 Summary

13.2.1 In any acquisition or disposal involving private, public or listed public companies, the same key issues need to be addressed as dealt with in more detail in other chapters. To recap:

- structure, ie shares or assets;
- form of the consideration;
- raising of finance;
- due diligence;
- contractual protection, eg warranties.

13.2.2 Where the vendor is a publicly listed company there will need to be some differences in approach to these key issues:

- **due diligence** – there is more information about a listed company vendor in the public domain because of its status as a listed company;
- **contractual protection** – very limited (if any) warranties will be available in the case of a listed company target as the shareholders have had little or no input in the management of the company;

- **consideration and funding** – if the listed company is the purchaser, the issue of further securities by means of a placing or rights issue may be considered to fund the acquisition, or shares in the listed company purchaser may be offered as consideration instead of cash.

13.2.3 As well as these differences, there are a number of other considerations to take into account when an acquisition or disposal involves a listed company or a subsidiary undertaking of the listed company:

- the requirements of the Listing Rules or the AIM Rules as they apply to the transaction:
  - the classification of the transaction and the consequences for the listed company of that classification;
  - disclosure of the transaction;
  - restrictions on directors of the listed company dealing in the company's shares together with the insider dealing legislation;
  - requirements of the Listing Rules or AIM Rules in respect of share issues;
  - where the consideration (or the funding for the consideration) is in the form of new shares to be listed, listing particulars or a prospectus will be required;
- the requirements of any institutional investors;
- additional requirements under the Companies Act 1985 (CA) applicable to public companies;
- if the quoted company is the target of an acquisition, the Takeover Code and Substantial Acquisition Rules (SARs).

13.3 Class tests

13.3.1 Classification of the transaction and its effect for a company on the Official List and the provisions for the classification of transactions involving listed companies (principally meaning acquisitions and disposal) are found in chapter 10 of the Listing Rules. The provisions apply whether the acquisition or disposal is of shares or assets and whether the listed company is vendor or purchaser.

13.3.2 Transactions are categorised for the purposes of the Listing Rules according to their size in relation to the listed company by reference to a number of percentage ratio tests.

13.3.3 There are five percentage ratio tests, based on assets, profits, turnover, consideration to market capitalisation and gross capital. Each involves a comparison between the size of the transaction and the listed company.

PERCENTAGE RATIO TESTS

- **Assets** –the gross assets which are the subject of the transaction divided by the gross assets of the listed company. The gross assets of the listed company are defined by the Listing Rules as the total fixed assets of the listed company plus the total current assets of the listed company. If the transaction involves the acquisition or disposal of shares in an undertaking, the net assets of that undertaking must be consolidated in the accounts of the listed company for the purpose of the test or (on disposal) the net assets of that undertaking should be discounted and no longer consolidated in the accounts of the listed company for the purpose of the test. The purpose of this adjustment is to ensure that the assets which are the subject of this transaction mean the value of 100 per cent of the relevant undertaking's assets irrespective of what interest is actually acquired or disposed of. In all other cases involving shares, the assets that are the subject of the transaction are, for an acquisition, the consideration together with any liabilities that may be assumed and, for disposal, the assets attributed to that interest in the company's accounts. Where the acquisition or disposal is of assets rather than shares, the value on an acquisition is the consideration or, if greater, the book value of those assets. In the case of a disposal of assets, it means the book value of the assets.

- **Profits** – the profits attributable to the assets which are the subject of the transaction divided by the profits of the listed company. Profits is defined by the Listing Rules as profits after deducting all charges except tax and extraordinary items. In the case of an acquisition or disposal of an interest in a company which, as a result, is to be included or removed from the consolidated accounts of the company, then profits means 100 per cent of the profits of the undertaking irrespective of what interest is acquired or disposed of. The assessment of the assets subject to the transaction is the same as in the assets test.

- **Turnover** – the turnover attributable to the assets which are the subject of the transaction divided by the turnover of the listed company. The Listing Rules do not provide any express guidance on the calculation of turnover. Therefore, turnover will be the sum of the trading receipts as determined by the company's accountants.

- **Consideration to market capitalisation** – the consideration divided by the aggregate market value of all the ordinary shares of the listed company. The consideration is the amount paid to the vendors but the UKLA may require the inclusion of further amounts, for example where the purchaser agrees to discharge any liabilities, including the repayment of inter-company or third party debt as part of the terms of the transaction. Where the transaction involves an element of deferred consideration then the consideration is the maximum total consideration payable or receivable under the agreement. Where the total consideration is not subject to any maximum the transaction will be treated as a class one transaction, notwithstanding the class into which it otherwise would fall. In calculating the aggregate market value of all the ordinary shares of the listed company, the price is that at the close of business on the last date immediately preceding the announcement of the transaction.

- **Gross capital** – the gross capital of the company or business being acquired divided by the gross capital of the listed company. This percentage ratio test applies only in the case of an acquisition of a company or business. The gross capital of the company or business being acquired means the aggregate of the consideration payable and the liabilities being assumed. The gross capital of the listed company is its liabilities together with its aggregate market value.

13.4 Classification

13.4.1 The purpose of performing the various percentage ratio tests is to ascertain the classification of the transaction and the formalities required by the Listing Rules as a consequence of such classification. Chapter 10 of the Listing Rules divides transactions into:

- **class one** – a transaction where any percentage ratio is 25 per cent or more;
- **class two** – a transaction where any percentage ratio is 5 per cent or more but each is less than 25 per cent;
- **class three** – a transaction where all percentage ratios are less than 5 per cent;
- **reverse takeover** – acquisition by a listed company of a business, an unlisted company or assets where any percentage ratio is 100 per cent or more or which would result in a fundamental change in the business or in a change in board or voting control of the listed company.

13.4.2 Where an acquisition or disposal is classified as a class one transaction the following is necessary:

- the company must notify a regulatory information service without delay after the terms of the transaction are agreed prescribing details of the transaction;
- an explanatory circular must be sent to shareholders;
- shareholder approval must be obtained to the transaction (by ordinary resolution);
- the transaction must be conditional upon shareholder approval being obtained.

The Listing Rules set out the information that must be included in the announcement and circular to shareholders. Private individuals or companies who intend to enter into a transaction with a listed company must be aware that details of the transaction will be made public, which may run contrary to their desire to keep private information such as the consideration being paid.

13.4.3 A class two transaction does not require an explanatory circular to be sent to shareholders nor shareholder approval. Instead, the only requirement is that the company must notify a regulatory information service without delay after the terms of the class two transaction are agreed. Paragraph 10.3.1 of the Listing Rules sets out the specific details required in the announcement (the same details are required for an announcement of the class one transaction).

13.4.4 There is no requirement for an announcement of a class three transaction unless:

- the company intends to make any other form of announcement; or
- in the case of the purchaser, the consideration includes the issue of shares which will be listed.

The Listing Rules set out the requirements for any necessary announcement, however less information is required than for a class one or class two announcement.

13.4.5 Upon the announcement of a reverse takeover that has been agreed or is in contemplation, the UKLA will suspend listing of the listed company's shares. The company must then prepare a class one circular, obtain the prior approval of shareholders to the transaction and, if the company wishes to be listed following completion of the transaction, prepare listing particulars as though the company were a new applicant. The listing will be restored on publication of the circular and the listing particulars.

13.4.6 In the case of a reverse takeover, the transaction will be treated as a class one transaction if the following conditions are satisfied:

- the subject of the acquisition is a similar size to that of the acquiring company;
- the subject of the acquisition is in a similar line of business to that of the acquiring company;
- the undertaking that is the subject of the acquisition complies with the conditions for listing set out in chapter 3 of the Listing Rules;
- there will be no change of board or voting control as a result of the transaction.

13.5 Classification of the transaction for companies listed on AIM

13.5.1 The AIM Rules contain five tests, which are broadly similar to those found in the Listing Rules. The classification of the transaction is, however, different. If any of the class tests gives a result of 10 per cent or more, the transaction is a 'substantial transaction'. The effect of this is that the company must notify LSE without delay as soon as the terms of any substantial transaction are agreed, disclosing the information specified by the AIM Rules. There is no specific obligation under the AIM Rules for shareholder consent to such a transaction or even notification to shareholders, however, if shares are being issued by the AIM company as consideration, shareholder consent may be required to effect an increase in authorised share capital or to give directors sufficient authority to allot the shares in connection with the transaction.

13.5.2 In the event of a reverse takeover (which is the same definition as the Listing Rules), any agreement that would effect a reverse takeover must be:

- conditional on the consent of its shareholders;
- notified without delay, disclosing the information specified by the AIM Rules;
- accompanied by the publication of admission documents in respect of the proposed enlarged entity convening the required general meeting for shareholder consent.

13.5.3 Where shareholder approval is given for the reverse takeover, trading in the securities of the AIM company will be cancelled. If the enlarged entity seeks admission, it must make an application in the same manner as any other company applying for admission of its securities for the first time.

13.5.4 It should be noted that under the AIM Rules transactions in a 12 month period must be aggregated for the purposes of classification where they are entered into with the same or connected persons, involve the acquisition or disposal of securities or an interest in one particular business, or together lead to a principal involvement in any business activity or activities which did not previously form a part of the AIM company's principal activities.

13.6 Disclosure

13.6.1 Listed companies are under a general duty to disclose to UKLA without delay any major developments in their activities which are not public knowledge but which may have a substantial effect on the company's share price. The same obligations apply to companies listed on AIM. There is an exception for matters in the course of negotiation (eg an acquisition or disposal), which do not need to be notified until the negotiations are complete unless there has been or is likely to be a breach of confidentiality, at which point an announcement would be required.

13.6.2 Companies are under an express responsibility to ensure that any information released to the regulatory information service is not misleading, false, deceptive or materially incomplete.

13.7 Companies Act requirements

13.7.1 Sections 198 to 208 CA require the disclosure of shareholdings in public companies where the holding reaches the notifiable level of 3 per cent. This will be relevant in the build up to an acquisition if the purchaser is stake building in a public company target. Where the public company is listed, the Listing Rules require the information of major shareholdings to be forwarded onto the UKLA. Where the shareholding reaches 15 per cent or more in a listed company, disclosure is required under the SARs issued by the Panel on Takeovers and Mergers (see paragraph 13.9).

13.8 Listing particulars/prospectus

13.8.1 If the listed company is seeking a listing for further securities, either as consideration for the transaction by means of a placing or rights issue or to fund the consideration, a listing document may be required. The information to be included in the listing document is detailed in chapters 5 and 6 of the Listing Rules. There is a distinction drawn by the Listing Rules as to whether a prospectus or listing particulars need to be produced.

13.8.2 Paragraph 5.1 of the Listing Rules states that when an issuer applies before admission for listing of its securities that are to be offered to the public in the UK for the first time, a prospectus must be prepared. In other cases the requirement is to draw up listing particulars or a prospectus. There are various exclusions to this, for example if the new issue increases the shares of a class already listed by less than 10 per cent there is no need for a full listing document.

13.9 Takeover Code and Substantial Acquisition Rules

13.9.1 Where the target of an acquisition is a UK public company, the Takeover Code will apply on a share acquisition. Where the Code applies, the timetable and procedure of the acquisition are made subject to its regulations. Specialist advice should be taken in relation to the application of the Takeover Code.

13.9.2 If the target is a UK listed public company then the SARs will also apply in the period leading up to an offer for the entire issued share capital of the target. In basic terms, the SARs regulate the speed and formality of stake building in the run up to a full offer. Again specialist advice should be taken in this regard.

13.10 Timing

13.10.1 One of the principal effects on the timetable when dealing with a listed company is that if any fundraising is required through a placing or rights issue, or consideration shares are to be issued then a split exchange and completion will be required.

13.10.2 In the case of a public company carrying out a fundraising exercise, the sale and purchase agreement would be conditional on the outcome of the fundraising and also shareholder approval, should it be required. In the case of the issue of consideration shares, the agreement would be conditional on shareholder approval should it be required and admission of the consideration shares to the relevant exchange. In both instances this requires amendment to the sale and purchase agreement as set out in the sample document 6 (page 166).

CHAPTER 14

Completion and Beyond

14.1 Completion meeting

14.1.1 Completion of acquisitions (in particular buy-outs with VC and bank funding) is often lengthy and continues well into the night and beyond. This is often due to last minute negotiations and the fact that late changes to the terms or late arrival of information can have considerable impact on the documents involved. It is often true that conclusion of the deal will only be achieved through a face to face meeting where all parties commit to stay until the matter is finalised.

14.1.2 Documents relating to the acquisition and funding arrangements will be tabled, checked, agreed and then executed at the completion meeting. There is therefore a vast quantity of paper. One of the lawyers' tasks is to ensure that the papers are properly organised, checked and properly executed. It will often be difficult for MBO teams to read each draft of all the documents and they are particularly reliant upon their advisors in these circumstances. In any event, vendors and purchasers will rely on their lawyers to read the documents and explain the key issues.

14.1.3 Completion will take place when all documents have been executed and the parties to the various transactions agree (usually through their lawyers) that completion should take place. At that point, the documents are dated and all those arrangements are legally binding.

14.1.4 Following the completion meeting, a number of tasks will need to be carried out by the parties and their advisors, which are briefly outlined in this chapter.

14.2 Share sale

14.2.1 The transfers of the shares in the target will be subject to stamp duty at 0.5 per cent of the consideration. Where this is a fixed sum payable in cash, the share transfers can simply be sent to the Inland Revenue (IR) with appropriate payments. In other cases, for example where there are consideration shares, the value of that consideration will need to be adjudicated by IR. This involves submitting the transfers with a letter explaining the circumstances and giving evidence to support the valuation of the consideration.

14.2.2 When the share transfers have been stamped, the transfers should be entered into the target's register of members. It is a criminal offence for the directors to allow transfers to be registered unless they are properly stamped or certified as exempt from stamp duty.

14.2.3 The transfers should be approved for registration by the board of directors of the company, in accordance with the articles. See for example the completion board minutes for the target company included in sample document 17 (page 258). This approval can take place 'subject to stamping' at the completion meeting.

14.2.4 There are likely to be a number of returns to be made to Companies House as a result of the transaction. These include filing:

- the financial assistance whitewash papers, being the shareholder resolutions, statutory declaration and auditors' report on that declaration;
- any new articles adopted in respect of the target or purchaser, together with the resolutions adopting them;
- any new charges granted over the assets of the target or purchaser, together with form 395, both of which must be submitted within 21 days of creation of the charge, failing which the charge will be void.

14.3 Business purchase

14.3.1 Stamp duty land tax will be payable on the transfer of any freehold or leasehold property, according to the value of property, at the following rates:

- £0 to £150,000 – nil
- £150,000 to £250,000 – 1 per cent
- £250,001 to £500,000 – 3 per cent
- £500,001 and above – 4 per cent

14.3.2 Transfers of property, following stamping, will need to be registered at HM Land Registry within the appropriate time limits.

14.3.3 Transfers of registered intellectual property rights will need to be registered with the relevant authorities.

14.3.4 Where the purchaser is a company, there may be forms and resolutions to be filed at Companies House, in particular:

- registration of charges with form 395, as mentioned above;
- changes to the directors and other statutory particulars of the purchaser.

14.4 Documents

14.4.1 All original documents would usually be prepared in duplicate (assuming they are made between two principal parties). In this case, the lawyers for each party would take away those documents from the completion meeting and store them safely in their respective deeds room.

14.4.2 Funders (or their lawyers) will usually want to retain original documents relating to their funding. The bank will in particular need to take original security documents for registration and then safe-keeping.

14.4.3   A bible of documents would be prepared on most acquisitions. This is a set of copies of all the principal acquisition documents with an index, which is distributed to the parties and their advisors for future reference. These bibles can be quite voluminous and take some time to prepare, but it is a good idea for the bible to be compiled immediately following completion and then distributed as soon as possible so that the parties can refer to the agreements and their ongoing obligations under them.

14.4.4   Bibles are usually prepared in paper form in lever arch files. Many law firms now produce them in the form of CD ROMs, which are much more compact and enable the parties to view and print documents on their computers. However, many clients request lawyers to produce both paper copies and CD ROMs, partly defeating the original purpose.

14.4.5   It may be necessary, particularly on a business purchase, to change the stationery of the vendor and/or the purchaser, where there has been a change to the corporate name or registered office. In the case of Newco, this will usually involve its first stationery, which should set out the following:

- the full corporate name, whether or not other trading names are used on the stationery;
- the registered number and the fact that the company is registered in England and Wales;
- the registered office of the company;
- if the company decides to name the directors on the stationery, all their names must appear.

14.4.6   Where employees have transferred to the purchaser under TUPE, the purchaser should write to each employee confirming the transfer has taken place and identifying itself as the new employer.

14.4.7   Pension arrangements may require considerable post completion work in establishing new arrangements for dealing with the transfer of funds or changes to the trustees.

14.4.8   Professional advisors will render invoices and seek payment for fees in relation to the acquisition, which should be in line with quotations or budgets agreed in advance of completion.

14.5 Integration

14.5.1   The key task of the purchaser will be to take control of the affairs of the target. This is likely to include introducing new management systems in relation to administration, financial reporting, human resources and operations.

14.5.2   The purchaser will probably communicate with key customers and suppliers of the target to ensure continuity and keep them informed.

14.5.3   It may be necessary to integrate the target with an existing business and to reorganise the structure of the purchaser's group. All of this should be planned before completion so that it can, so far as possible, be included in any necessary approvals or legal steps.

Sample Documents

The following sample documents, referred to in the earlier part of the book, are reproduced in the following pages. They are also included on the accompanying CD, so that readers may tailor them to their own requirements.

Readers should note that preliminary material such as tables of contents and title pages have been omitted. They are, however, included on the CD.

Document 1
Confidentiality Undertaking

From: [Name and address]

Date [ ] 200[ ]

To [Name and address of proposed purchaser]

Dear [ ]

CONFIDENTIALITY UNDERTAKING

You have expressed an interest in pursuing the possibility of acquiring all or part of the entire issued share capital or business of [ ] Limited and its subsidiaries ('the Company') from its shareholders ('the Shareholders'). In this letter the proposed acquisition of the entire share capital of the Company is referred to as the 'proposed transaction'.

In consideration of our making available to you and your advisors certain information, you on behalf of yourselves and your advisers hereby agree and undertake to the Company and the Shareholders:

1   All information of whatsoever nature (whether oral, written or in any other form) containing or consisting of material of a technical, operational, administrative, economic, marketing, planning, business or financial nature or in the nature of intellectual property of any kind or of any other nature and relating to the Company, including the existence and the contents of this letter (which information is referred to in this letter, collectively and individually as 'Confidential Information') which is disclosed to you and/or to your representatives shall be held in complete confidence by you and by your advisors and representatives and shall not, without our prior written consent, be disclosed to any other person, nor used for any purpose, other than in connection with the evaluation and negotiation of the proposed transaction.

2   This obligation to maintain the confidentiality of and not use the Confidential Information shall continue to apply whether or not you complete the proposed transaction. However, your obligation does not apply to Confidential Information:
    2.1   all of which is generally available to third parties (unless available as a result of a breach of this undertaking);
    2.2   all of which is lawfully in your possession (as evidenced by your written records) and was not acquired directly or indirectly from us;
    2.3   which relates to the Company and has become your property following successful completion of the proposed transaction; and/or
    2.4   the disclosure of which is required by any applicable law or by any supervisory or regulatory body to whose rules you are presently subject.

3   The exceptions in paragraph 2 above shall not however apply to:
    3.1   Confidential Information merely because it is embraced by more general information which falls within any one or more of such exceptions; or
    3.2   any combination of features merely because individual features (but not the combination itself) fall within any one or more of such exceptions.

4   You will not disclose Confidential Information to any person other than those of your advisors or in relation to any company controlled by you (which is intended to be involved in the proposed transaction), its directors, officers, employees, advisers and representa-

tives who are directly concerned with the appraisal of the proposed transaction and who need to know such Confidential Information. You will, on written demand from us, supply us with a list of those persons within your company and/or any company controlled by you (giving their names and details of positions held by them) and of your advisers and representatives who are likely to be directly concerned with your appraisal of the proposed transaction and to whom Confidential Information is to be or has been disclosed.

5   No announcement or disclosure of your interest in the proposed transaction will be made or solicited by you or on your behalf without our prior written consent unless such announcement or disclosure is required by law or by any supervisory or regulatory body to whose rules you are subject.

6   If any proceedings are commenced or action taken which could result in you or your advisers or representatives becoming compelled to disclose Confidential Information, you will immediately notify us of such proceedings or action in writing and you will take all available steps to resist or avoid such proceedings or action, including all steps that we may reasonably request and keep us fully and promptly informed of all matters and developments relating thereto. If you or any person to whom Confidential Information has been disclosed are legally obliged to disclose Confidential Information to any third party you will procure that they and/or you disclose only the minimum amount of information consistent with satisfying such obligation. Furthermore, you will seek a written undertaking from such third party to respect the confidential nature of the information disclosed and will give us prior written notice of the information proposed to be disclosed and a copy of the proposed disclosure and confirmation that your legal advisers' opinion is that such disclosure is required, and you will take into account any reasonable comments we may have in relation to the contents of the proposed disclosure.

7   You and your advisers and representatives will immediately upon receipt of a written demand from us:
    7.1   return to us all Confidential Information (including any and all copies thereof or of any part thereof in whatever media they exist);
    7.2   expunge all Confidential Information from any computer, word processor or other similar device into which it was programmed or in which it is stored by you or on your behalf or by your representatives or on their behalf; and
    7.3   destroy all notes, analyses or memoranda containing any part of the Confidential Information prepared by you or on your behalf or by your advisers or representatives or on their behalf.

8   You, your advisers and your representatives will only copy, reproduce or distribute in whole or in part Confidential Information:
    8.1   with our prior written consent; or
    8.2   for the purpose of supplying Confidential Information to persons to whom disclosure is permitted pursuant to paragraph 4.

9   During the period of twelve months commencing on the date of this letter you will not, without our prior written consent, directly or indirectly initiate or accept or engage in any discussions or contacts of any kind with any of our employees or agents engaged in or associated with the activities of the Company other than in the ordinary course of your business.

10   During the period of twelve months commencing on the date of this letter you will not, without our prior written consent, directly or indirectly, solicit any person who is employed by us and engaged in or associated with the activities of Company to terminate such employment.

11 You will procure that your employees, agents, advisers and representatives each act, or omit to act, as if he or she had agreed with us in the same terms mutatis mutandis as this letter. You will also procure that each person to whom disclosure of Confidential Information is made by you or on your behalf or in the course of representing you or advising you is made aware of and adheres to the terms of this letter.

12 You will indemnify us and keep us indemnified against any loss (including lost profits or business), damage (including damage to staff, goodwill and reputation), consequential loss, claims, actions, liabilities or any other adverse affects resulting from any breach of the terms of this undertaking by you or any of the persons referred to in paragraph 4 above.

13 Financial compensation would not normally be an adequate remedy for a breach of this undertaking and you confirm your view and agreement that we should be entitled to equitable relief including injunctive relief to the maximum extent available under any applicable law in respect of any breach of this undertaking.

14 You will, on written demand from us, certify to us in writing that you have complied with your obligations under this letter.

15 You will make all requests for Confidential Information and all inquiries relating to the proposed transaction only to [ ] at the Company in the private and confidential manner specified by him/her.

16 The furnishing of Confidential Information to you or your advisers or representatives will not constitute an offer nor the basis of any contract or representation which may be relied upon by you.

17 We do not make nor are we to be taken as making any representation or warranty, whether express or implied as to accuracy or completeness or otherwise of Confidential Information, and that we will have no liability for the use of Confidential Information by you or on your behalf or by your representatives or your advisers or on their behalf.

18 No failure or delay by us in exercising any right, power or privilege to which we are entitled shall operate as a waiver nor shall any single or partial exercise of any such right, power or privilege preclude any other or further exercise. The terms of this letter and your obligations and acknowledgements which you accept by signing and returning a copy of this letter may only be waived or modified by an agreement in writing between you and us.

19 You are acting as principal not as an agent or broker for any other person and agree and confirm that you will be responsible for any costs incurred by or on your behalf.

20 In furnishing Confidential Information, we undertake no obligation to provide you with access to any additional information or to update any Confidential Information or to correct any inaccuracies therein which may become apparent and we reserve the right, without advance notice, to change the procedure for the possible sale of the Company or to terminate negotiations at any time prior to the signing of any binding agreement therefor.

21 All of the rights and benefits of this undertaking shall inure to the benefit of and be enforceable by the eventual purchaser of the Company and that, accordingly, we may assign in whole or in part our rights under this letter to any such purchaser who may enforce the same to the same extent and in the same manner as we can enforce the terms and provisions of this letter. The rights and obligations of this undertaking may not be assigned or transferred by you.

22 If any provision of this letter is prohibited or unenforceable in any jurisdiction in relation to us or you, the prohibition or unenforceability will not invalidate the remaining provi-

sions or affect the validity or enforceability of the provision in relation to any other party or in any other jurisdiction.

23 The terms of this letter and your obligations and undertaking thereunder shall be governed by and construed in accordance with English law. You hereby submit to the non-exclusive jurisdiction of the English courts.

24 Your signing and returning a copy of this letter constitutes your acknowledgement and agreement to the terms of this undertaking.

Please indicate your acceptance of the above by signing and returning the enclosed copy of this letter.

Yours faithfully

....

for and on behalf of

[   ] **Limited**

and its Shareholders

I/We fully understand the above letter, and accept that I/we shall be bound by the undertakings, acknowledgements and agreements set out therein and on the reliance of such acceptance I/we request you to provide me with the Confidential Information.

....

[   ]

Document 2
Data Room Rules

[To be typed on Seller's or sales agents'/financial advisers' letterhead]

To: [Purchaser]   [Date]

    [Address]

Re: [Target] Due Diligence Procedure

1 **INTRODUCTION**

    1.1   On behalf of the [shareholders in Target] [Seller] we have arranged for you to inspect the documents regarding [Target] set out in the index attached to this letter (the 'Documents'). [You will see from the index that some of the documents are not yet available but will become available in due course.] [In addition,] further documents may be added to the index, in which event a revised index will be distributed.

    1.2   The Documents are available in a Data Room in our offices at [   ]. To facilitate your visit we set out below details of some of the administrative arrangements regarding access, photocopying, telephone/fax facilities and refreshments. You will also be asked to sign a letter of agreement to abide by the Data Room rules in the form of the attached letter.

    1.3   [One member of the staff of [ ] will be in full attendance in the Data Room during your visit, to whom requests for assistance/facilities should be made.] If you require facilities which are not listed below please ask. All requests for assistance/facilities should be to one of the following members of staff:

    [   ] [*extension*]

    I   ] [*extension*]

    1.4   Please remember to sign out at reception before leaving. Your co-operation is appreciated.

2 **ACCESS**

    2.1   If you wish to inspect the documents, please make an appointment with and notify [ ] of the names and positions of those persons in your team proposing to attend and the names of their respective employers. A team leader must be designated who will represent your Company on all questions and requests submitted during your visit.

    2.2   Only your directors, officers and employees, and representatives of your advisers will be allowed to attend.

    2.3   On arrival you will be asked to sign a register and quote the reference number which [appears on this letter] [was contained in a letter from [financial advisers] confirming this visit].

    2.4   The opening times of the Data Room are 9.00 am to 5.00 pm Monday to Friday from [date] to [date]. The Data Room must be vacated at 5.00 pm.

    2.5   The Data Room accommodates a maximum of [ ] people. Writing materials are provided in the Data Room, and members of your team may take into the Data Room calculators [, lap-top computers] and writing instruments only. Other items, such as briefcases, should be left at reception.

    2.6   On vacating the Data Room each member of your team must report to reception and sign out. Your team leader will be asked to confirm that all information in the

Data Room has been returned to its original location before the last member of the team signs out.

2.7   Visitors' badges must be worn at all times.

2.8   You are not permitted to enter any parts of the building other than the Data Room and the public areas of the building.

3   COPYING DOCUMENTS

3.1   [You will not be allowed to copy or remove any of the documents from our offices nor to use any recording devices whatsoever including, without limitation, tape recording or dictating machines, scanners or optical character readers or digital cameras. If, exceptionally, you feel you need a copy of a document (or extract) we will seek the Seller's consent to such a copy being made and provided to you at your expense. There are, however, some documents which may not be photo-copied under any circumstances. These documents are marked with an asterisk in the index. In general, however, at this stage copies will not be given of any docu-ment [or extract] in the Data Room].

OR

[If you require copies of documents in the Data Room we will endeavour to meet your reasonable request. The procedure is as follows:

    3.1.1   complete a photocopying form (copies of which are available in the Data Room) and specify:

        (a) your reference number;

        (b) the documents to be copied by reference to their number on the index;

        (c) the address to which they are to be sent in cases where a large number of documents are to be copied, which will take at least 24 hours.

    3.1.2   notify one of the persons mentioned in paragraph 1.3, who will make the necessary arrangements.

3.2   If you want only a small number of documents copied, it may be possible to com-plete this during your visit. Again, it will be necessary to complete a form and request assistance as set out in paragraph 3.1.

3.3   A charge of [20p] per page will be made. Invoicing of charges is set out at paragraph 9.

3.4   There are some documents that may not be copied under any circumstances. These are marked with an asterisk on the index.]

4   [FAX FACILITIES

4.1   If during your visit you need to send any faxes, the procedure is as follows:

    4.1.1   complete a fax front sheet (copies of which are available in the Data Room) and specify your reference number;

    4.1.2   notify one of the persons mentioned in paragraph 1.3, who will make the necessary arrangements.

4.2   A charge of [20p] per page will be made. Invoicing of charges is set out at paragraph 9.]

5   TELEPHONE

There is a telephone in the Data Room which will take incoming calls. The telephone number is [ ] extension [ ] Outside calls may be made by dialling [ ] for assistance. The cost of calls will be charged to you.

6   REFRESHMENTS

6.1   Tea and coffee may be ordered by notifying the receptionist of your requirements on arrival. A supply of mineral water is available in the Data Room.

6.2   A sandwich lunch will be provided on request; this should be ordered through the receptionist on arrival.

6.3   The provision of refreshments (other than tea, coffee and mineral water) will be charged to you.

7   FUNCTION OF DATA ROOM

7.1   If you proceed to sign a binding purchase agreement with the [shareholders in Target] [Seller], the documents in the Data Room will be treated as having been disclosed against any warranties [and indemnities] contained in the purchase agreement.

7.2   Neither the [shareholders in Target] [Seller] nor any of their advisers nor [Target] shall have any obligation to you except insofar as these are expressly contained in any binding purchase agreement ultimately entered into between you and the [shareholders in Target] [Seller].

7.3   The [shareholders in Target do] [Seller does] not propose to give any warranties save as to title to shares. Accordingly, you should approach the Data Room process as being your only opportunity to conduct a due diligence exercise with respect to the potential purchase. Any subsequent proposal which is subject to due diligence will not be permitted.]

8   CONFIDENTIALITY

We draw your attention to the terms of the confidentiality agreement dated [ ] which you signed and delivered to the Seller (the 'Confidentiality Agreement'). We would also remind you that you are responsible for ensuring that those who conduct the inspection will adhere to the terms of the undertaking as if they were a party to it. All information in the Data Room is confidential and is provided to you solely for the purpose of an evaluation of a possible purchase of shares in [Target]. If you have any questions please contact [ ]. Members of your team will be admitted to the Data Room only if we are satisfied that each member is covered by the terms of the Confidentiality Agreement. A copy of the Confidentiality Agreement must be sent to us at least one business day before your appointment to visit the Data Room.

9   CHARGES

All charges you incur (plus VAT) will be invoiced to you following your visit. Payment must be made in full within 30 days of invoicing.

10   QUESTIONS

10.1   Questions may be submitted by your team leader only.

10.2   Questions of an administrative nature will be dealt with by [ ] of our offices.

10.3   Questions of a substantive nature may be accepted provided they are in writing, and submitted to [ ] within [ ] days of the visit.

Yours faithfully

[Letterhead of Seller]

To: [Name of Potential Buyer]

[Date]

Dear Sirs

In consideration of our granting you access to the Data Room situated at [   ] (**the 'Data Room'**) you agree, by signing and returning to us the attached copy of this letter, as follows:

1   not to remove any document from the Data Room;

2   not to mark, amend, deface or otherwise damage any document in the Data Room;

3   not to re-arrange the order in which the documents appear in the Data Room;

4   not to copy any documents in the Data Room otherwise than in accordance with arrangements specified in writing by [ ];

5   to notify [ ] immediately if any document is found to be missing or incomplete;

6   to submit to any reasonable security regulations and procedures notified from time to time;

7   to comply fully with any instructions concerning admission to and vacation of the Data Room notified to you by [ ].

You further acknowledge that the documents contained in the Data Room are subject to the Confidentiality Agreement exchanged between us dated [ ].

Yours faithfully

for and on behalf of [the Seller]

[To be typed on copy]

To: [The Seller]

Dear Sirs

We confirm our agreement to the terms and conditions set out in the original of the above copy letter in consideration of your granting us access to the Data Room.

Yours faithfully

for and on behalf of [the Buyer]

Document 3
Lock-out Agreement

THIS AGREEMENT is made the   day of   200[ ]

PARTIES

(1) [ ] of [ ] ('the Purchaser')
(2) [ ] of [ ] ('the Vendor')

BACKGROUND

(A) The Purchaser and the Vendor have entered into negotiations for the purchase by the Purchaser from the Vendor of the business relating to [ ] carried on by the Vendor ('**the Business**').

(B) The negotiations have reached the point where the Purchaser will incur significant costs (both legal and otherwise) in connection with this proposed purchase including (but without limitation) the costs of investigating the assets and rights used in the Business and the affairs of the Vendor generally.

OPERATIVE PROVISIONS

1 **Interpretation**

In this Agreement:

1.1   the following expressions have the following meanings unless inconsistent with the context:

Expression	Meaning
'the Lock-Out Date'	[*Date*] or such later date as the parties agree in writing [or such earlier date on which the Purchaser gives notice to the Vendor that it no longer wishes to proceed with the proposed transaction];
'a Relevant Disposal'	a sale or other disposal of the Business as a going concern or of any material assets or rights used in the Business or any material portion of the assets or undertaking of the Vendor

1.2   references to persons will be construed so as to include bodies corporate, unincorporated associations and partnerships.

2 **Vendor's undertakings**

In consideration of the Purchaser continuing negotiations for the purchase of the Business from the Vendor and the sum of £1 paid by the Purchaser to the Vendor (receipt of which the Vendor acknowledges) the Vendor agrees, undertakes and represents that:

2.1   the Vendor will not at any time prior to the Lock-Out Date discuss, negotiate, arrange, agree or conclude any Relevant Disposal with any person other than the Purchaser [except in the ordinary course of the Business];

2.2   the Vendor has terminated all discussions or negotiations which the Vendor may have entered into with any persons other than the Purchaser relating to a Relevant Disposal;

2.3   the Vendor will not and will procure that the Vendor's advisors will not at any time prior to the Lock-Out Date and except in the ordinary course of the Business make any information concerning the Vendor or the Business available to any person other than the Purchaser and its advisers;

2.4 [the Vendor will co-operate with the Purchaser and the Purchaser's advisers as reasonably necessary to enable a purchase of the Business by the Purchaser to be completed prior to the Lock-Out Date including the provision of any information regarding the Business which is reasonably required by the Purchaser or the Purchaser's advisers for that purpose].

3 **Indemnity**

In the event of a breach by the Vendor of the undertakings contained in clause 2 [or in the event that the Vendor withdraws from negotiations with the Purchaser before [or after] the Lock-Out Date], the Vendor will:

3.1 reimburse to the Purchaser on demand and indemnify it against the cost of all legal, accountancy, actuarial, pensions, property, environmental and financial advice and due diligence obtained by the Purchaser in connection with the proposed acquisition, whether such costs were incurred or advice obtained before or after the date of this agreement;

3.2 pay to the Purchaser on demand a sum equal to the amount of the Purchaser's internal management costs and expenses incurred in investigating and negotiating the proposed transaction both before and after the date of this agreement [which sum is agreed by way of liquidated damages and not by way of penalty to be £[ ]].

4 **Severability**

The Vendor agrees that the undertakings set out in clause 2 above are separate and severable and enforceable accordingly and if one or more of such undertakings or part of an undertaking is held to be unlawful or in any way unenforceable the remaining undertakings or remaining part of the undertaking shall continue in full force and effect and bind the Vendor.

5 **General**

5.1 This Agreement will be binding on and will enure for the benefit of each party's successors, assigns and personal representatives (as the case may be).

5.2 Failure or delay by any party in exercising any right or remedy under this Agreement will not in any circumstances operate as a waiver of it, nor will any single or partial exercise of any right or remedy in any circumstances preclude any other or further exercise of it or the exercise of any other right or remedy.

5.3 Any waiver of any breach of, or any default under, any of the terms of this Agreement will not be deemed a waiver of any subsequent breach or default and will in no way affect the other terms of this Agreement.

5.4 The Purchaser may release, or compromise the liability of, or grant time or any other indulgence to, any person who is a party to this Agreement without in any way prejudicing or affecting the liability of any other person who is a party to this Agreement.

5.5 The headings to the clauses of this Agreement will not affect its construction.

5.6 The rights and remedies expressly provided for by this Agreement will not exclude any rights or remedies provided by law.

5.7 This Agreement may be executed in any number of counterparts, and by the parties on separate counterparts, each of which so executed and delivered will be an original, but all the counterparts will together constitute the same agreement.

5.8 The formation, existence, construction, performance, validity and all aspects whatsoever of this Agreement or of any term of this Agreement shall be governed by English law.

The English courts shall have jurisdiction to settle any disputes that may arise out of or in connection with this Agreement. The parties agree to submit to the said jurisdiction.

EXECUTED as a **DEED** by [ ]   )
acting by:)
)

....
Director

....
Director/Secretary

EXECUTED as a **DEED** by [ ]   )
acting by:)
)

....
Director

....
Director/Secretary

Document 4
Heads of Agreement (Share Acquisition)

THESE HEADS OF AGREEMENT are made [   ] day of [   ] 200[   ]

BETWEEN:

(1) [   ], [   ] and [   ] ('the Vendors');

(2) [   ] **LIMITED** (Company number [   ]) a new company formed by the Management Team for the purpose of the acquisition of the entire issued share capital of the Company and its subsidiaries ('the Purchaser');

(3) [   ], [   ] and [   ] ('the Management Team').

WHEREBY IT IS AGREED as follows:

1 Interpretation

'Company'	[ ] Limited (company number [ ]).
'Completion'	Completion of the sale and purchase of the entire issued share capital of the Company and its subsidiaries contemplated by these Heads of Agreement.
'Exclusivity Period'	The period commencing on the date of signing of these Heads of Agreement and expiring on [ ] 200[ ].
'Relevant Event'	Shall mean in respect of all or any one or more of the Purchasers and/or the Company and/or its/their subsidiaries:

        (i)   a sale of any or all of the issued share capital;

        (ii) a sale of any or all of the business and assets;

        (iii) flotation;

        (iv) any other event pursuant to which there is a return of capital to shareholders.

2 **Status**

   2.1   Matters dealt with in paragraphs 10, 11, 12 and 13 are intended to and do, in fact, create legally binding obligations enforceable by and against the Purchaser and the Vendors (as the case may be).

   2.2   Except as set out in paragraphs 10, 11, 12 and 13 these Heads of Agreement are not intended to and do not create any legally binding obligations between the Purchaser and the Vendors and each party is free to withdraw from negotiations without liability at any time.

3 **Sale and purchase**

The Vendors will sell and the Purchaser will purchase the entire issued share capital of the Company and its subsidiaries.

4 **Consideration**

   4.1   Subject to paragraph 4.6 the consideration for the sale and purchase will be payment by the Purchaser to the Vendors of £[   ]. The consideration is to be discharged either in cash loan notes or preference shares (or a mixture) on a basis and in proportions to be agreed with the Vendors save that the overall cost to the Purchaser will not exceed the cash consideration price agreed.

   4.2   It is noted by the Purchaser without prejudice to the terms of paragraph 12.1 that following negotiations between [   ] and the Purchaser it has been established that

155

[ ] is only prepared to sell his shareholding in the Company if his allocation of the Consideration is a minimum of £[ ]. The balance of the consideration to be split equally amongst the other shareholders pro rata to their shareholding.

4.3   The loan notes, if required, will be:

    4.3.1   freely transferable without limit;

    4.3.2   bank guaranteed;

    4.3.3   redeemable at the option of the noteholders provided such notice does not expire earlier than six months after issue;

    4.3.4   will be redeemed one year from Completion;

    4.3.5   will carry interest at a commercial rate to be agreed payable quarterly.

4.4   The Vendors have expressed a wish to have a possible route to be involved with the Company after Completion to some small extent for sentimental reasons. Therefore the loan notes will carry the right to subscribe for preference shares. The number of preference shares will be capped at £[ ] in aggregate. It is suggested that these preference shares will be irredeemable and carry a coupon of 3%.

4.5   The preference shares, if required, will be:

    4.5.1   freely transferable;

    4.5.2   redeemable at any time after a year at holders' option;

    4.5.3   carry a coupon at a commercial rate to be agreed and paid quarterly;

4.6   The Purchasers will procure that [ ] Limited ('[ ]') enters into an option arrangement with the holders of the preference shares that they may put their shares to [ ] in exchange for cash at par.

4.7   If a Relevant Event occurs within 24 months of Completion pursuant to which the aggregate of the amounts to be received by the relevant Vendor(s) in connection with the Relevant Event plus the amount of all debt to be assumed by the Purchaser in connection with the Relevant Event is in excess of £[ ] then the Purchaser and/or the Management Team, whichever is the Vendor, shall make or procure that there is made a further payment to the Vendors of an amount equal to:

    4.7.1   if the Relevant Event occurs within 12 months of the date of Completion 15% of the excess value received by the relevant Vendor(s);

    4.7.2   if the Relevant Event occurs within 24 months of the date of Completion but not earlier than 12 months from the date of Completion 7.5% of the excess value received by the relevant Vendor(s).

4.8   Options over shares in the Company granted to employees prior to Completion will not be subject to rollover, but will be allowed to lapse. Compensation payments will be negotiated on an individual basis.

4.9   [ ] may roll over his shares into new shares in the Purchaser.

5   Pre-Completion

5.1   Prior to Completion the businesses of the Company and its subsidiaries will be carried on in the ordinary course. The Purchaser will acquire the Company and its subsidiaries which will include all existing overdrafts, HP liabilities and deferred consideration liabilities arising from sale and purchase agreements entered into within the period of two years prior to Completion. The Vendors will not receive from the Company and/or its subsidiaries after the date of signing of these Heads of Agreement any payments other than payments for their services under their existing contracts of employment or consultancy agreement with the Company and its subsidiaries.

5.2   The Vendors will acquire from the Company and its subsidiaries all assets which are personal to the Vendors at the higher of book value or market value thereof together with rights and patents attaching to [ ] for £1.

6   Completion of sale and purchase agreement

6.1   The terms contained in these Heads of Agreement will be incorporated into a formal sale and purchase agreement which will contain inter alia:

    6.1.1   appropriate warranties and indemnities concerning the Company and its affairs (having regard to the level of involvement the Management Team has in the administration and running of the Company and its subsidiaries) in favour of the Purchaser;

    6.1.2   a restrictive covenant for three years in favour of the Purchaser and the Company preventing the Vendors or any other company, firm or person with which they are connected competing with the Company or soliciting any of its customers or employees.

6.2   The Purchaser and the Vendors will co-operate and work together towards execution of legally binding documentation for the purchase of the Company on or before [ ] 200[ ].

7   Due diligence

The Purchaser is to undertake any financial or legal due diligence which it wishes to pursue immediately following the execution of these Heads of Agreement with a view to such matters being completed by [ ] 200[ ].

In addition commercial due diligence will be undertaken, however the method of approaches made to customers or suppliers will be agreed in advance with [ ] and [ ].

8   Completion

8.1   Completion of the acquisition of the entire issued share capital of the Company and its subsidiaries is subject to:

    8.1.1   satisfactory finalisation of funding arrangements by the Purchaser;

    8.1.2   a formal contract being agreed between the Vendors and the Purchaser which will be drawn up by solicitors acting for the Purchaser and approved by the Vendors' solicitors;

    8.1.3   the satisfactory outcome of the due diligence review by the Management Team and on behalf of its financial backers.

9   Previous arrangements

These Heads of Agreement supersede any and all previous offers made by or for and on behalf of the Management Team and/or the Company, which are hereby withdrawn.

10   Exclusivity

In consideration of the Purchaser entering into these Heads of Agreement the Vendors agree that they will not during the Exclusivity Period seek or invite any offer or proposal for the sale of the Company and/or its subsidiaries (or the sale of the assets and undertaking of the Company) from any party other than the Purchaser nor will they respond to any offer or proposal which has been made to them (otherwise than to reject the offer or indicate that it cannot be progressed) nor will they make any offer or proposal to a third party or hold any discussions with or provide information to any other party in relation to any such offer or proposal or any indications of interest in relation to such offer or proposal.

11   Announcements and confidentiality

11.1   Save as set out in paragraph 11.3 the Vendors, the Purchaser and the Management Team agree to keep strictly confidential the existence and terms of these Heads of Agreement and neither the Vendors, the Management Team, the Purchaser nor their respective officers, employees or professional advisers will disclose (either in whole or in part) the contents or existence of the negotiations regarding this proposal or of these Heads of Agreement to any person (other than their respective professional advisers) or as may be required by law or any competent regulatory authority.

11.2 Subject to paragraph 11.3 each party shall treat as strictly confidential all information already received by it/them or received or obtained as a result of entering into these Heads of Agreement and/or negotiation of the legally binding agreement ('the Agreement') envisaged by it and which relates to:

    11.2.1 the negotiations relating to these Heads of Agreement and/or the formal sale and purchase agreement or any document referred to in these Heads of Agreement and/or the formal sale and purchase agreement;

    11.2.2 the provisions or subject matter of these Heads of Agreement and/or the formal sale and purchase agreement or any document referred to in these Heads of Agreement and/or the formal sale and purchase agreement;

    11.2.3 the business and affairs of the Company and its subsidiaries (save for information already in the public domain or which subsequently comes into the public domain other than by a breach by the relevant party of its obligations hereunder).

11.3 A party may disclose information which would otherwise be confidential if and to the extent:

    11.3.1 required by the law of any relevant jurisdiction or by any recognised investment exchange or by any regulatory or government body to which either party is subject or submits; or

    11.3.2 the information is disclosed on a strictly confidential basis to that party's professional advisers, auditors and bankers for the purpose of advising that party in connection with these Heads of Agreement and/or the formal sale and purchase agreement; or

    11.3.3 the other party is given prior written consent of all the other parties to the disclosure.

12 Costs

12.1 If during the Exclusivity Period the Vendors withdraw from negotiations with the Purchaser for the sale of the Company other than as a result of a prior breach of these Heads of Agreement by the Purchaser then the Vendors will pay to the Purchaser promptly on demand an amount not to exceed £[ ] (including VAT) and in any event not to exceed the costs actually payable by the Purchaser to [ ]. It is anticipated that abort fees will be negotiated by [ ] with the professional firms involved. It is confirmed that any claim against the shareholders would be limited to circumstances where the Vendors withdraw from negotiations at a time when [ ] were prepared to complete the transaction on the terms set out in these Heads of Agreement. It is further agreed that should [ ] amend the percentage of equity of Newco given to the Management Team below 60% and the Management Team decides to withdraw from the transaction then the costs of [ ] will not be met by the Vendors.

12.2 Otherwise, on Completion the Vendors and the Purchaser will bear and pay their own legal and professional fees and expenses.

13 Governing law

13.1 These Heads of Agreement and the transactions contemplated by them shall be governed by English law.

13.2 The parties irrevocably agree that English courts shall have jurisdiction in relation to any matters arising out of or in connection with these Heads of Agreement and the transactions contemplated by them and for those purposes hereby irrevocably submit to the non exclusive jurisdiction of those courts.

14 **Acceptance**

Acceptance of the terms of these Heads of Agreement is signified by the parties signing below.

....

[ ]   [ ]

....

[ ]   [ ]

on his own behalf and on behalf of the Purchaser

....

[ ]   [ ]

Document 5
Questionnaire (Share Acquisition)

Note of preliminary documents and information required relating to

[ ]

[ ]

and

[ ]

Definitions contained in the Heads of Agreement relating to Project [ ] shall carry the same meaning in this request for information.

This request for information is made as part of the Purchaser's evaluation of the Company and is to be interpreted as being in respect not only of the Company but also any subsidiaries, associated companies and holding companies of the Company. If there are any such companies, please regard each of the following enquiries as relating to each such entity in addition to the Company.

Please supply the following information and, where relevant, copy documents. Where a full understanding of the position cannot be obtained from the copy documents alone please provide an explanation.

In order to limit the necessity for further information requests please make your replies as detailed as possible.

1 **General**
   Please supply copies or details of:
   1.1   all subsidiary and associated Companies and any interests held in other companies or firms;
   1.2   the Memorandum and Articles of Association together with all ordinary and special resolutions required to be annexed thereto;
   1.3   the authorised and issued share capital;
   1.4   the date of Incorporation together with the Certificate of Incorporation, both originally and on change of name;
   1.5   the names and addresses of shareholders in the Company, showing the number of shares held and stating whether held beneficially or otherwise and details of any contracts for the issue of shares or options to call for the issue of shares;
   1.6   any individuals under a disability (eg infant or bankrupt) or for whom probate or letters of administration awaited;
   1.7   the directors' and secretary's names and addresses;
   1.8   the situation of registered office;
   1.9   the accounting reference date;
   1.10 the audited accounts since incorporation or (if shorter) for the last three years.
   1.11 the management accounts subsequent to last audited accounts.

2 **Properties**
   Please supply the following information:
   2.1   descriptions (to include all relevant details of the leases) of all properties owned by the Company;
   2.2   dates of purchase or acquisition of interest in the above properties, cost, present market values and any recent valuation thereof;
   2.3   who currently holds the title deed to the above properties;

2.4 the premises from which the businesses operate

2.5 in the case of leaseholds, copies of the leases and any sub-leases or tenancy agreements or of any licences relating to or outstanding notices affecting any property;

2.6 whether any properties are held through nominees;

2.7 copies of plans of the properties;

2.8 copies of any planning permissions;

2.9 copies of any mortgages or charges affecting any property;

2.10 whereabouts of title deeds and name and address of solicitors who acted on the purchase of freehold and grants of leasehold;

2.11 copies of title deeds or loans of the originals;

2.12 particulars of any positive or restrictive covenants relating to the use of any land or buildings of any of the Companies;

2.13 particulars of any continuing liabilities for the payment of rent and/or any other liability under any lease which at any time has been assigned;

2.14 any contract for the supply to any premises of the Company of services such as gas, electricity and water which have any unusual or special terms or any contract for the disposal of trade effluence. Does the Company foresee any difficulty in the disposal in the future?

2.15 copies of any environmental reports/audits carried out for or on behalf of the Company.

3 **Investments**

Please supply details of any listed and unlisted investments and investments in associated companies including date of acquisition, cost, present market values or any recent valuations, percentage of equity held and other major shareholders.

4 **Taxation**

Please supply the following information:

4.1 copies of latest agreed computations, details of agreed liabilities compared with provisions in the accounts for the last three years, details of any unusual items in the computations and any unusual arrangements with the Revenue;

4.2 are there any potential liabilities for tax or capital gains?

4.3 basis adopted for calculating deferred tax liabilities. Are there any contingent liabilities in respect of balancing charges or capital gains?

4.4 is the Company a close Company? Have the distribution provisions been complied with?

4.5 are the Companies a member of a VAT group? Details of VAT provisions. Are returns submitted regularly?

4.6 stage reached with the Inland Revenue for any liability not yet agreed and the reasons for any disputed items;

4.7 details of any tax clearances obtained and copies of any tax indemnities taken or given;

4.8 details of any stamp duty relief or capital duty relief obtained by the Company (together with any certificates given to the Inland Revenue Office or Controller of Stamps in respect of such relief from capital duty);

4.9 details of any intra-group transfers of assets during the last six years (other than on trading accounts);

4.10 details of any arrangements for the transfer of group relief or surrender of ACT;

4.11 details of any covenants for annual payments by any of the Companies which may be in force;

4.12 details of any donations to charities during the last six years or loans made to any third parties;

4.13 have any of the Companies taken any regional development grants or other forms of governmental financial assistance?

4.14 will there be any group relief surrendered as a result of the proposed acquisition of the Companies?

4.15 have any of the Companies been a party to any deprecatory transactions or the like?

5 **Trading agreements**

Please supply copies or details of:

5.1 any written or oral sales, agency or distributorship agreements;

5.2 standard terms and conditions of purchase and sale;

5.3 any contracts for the sale or purchase of any goods which have more than six months to run. Details of any other long-term commercial or other contracts, capital commitments and contracts incorporating unusual terms with customers or suppliers and including supply contracts and manufacturing agreements;

5.4 any hire purchase and credit sale contracts;

5.5 any agreement or arrangement with one or more competitors (whether written or unwritten or whether intended to be legally enforceable or not) which relates to the prices or conditions of sale under which any goods of the Companies are to be sold or any materials are to be acquired or any services are to be rendered by the Companies;

5.6 all contracts which now subsist or which have at any time during the last five years subsisted between any of the Companies and the Vendors or any company, consortium or other body controlled by the Vendors of which the Vendors are a member (for this purpose 'contract' shall be interpreted widely and shall include any course of dealing) in particular is there any indebtedness between any company within the group of Companies of which the Company is a member and any of the Vendors and if so, is it to be repaid?

5.7 major customers, ie those accounting for more than 5% of turnover, and value of sales to each in the last three years;

5.8 major suppliers, ie those accounting for more than 5% of the goods and materials purchased, and the value of purchases from each in the last three years;

5.9 dealings with overseas Companies. List of all overseas markets directly or indirectly supplied, with value of sales to each country in the last three years;

5.10 all motor vehicles owned, leased, hired, purchased or used by the Company;

5.11 trade associations of which any of the Companies are a member and any rules or codes of conduct of such associations (whether a member or not) with which the Companies are expected to comply or do in fact comply;

5.12 all contracts relating to the acquisition or disposal of the Companies, businesses or fixed assets during the last six years;

5.13 any agreement to which any of the Companies is a party, the terms of which are subject to termination or early termination or alteration of the effective terms thereof in the event of any change in the beneficial ownership of the shares of the Company or in the event of the Company becoming a public company or its shares or the shares of its parent or holding company becoming quoted on any recognised stock exchange;

5.14 any restrictions on the operation of or any alteration to the scope of the Companies' business, with particulars;

5.15 any agreements relating to any joint venture to which any of the Companies is a party;

5.16 any material change in any of the Companies' business or in the manner of carrying it on during the last three fiscal years (eg changes in pricing of Companies' products);

5.17 any special licences or consent held by any of the Companies under which the businesses are carried on, in particular any authorisations under the Consumer Credit Act 1974 or the Data Protection Act 1998;

5.18 any monopoly or merger investigations or investigations into any alleged anti-competitive practices in which the Companies have been involved or which have affected the business of such Companies;

5.19 any contract, agreement or arrangement which has been or ought to be registered either in the Office of Fair Trading under any provisions of the Competition Act 1988 or under Article 81 or 82 of the Treaty of Rome;

5.20 the 20 largest contracts in terms of turnover;

5.21 any collateral terms, waivers or guarantees affecting any of the Companies' contracts;

5.22 all credit notes outstanding in respect of contracts exceeding 5% of the book debts shown in the last audited accounts of the Companies;

5.23 any arrangements that the Companies have, contractual or otherwise, with any finance house and the particulars of all terms of such arrangements.

5.24 claims of returns for goods supplied to customers in the last two years.

6 **Employees and pension schemes**

6.1 For all employees please supply copies or details of:

6.1.1 name, age, length of service, position held, qualifications;

6.1.2 emoluments over the last three years showing salaries, fees, bonuses, benefits, etc, and any profit sharing arrangement;

6.1.3 the standard written particulars of employment;

6.1.4 all service agreements;

6.1.5 any employees who are likely to terminate employment in the event of sale of the Company.

6.2 Please supply details of all pension or life assurance, sick pay and disability schemes operated by the Company for its employees and in which employees of the Companies participate including, for each of the pension and/or life arrangement schemes, the following information and/or copies of the following documentation:

6.2.1 all trust deeds and rules including consolidated copy, if available;

6.2.2 all explanatory booklets relating thereto;

6.2.3 the report of the most recent actuarial valuation or fund review of the scheme (whether in draft or final form) and any subsequent written recommendations of an actuarial nature;

6.2.4 confirmation of the Inland Revenue's approval to the scheme;

6.2.5 all relevant contracting out certificates;

6.2.6 all members, and details of employees' current contribution levels;

6.2.7 any proposed amendment to the scheme that has been announced or is being considered;

6.2.8 any discretionary increases to pensions or payments in deferment under the scheme granted in the previous five years;

6.2.9 any discretionary practices which may have led any person to expect additional benefits in a given set of circumstances (by way of example (but without limitation) on retirement at the behest of the Companies or in the event of redundancy);

6.2.10 all voluntary pension payments and the current arrangements (whether legally binding or not) and making of any pension or ex gratia payments to employees or former employees not covered in the reply.

6.3   Please provide particulars of labour relations with management and unions, union representation, strike experience and other disturbances.

6.4   For all employees please supply copies or details of:

    6.4.1   benefits such as holiday pay arrangements, amenities, welfare services, canteen and recreational facilities and assisted mortgages;

    6.4.2   terms of employment of anyone who must receive more than three months' notice of termination;

    6.4.3   any trade union recognised to any extent by any of the Companies together with a copy of collective agreements;

    6.4.4   any share option, share incentive or profit related pay arrangements with which any of the employees, including directors, are eligible to participate and copies of all relevant documentation together with full details of all rights granted thereunder to employees and directors of the Companies;

    6.4.5   ex gratia payments made in the last 12 months;

    6.4.6   any current or former employees in respect of whom the directors of any of the Companies consider to be under a moral obligation to provide retirement, death, accident, sickness or disability benefits.

7 Plant and equipment

Please supply copies or details of:

7.1   the main categories and apparent condition;

7.2   any plant not used or obsolete;

7.3   any recent valuations, the basis of the valuation and details of replacement cost;

7.4   any plant register, if kept;

7.5   the Company's policy in relation to its equipment;

7.6   a Valuation for insurance purposes.

8 Intellectual property

Please supply copies or details of any agreements relating to intellectual property to which the Company is a party, and in particular, of:

8.1   all patents owned by or used by the Company, including copies of all registrations and applications;

8.2   all trade marks and registered designs owned or used by the Company and copies of all registrations, applications, licences etc, including details of actual use in the last three years;

8.3   all copyright including software owned by or used by the Company;

8.4   all design rights owned by or used by the Company;

8.5   all business names and logos used by the Company;

8.6   any confidential know-how or information used by the Company, and any licences relating to use;

8.7   any confidentiality agreements entered into by the Company;

8.8   intellectual property for which the Company has or is applying to be registered as proprietor and any procedural steps, payments or obligations which fall due or are to be performed thereunder;

8.9   any licences or authorisations to use, in any way, the intellectual property owned by or licensed to the Company;

8.10   any intellectual property disclosed to any person other than in the ordinary course of business and details of whether valid confidentiality undertakings were obtained from the recipient;

8.11   any agreements entered into by the Company for the provision or acquisition of technical information or assistance;

8.12 any actual or potential (or any grounds which may give rise to a) claim, dispute, action, opposition, infringement or other restrictions or arrangements of any nature in respect of any intellectual property owned, used or licensed by the Company;

8.13 the use by any other person of any of the intellectual property owned, used by and/or licensed to the Company;

8.14 the Company's entitlement to use, without payment or other consideration, all know-how and technical information used by it and all information concerning the products, methods and processes used by the Company;

8.15 any overlap between the intellectual property above and that used in the business retained by the Vendor;

8.16 any known infringements by the Company.

9 Banking and finance

Please provide copies or details of:

9.1 the name and branch address of all banks at which the Company has an account, and account numbers; all existing mandates; any pooled banking arrangements and particulars as to proposals for the separation of the Company from them;

9.2 agreed overdraft limits, any amount currently outstanding on overdraft to the Company's bankers and an estimate of the amount that will be outstanding at completion;

9.3 any debentures, debenture stock, term loans or other financing arrangements and copies of all deeds, agreements etc relating thereto;

9.4 all guarantees and indemnities given by or in respect of the Company (including intra-group arrangements).

10 Insurance

Please supply copies or details of:

10.1 all insurances (receipts for last premiums to be produced);

10.2 any outstanding or unsettled insurance claims:

10.3 any insurance claims made in the past three years.

11 Litigation

Please supply particulars of any material claims, actions, prosecutions and arbitrations – current, threatened, pending or potential.

12 Guarantees

Please provide details of any guarantees or indemnities or suretyships:

12.1 given or undertaken by the Company;

12.2 given or undertaken by any shareholder in favour of the Company.

13 Loans

Please supply details of all loans made by the Company to any of its Directors or members and all loans made to the Company by any of its Directors or Members.

14 Miscellaneous

Please supply the following information:

14.1 any reports commissioned for this transaction or otherwise relevant;

14.2 details of any United Kingdom or overseas bodies that need to consent to this transaction.

Document 6
Share Acquisition Agreement

DATE: 200[ ]

PARTIES:

(1) THE PERSONS whose names and addresses appear in Schedule 1 of this Agreement;

(2) [   ] LIMITED a company incorporated and registered in England (number [   ]), whose registered office is at [   ].

INTRODUCTION:

(A) The Vendors are the registered holders and beneficial owners of the Shares.

(B) The Vendors have agreed to sell and the Purchaser has agreed to purchase the Shares on and subject to the terms and conditions contained in this Agreement.

1   **Definitions**

In this Agreement the following definitions will apply:

'Accounts'	The audited financial statements of the Company [ ] [and [each/the] Subsidiary and the audited consolidated financial statements of the Company, in each case] for the period ended on the Accounts Date, including the notes to such statements
'Accounts Date'	[ ] 200[ ]
'Agreed Form'	In a form agreed between the parties and, for the purposes of identification only, initialled by or on behalf of each of them
'Auditors'	[ ] of [ ]
'Bank'	[ ]
'Business Day'	Any day (other than a Saturday, Sunday or public holiday) on which banks in the City of London are generally open for business
'CA'	The Companies Act 1985
'Company'	[ ] Limited, brief details of which are set out in Schedule 2
'Completion'	Completion of this Agreement in accordance with Clause 5
'Completion Accounts'	The unaudited [consolidated] profit and loss account of the Company for the period from the Accounts Date to the date of Completion, [an unaudited] [a consolidated unaudited] balance sheet as at the date of Completion and the notes relating to such accounts and balance sheet, to be prepared pursuant to Clause 6.2
'Connected Person'	Has the same meaning as in section 839 of ICTA
'Consultancy Agreement'	The consultancy agreement in the Agreed Form to be entered into at Completion between [the Purchaser] (1) and [ ] (2)
'Disclosed Scheme'	[identify scheme]
'Disclosure Letter'	The letter of the same date as this Agreement from the Vendors to the Purchaser which contains certain disclosures to the Warranties [and the Tax Warranties]

166

'Environmental Laws'	All statutes, rules, regulations, statutory instruments, treaties, directives, directions, by-laws, codes of practice, circulars, guidance notes, orders, notices, demands or injunctions of any governmental authority or agency or any regulatory or other body, or any common law duty care, in any jurisdiction in relation to Environmental Matters
'Environmental Licences'	Every licence, registration, permit, authorisation, approval, consent or like matter relating to Environmental Matters which are necessary or desirable in connection with the commencement and continuation of the use of the Property or any process or activity carried on at the Property, including any conditions or limitations imposed from time to time on such licence, registration, permit, authorisation, approval or consent and any subsequent amendment or alteration

'Environmental Matters'

Any of the following:

(i) the release, emission, entry or introduction of any Relevant Substance into the air including, without limitation, the air within buildings and other natural or man-made structures, whether above or below ground;

(ii) the discharge, release or entry into water (whether natural or artificial, above or below ground) including, without limitation, into any river, water course, lake, loch, pond, or reservoir or the surface of the river bed or of other land supporting such waters, ground waters (as defined in section 1(12) of the Environmental Protection Act 1990), sewer or the sea;

(iii) the release, deposit, keeping or disposal of any Relevant Substance in or on land, whether or not covered by the sea or other waters;

(iv) the deposit, disposal, keeping, treatment, importation, exportation, transportation, handling, processing, manufacture, collection, sorting or presence of any Relevant Substance;

(v) any deposit, disposal, keeping, treatment, importation, production or carrying of any waste, including without limitation, any substance which constitutes scrap material or any effluent or other unwanted surplus substance arising from the application of any process or activity (including making it re-usable or re-claiming substances from it) and any substance or article which requires to be disposed of as being broken, worn out, contaminated or otherwise spoiled;

(vi) nuisance, noise, defective premises, health and safety at work, industrial illness, industrial injury due to environmental factors, environmental health problems, the conservation, preservation and protection of the natural or built environment or of man or any living organisms supported by the environment;

(vii) any other matter whatsoever affecting the environment or any part of it.

'EPA'	The Environmental Protection Act 1990
'Expert'	An independent firm of chartered accountants appointed: (i) by agreement between the Vendors and the Purchaser; or (ii) if the Vendors and the Purchaser cannot agree upon an appointee within ten Business Days of a request served by either of them so to do, by the President for the time being of the Institute of Chartered Accountants in England and Wales upon the application of either the Vendors or the Purchaser.
'ICTA'	The Income and Corporation Taxes Act 1988
'Intellectual Property'	Patents, trademarks, service marks, registered designs, utility models, applications for any of them (and the right to apply for any of them in any part of the world), copyright, inventions, confidential know-how, internet domain names and business names (whether registerable or not) in any country
'Last Actuarial Valuation'	The last actuarial valuation or funding review of the Disclosed Scheme received, whether in draft or final form, prior to the date of this Agreement
'Management Accounts'	The unaudited management accounts of the Company [and [each/the] Subsidiary and the unaudited consolidated management accounts of the Company, in each case] for the period from the Accounts Date to the Management Accounts Date
'Management Accounts Date'	[ ] 200[ ]
['Net Asset Value'	The aggregate value, as at Completion of the share capital and reserves of the Company as shown in the Completion Accounts]
['Net Profits'	The [consolidated] net profits (or losses) of the Company for the period from the Accounts Date to Completion, as shown by the Completion Accounts, calculated: (i) after deducting all expenses of the Company including, without limitation, directors' remuneration (whether by way of fees, salary, commission or otherwise) and depreciation; (ii) before deducting any Tax on profits or gains; and (iii) before taking into account profits or losses of a capital nature arising on a disposal of fixed assets, investments or any other assets of the Company.]
'Planning Acts'	The same meaning as in section 336 of TCPA
'Planning Permission'	A permission under the TCPA
'Prohibited Activities'	The [*identify the nature of activities*], as undertaken by the Company in the [*insert time, eg 12 months*] prior to Completion
'Property'	The [freehold/leasehold] property of the Company, brief details of which are set out in Schedule 4
'Purchaser'	[ ] Limited
'Purchaser's Group'	From time to time, the Purchaser, any holding company or subsidiary of the Purchaser and any subsidiary of any holding company of the Purchaser

'Purchase Price'	£[　] [subject to adjustment in accordance with Clause 6.2]
'Purchaser's Solicitors'	[　] of [　]
'Recognised Investment Exchange'	Has the same meaning as in section 285 of the Financial Services and Markets Act 2000
'Relevant Substance'	Any hazardous, dangerous, toxic, poisonous, noxious, offensive, radioactive, flammable, explosive, infectious or polluting substance including, without limitation, asbestos, polychlorinated biphenyls or terphenyls (PCBs or PCTs), petroleum (including crude oil, any fractions of crude oil and any petroleum produce and distillates), radon gas, batteries and any other substance or waste described or listed in or pursuant to any Environmental Laws as hazardous, dangerous, special, toxic, radioactive, noxious or offensive and any other substance which is included under or regulated by or pursuant to any Environmental Laws relating to matters which come within the scope of the definition of Environmental Matters or anything made using any of those substances
'Service Agreements'	The service agreements in the Agreed Form to be entered into at Completion between the [Purchaser] (1) and [each of the Vendors respectively] (2)
'Shares'	The entire issued share capital of the Company
'Subsidiar[y/ies]'	[: (i) [　] Limited, company number [　] [; and (ii) [　] Limited;] brief details of [each of] which [is/are] set out in Schedule 3
'Target Group'	The Company and [　] [each of] the Subsidiar[y/ies];
'Tax'	(i) All forms of taxes, duties, imposts and levies in the nature of taxes, whenever created or imposed, and whether of the United Kingdom or elsewhere including, without limitation, income tax, corporation tax, advance corporation tax or any amount to be deducted or withheld from or accounted for in respect of any payment, capital gains tax, inheritance tax, VAT, Customs & Excise duties, stamp duty, stamp duty reserve tax and national insurance and social security or similar contributions, general and business rates and any other taxes, charges, rates, imposts, duties, levies similar to, corresponding with or replaced by any of the above (ii) All penalties, fines, charges and interest relating to tax (as within paragraph (i)) or to any return or information required to be provided for the purposes of such tax
'Tax Covenant'	The covenants relating to Tax contained in Part 2 of Schedule 6
'Tax Warranties'	The warranties relating to Tax contained in Part 3 of Schedule 6
'TCPA'	The Town and Country Planning Act 1990
'VAT'	Value added tax

'VATA'	The Value Added Tax Act 1994
'Vendors'	The persons listed in Schedule 1
'Vendors' Solicitors'	[ ] of [ ]
'Warranties'	The representations and warranties set out in Schedule 5.

2   **Interpretation**

2.1   The headings and table of contents in this Agreement are inserted for convenience only and shall not affect its interpretation or construction.

2.2   References in this Agreement to Clauses and Schedules are, unless otherwise stated, references to the Clauses of and Schedules to this Agreement. References to paragraphs are, unless otherwise stated, references to the paragraphs of Schedules to this Agreement.

2.3   The Schedules form part of this Agreement and shall have the same force and effect as if expressly set out in the body of this Agreement.

2.4   Words and expressions defined in the CA shall, unless they are otherwise defined in this Agreement or the context otherwise requires, bear the same meaning in this Agreement.

2.5   References in this Agreement to statutes shall include any statutory modification, re-enactment or extension of such statute and any orders, regulations, instruments or other subordinate legislation made pursuant to such statute.

2.6   In this Agreement, references to:

2.6.1   the masculine gender shall include the feminine and neuter and vice versa;

2.6.2   the singular shall include the plural and vice versa;

2.6.3   'persons' shall include bodies corporate, unincorporated associations and partnerships.

2.7   [References in clauses 7 and 8, the Warranties, the Tax Warranties and the Tax Covenant to 'the Company' shall, where the context permits, be deemed to include a reference to the Company and [each of] the [Subsidiar[y/ies]].]

2.8   References to encumbrances include any mortgage, charge, pledge, lien, assignment, hypothecation, security interest, title retention or other interest.

3   **Sale and purchase of shares**

3.1   The Vendors agree to sell and the Purchaser agrees to purchase all the Shares, free from all encumbrances and with the benefit of all rights and advantages attaching to them as at Completion.

3.2   The Shares are sold by the Vendors with full title guarantee.

3.3   The Purchaser shall not be obliged to complete the purchase of any of the Shares unless the sale and purchase of all of the Shares is completed at the same time.

3.4   Each of the Vendors:

3.4.1   waives any right of pre-emption over or in respect of the Shares (or any of them) which may have been conferred on him, whether under the articles of association of the Company or otherwise;

3.4.2   undertakes to procure that any right of pre-emption over any of the Shares which may be vested in any other persons is waived.

4   **Consideration**

4.1   The consideration for sale and purchase of the Shares shall be the Purchase Price. This shall be apportioned between the Vendors on the basis set out in Schedule 1.

4.2   The Purchase Price shall be paid[, subject to adjustment pursuant to Clause 6,][in full upon Completion][as follows:

4.2.1   £   upon Completion; and

4.2.2 £[   ] on [   ].]

4.3 The Vendors authorise the Purchaser to pay all sums due under this Agreement to the Vendors' Solicitors on their behalf. The receipt of the Vendors' Solicitors will give a full and valid discharge to the Purchaser and the Purchaser shall not be obliged to see to the application of such monies as between the Vendors.

5 Completion

Completion of the sale and purchase of the Shares shall take place at the offices of the Purchaser's Solicitors immediately following exchange of this Agreement. On Completion:

5.1 the Vendors shall deliver to the Purchaser:

5.1.1 duly executed transfers of the Shares in favour of the Purchaser (or such other person as the Purchaser directs);

5.1.2 the certificates for the Shares (or a duly executed indemnity in a form acceptable to the Purchaser in respect of any missing, lost or destroyed certificates);

5.1.3 duly executed transfers of any shares in the capital of the [Subsidiar[y/ies] not registered in the name of the Company in favour of the Company (or such other person as the Purchaser directs);

5.1.4 the certificates for the shares in the capital of [each of] the [Subsidiar[y/ies] (or a duly executed indemnity in a form acceptable to the Purchaser in respect of any missing, lost or destroyed certificates);

5.1.5 the common seal, certificate[s] of incorporation, any certificate of incorporation on change of name and statutory books of the Company [and [each of] the [Subsidiar[y/ies]] made up to the date of Completion;

5.1.6 the written resignations in the Agreed Form of the directors and secretary of the Company [and [each of] the [Subsidiar[y/ies]];

5.1.7 the written resignation in the Agreed Form of the Auditors from their office as auditors of the Company [and [each of] the [Subsidiar[y/ies]];

5.1.8 such waivers or consents as the Purchaser may require to enable the Purchaser or its nominee to be registered as the holder of the Shares;

5.1.9 the title deeds to the Property;

5.1.10 certificates as to the balances in the bank accounts of the Company [and [each of] the [Subsidiar[y/ies]] as at the close of business on the Business Day immediately prior to Completion, and a statement reconciling such balances with the cash book of the Company [and the relevant Subsidiary] as at Completion;

5.1.11 the Service Agreements duly executed by [each of the Vendors respectively];

5.1.12 the Consultancy Agreement duly executed by [   ];

5.1.13 all company credit cards [held by the Vendors or their connected persons];

5.1.14 [vehicle registration documents for all motor vehicles (if any) of the Company [and [each of] the [Subsidiar[y/ies]];

5.1.15 powers of attorney in the Agreed Form in relation to the exercise of rights attaching to the Shares during the period commencing on Completion and ending on the date upon which the Purchaser or its nominee is registered as the holder of the Shares.

5.2 the Vendors shall procure that a board meeting of the Company [and [each of] the [Subsidiar[y/ies]] is held at which:

5.2.1 existing authorities and instructions to bankers in respect of the operation of the [Company's][relevant company's] bank accounts are revoked and new authorities and instructions are issued in such terms as the Purchaser may require;

5.2.2 such persons as the Purchaser may nominate as directors and secretary are appointed;

5.2.3 the share transfers referred to in Clause 5.1.1 [or Clause 5.1.3 as the case may be] are approved, subject only to stamping;

5.2.4 its registered office is changed to [   ];

5.2.5 [   ] are appointed as its auditors;

5.3 the Vendors shall each repay (or procure the repayment of), in cleared funds, all amounts owed by them or their connected persons to the Company [or [the/any] Subsidiary];

5.4 the Purchaser shall then:

5.4.1 pay [   ] [£[   ] on account of] the Purchase Price to the Vendors' Solicitors; and

5.4.2 deliver to the Vendors a counterpart of the Service Agreements and the Consultancy Agreement each duly executed by the Purchaser.

6 **Completion Accounts**

6.1 Following Completion the Completion Accounts shall be prepared in accordance with Schedule 6.

6.2 Within five business days of agreement or determination of the [Net Asset Value/Net Profits] pursuant to Schedule 6:

6.2.1 the Vendors will repay to the Purchaser an amount equal to the amount (if any) by which the [Net Asset Value/Net Profits] are less than £[   ]; or

6.2.2 the Purchaser will pay to the Vendors an amount equal to the amount (if any) by which the [Net Asset Value/Net Profits] are more than £[   ].

6.3 Any payment made pursuant to Clause 6.2 is to be in cash and shall be made by way of an adjustment to the Purchase Price.

7 **Warranties**

7.1 The Vendors represent and warrant to the Purchaser in the terms of the Warranties and the Tax Warranties as at Completion.

7.2 [Without prejudice to any right or remedy which the Purchaser may otherwise have at law or in equity for breach of the Warranties or the Tax Warranties, the Vendors agree to pay to the Purchaser, on demand, an amount equal to the higher of:

7.2.1 any depletion in the value of the assets or increase in the liabilities of the Company; and

7.2.2 any diminution in value of the Shares;

(in each case) to the extent that it arises as a result of or in connection with any breach of any of the Warranties or the Tax Warranties, together with all costs, claims and expenses incurred in connection with such breach or the rectification of such breach.]

7.3 The Warranties and the Tax Warranties are given subject to matters fully and fairly disclosed in the Disclosure Letter. No other information of which the Purchaser, its agents or advisers may be aware, or any investigations carried out by them, shall prejudice or limit the extent of any claim made, or operate to reduce the amount recoverable, by the Purchaser under the Warranties or the Tax Warranties.

7.4 Each of the Warranties, the Tax Warranties and the obligations contained in the Tax Covenant are intended to give rise to separate and independent obligations. Unless otherwise stated, none of the Warranties, the Tax Warranties nor the Tax Covenant are to be limited by reference to any other Warranty, Tax Warranty or provision in the Tax Covenant.

7.5 [The Vendors acknowledge that, in reliance upon the Warranties, the Tax Warranties, the Disclosure Letter and the Tax Covenant, the Purchaser may advance or procure the advance of monies to the Company, guarantee its obligations to third parties and/or permit the Company otherwise to become indebted to the Purchaser or any member of the Purchaser's Group.]

7.6 The Vendors agree with the Purchaser (for itself and as trustee for the Company, its officers and employees) to waive any right which they may have in respect of any misrepresentation, inaccuracy or omission in any information or advice supplied or given by the Company, its officers or employees to the Vendors in enabling the Vendors to give the Warranties or the Tax Warranties, to prepare the Disclosure Letter and enter into the Tax Covenant.

7.7 The aggregate liability of the Vendors in respect of all claims made under the Warranties, the Tax Warranties and the Tax Covenant shall not exceed the Purchase Price [plus the amount of all costs and expenses incurred by the Purchaser in connection with such claims].

7.8 The Vendors shall not be liable in respect of any claim under the Warranties[, the Tax Warranties or the Tax Covenant] unless the aggregate liability of the Vendors in respect of all such claims exceeds £[   ]. If the aggregate liability of the Vendors in respect of all claims under the Warranties[, the Tax Warranties and the Tax Covenant] exceeds £[   ], the Vendors shall be liable for the full amount of all claims and not merely the excess over £[   ].

7.9 The Vendors shall not be liable in respect of any claim under or in connection with the Warranties or the Tax Warranties unless the Purchaser shall have given notice of such claim to the Vendors on or before:

7.9.1 in the case of any claim under the Tax Warranties, the seventh anniversary of the date of Completion; or

7.9.2 in any other case, [the expiry of [*number of months*] months from] [the second/third anniversary of] Completion.

7.10 The provisions of Clauses 7.6, 7.7 and 7.8 shall not apply in relation to any claim pursuant to the Warranties, the Tax Warranties or the Tax Covenant which arises as a result of or involves any fraud, dishonesty or wilful non-disclosure on the part of or involving the Vendors or their Connected Persons.

7.11 No claim may be made by the Purchaser for breach of the Warranties to the extent that such claim arises as a result of any change of law occurring after the date of this Agreement.

7.12 Any claim made by the Purchaser for breach of the Warranties shall take into account the extent to which the Purchaser or the Company has previously recovered compensation from a third party in relation to the subject matter of the claim.

7.13 No claim may be made under the Warranties to the extent that the Purchaser has previously made a claim and received compensation under the Warranties, the Tax Warranties or the Tax Covenant in respect of the same breach or subject matter.

8 Restrictions on the Vendors

8.1 The Vendors will, for a period of [*insert time, eg three*] months following Completion, provide such assistance and support as the Purchaser may reasonably require to enable it to achieve a smooth and orderly transfer of the ownership of the Company to the Purchaser.

8.2 The Vendors severally undertake to the Purchaser that they will not, without the prior written consent of the Purchaser, for a period of [*insert time, eg two*] years following Completion:

8.2.1   carry on or be engaged, concerned or interested, directly or indirectly in any Prohibited Activities within [a radius of [*number of miles*] miles from the Property/the United Kingdom];

8.2.2   solicit or knowingly accept any orders, enquiries or business in respect of any Prohibited Activities from any person who was, in the [*insert time, eg 12 months*] prior to Completion, a customer of the Company;

8.2.3   solicit or entice or endeavour to solicit or entice any of the [senior] employees of the Company [engaged in a managerial capacity or who have had direct contact with customers in the course of their duties] to cease working for the Company; or

8.2.4   interfere in the relationships between the Company and its suppliers and professional contacts.

8.3   The Vendors severally undertake to the Purchaser that they will not, without the prior written consent of the Purchaser, at any time after Completion:

8.3.1   hold themselves out as having any continuing involvement with the Company;

8.3.2   disclose or use (or authorise any third party to disclose or use) any confidential information concerning the accounts, financial or contractual arrangements or other dealings of the Company, save to the extent that disclosure of such information is required to satisfy any obligations imposed by law or the rules of any recognised investment exchange; or

8.3.3   use, whether as a company name, trading name or otherwise the name '[   ]' or any other name used by the Company in connection with its business activities (or any other names which are identical to or liable to be confused with such names).

8.4   The restrictions contained in Clauses 8.2 and 8.3 shall apply to any action carried out by the Vendors whether on their own behalf or jointly with or as agent, manager, director or shareholder of any other person.

8.5   Each of the restrictions contained in Clauses 8.2 and 8.3 are to be treated as separate obligations, independent of the others.

8.6   The parties consider the restrictions contained in Clauses 8.2 and 8.3 to be reasonable as between themselves and the public interest. If, however, any of them are found by a court to be unreasonable or unenforceable, but would be reasonable and enforceable if certain words were deleted, then the restrictions will apply with those words deleted.

9   Announcements

Save as required by law or the rules of any Recognised Investment Exchange, no announcement relating to the sale and purchase of the Shares shall be made by [the Vendors/either party] without the prior written consent of the [Purchaser/other].

10   Further assurance

The Vendors shall[, at the Purchaser's cost,] do and execute all such acts, things, deeds and documents as may be necessary or reasonably requested by the Purchaser to give effect to the terms, and provide to the Purchaser the full benefit, of this Agreement.

11   Notices

11.1   Any notice required to be given pursuant to this Agreement shall be in writing signed by, or on behalf of, the person issuing the notice. Notices may be served by personal delivery, prepaid first class post or facsimile transmission:

11.1.1   in the case of the Vendors, to the addresses set out in Schedule 1 or such other address for service in the United Kingdom as they may from time to time notify to the Purchaser; and

11.1.2 in the case of the Purchaser, to its registered office for the time being.

11.2 Notices served in accordance with Clause 11.1 shall be deemed to have been received:

11.2.1 if delivered personally, upon delivery;

11.2.2 if served by prepaid first class post, at the close of business on the second Business Day after posting;

11.2.3 if served by facsimile transmission, upon receipt of confirmation that the notice has been correctly transmitted (unless such transmission takes place on a day which is not a Business Day or after 5.00 p.m. on a Business Day, in which case notice will be deemed to have been received at 10.00 a.m. on the next Business Day).

11.3 In proving service by post, it will be necessary only to prove that the notice was properly stamped, addressed and posted.

12 Entire agreement

12.1 This Agreement (together with the Agreed Form documents) constitute the entire agreement between the parties with respect to the sale and purchase of the Shares. [OR]

[The parties acknowledge that this Agreement has been negotiated on the basis that:

12.1.1 this Agreement and the documents in the Agreed Form contain the entire agreement and understanding of the parties in connection with the sale and purchase of the Shares, and supersedes and extinguishes all previous agreements between the parties relating to such sale and purchase;

12.1.2 this Agreement has been freely negotiated between the parties, each of whom has received independent legal advice;

12.1.3 it is reasonable for each party to assume that, unless the other parties have asked for any oral representations to be continued within or incorporated into this Agreement, it is not relying upon the oral representation; and accordingly the parties agree that no party will in any respect be responsible for any oral representations made to any other party or their respective representatives during the course of negotiations leading to exchange of this Agreement whether under sections 2(1) or 2(2) of the Misrepresentation Act 1967 or otherwise, save to the extent that they are incorporated into this Agreement or have been made fraudulently.]

12.2 No variations to this Agreement shall be effective unless made in writing and signed by all of the parties to this Agreement.

12.3 If at any time any provision of this Agreement is or becomes unlawful, invalid or unenforceable in any respect, in any jurisdiction, than the legality, validity and enforceability of the remaining provisions of this Agreement, or in any other jurisdiction, shall not be impaired or affected in any way.

13 Costs

Each party shall bear the costs of its own financial, accounting and legal advice in relation to this Agreement.

14 Interest

If any moneys due under this Agreement are not paid in full on the due date for payment, they will bear interest at a rate [ ]% per annum above the base lending rate of the Bank from time to time in force, such interest to be paid monthly in arrears on the last business day of each month. Interest will accrue and be payable both before and after judgement and, if not paid when due, will be compounded and itself bear interest in accordance with this Clause 14.

15 Benefit and burden of this Agreement

15.1 This Agreement shall remain in full force and effect after Completion in respect of any matters, covenants or conditions which shall not have been done, observed or performed in full on or before Completion and the Warranties and all other obligations given or undertaken shall continue in full force and effect notwithstanding Completion.

15.2 This Agreement shall be binding upon and survive for the benefit of the personal representatives and successors-in-title of the parties.

15.3 The benefit of this Agreement is personal to the parties. Save as permitted under Clause 15.4, no party may assign the benefit or burden of this Agreement to any other person without the prior written consent of the other party.

15.4 The Purchaser may assign the benefit and burden of this Agreement to:

15.4.1 any other company which is, for the time being, a member of the Purchaser's Group; or

15.4.2 any bank or other provider of finance to a member of the Purchaser's Group as security for such finance.

16 Third party rights

Unless otherwise stated in this Agreement, no person, other than the Vendors and the Purchaser, may enforce or rely upon this Agreement under the Contracts (Rights of Third Parties) Act 1999. No party to this Agreement may hold itself out as trustee of any rights under this Agreement for the benefit of any third party unless specifically provided for in this Agreement.

17 Counterparts

This Agreement may be executed in any number of counterparts, each of which when executed and delivered shall be an original. All the counterparts shall together constitute one and the same agreement, which shall be deemed executed when counterparts executed by all of the parties to this Agreement are delivered.

18 Joint and several liability

18.1 Where any covenant, warranty, obligation or other liability is entered into under this Agreement by the Vendors it is, unless otherwise stated, entered into on a joint and several basis.

18.2 The Purchaser may release or compromise the whole or any part of the liability of any one or more of the Vendors under any provision of this Agreement, or grant to any Vendor time or other indulgence, without affecting the liability of any other Vendor. No waiver by the Purchaser of, or delay in enforcing, any of the provisions of this Agreement shall release any Vendor from full performance of his remaining obligations under this Agreement.

18.3 No failure to exercise or delay in exercising or enforcing any right, power or remedy under this Agreement shall constitute a waiver of such right, power or remedy. No partial exercise or enforcement or non-exercise or non-enforcement of any right, power or remedy under this Agreement shall in any circumstances preclude or restrict any further or other exercise or enforcement of such right, power or remedy or the exercise or enforcement of such right, power or remedy against any other Vendor.

18.4 The rights, powers and remedies provided in this Agreement are cumulative, and not exhaustive, of any rights powers and remedies provided by law.

19 Governing law

This Agreement shall be governed by and interpreted in accordance with English law. The parties agree to submit to the non-exclusive jurisdiction of the English courts in relation to any claim or matter arising under this Agreement.

IN WITNESS of which the parties have signed this Agreement on the date set out above.

Schedule 1

Vendors

(1) Name and Addresses	(2) Number of Shares Sold	(3) Purchase Price (£)
[]		
[]		
[]		
[]		
[]		
[]		
[]		
TOTAL		

Schedule 2

The Company

Name	[ ]
Number	[ ]
Date of Incorporation	[ ]
Place of Incorporation	England and Wales
Registered Office	[ ]
Authorised Share Capital	£[ ] divided into [ ] shares of [ ] each
Issued Share Capital	£[ ] registered as follows: Member No. of shares [ ] [ ]
Directors	[ ] [ ] [ ] [ ]
Secretary	[ ]
Accounting Reference Date	[ ]
Last Accounts Filed	[ ]
Last Annual Return Filed	[ ]
Auditors	[ ] of [ ]
Charges	**Date Registered Document Chargee** [ ] [ ] [ ]

Schedule 3

[Subsidiar[y/ies]

Name	[ ]
Number	[ ]
Date of Incorporation	[ ]
Place of Incorporation	England and Wales
Registered Office	[ ]
Authorised Share Capital	£[ ] divided into [ ] shares of [ ] each
Issued Share Capital	£[ ] registered as follows: Member No. of shares [ ] [ ]
Directors	[ ] [ ] [ ] [ ]
Secretary	[ ]
Accounting Reference Date	[ ]
Last Accounts Filed	[ ]
Last Annual Return Filed	[ ]
Auditors	[ ] of [ ]
Charges	Date Registered Document Chargee [ ] [ ] [ ]

REPEAT AS NECESSARY FOR MULTIPLE SUBSIDIARIES

Schedule 4

Property
Freehold

Description	Title Number

Leasehold

Description	Date of Lease	Present Rent	Title Number

Schedule 5

Warranties

1 **Capacity**

1.1 Each Vendor has the power to enter into and perform this Agreement and any other deeds and agreements to be entered into pursuant to this Agreement. This Agreement (and the agreements to be entered into pursuant to this Agreement) will, when executed, constitute obligations binding on the Vendors in accordance with their terms.

1.2 The execution and delivery of, and the performance by the Vendors of their obligations pursuant to, this Agreement (and any agreements to be entered into pursuant to this Agreement) will not conflict with, result in a breach of or give rise to a right of termination of any obligation under:

1.2.1 any contract, agreement or arrangement to which any of the Vendors or the Company is a party or subject; or

1.2.2 any order, judgement, ordinance, regulation or other restriction imposed by any regulatory body or court having jurisdiction over the Vendors or the Company.

2 **Information**

2.1 The information set out in Schedules 1[,/and] 2 [,/and 3[and 4]] is true, complete and accurate in all respects.

2.2 All information which has been given in writing by the Vendors and/or their professional advisers to the Purchaser and/or its professional advisers in the course of the negotiations leading to this Agreement including, without limitation, the information contained in or attached to the Disclosure Letter, is true, complete and accurate in all respects. The Vendors are not aware of any fact or matter not contained in the Disclosure Letter which renders any such information untrue, incorrect, incomplete or misleading.

2.3 As far as the Vendors are aware, all information relating to the Company which is material to be known by a purchaser for value of shares in the Company is contained in the Disclosure Letter.

2.4 No person is entitled to receive any commission, bonus, finder's fee or other payment or to receive any benefit upon the sale of the Shares (whether or not sold to the Purchaser).

2.5 No person, other than the Purchaser, has been provided with any confidential information relating to the Company, whether in relation to the sale of the Shares or otherwise.

2.6 The Company has not incurred, assumed or discharged any liability, including any liability for professional costs and expenses, in relation to the sale of the Shares.

2.7 The Vendors are not and have not in the five years prior to Completion been involved, engaged or interested in any other company or business which in any way overlaps or competes with or has in any way affected the trading results and performance of the Company.

3 **Ownership of Shares**

3.1 The Shares are fully paid or credited as fully paid and constitute the whole of the issued share capital of the Company. None of the Shares were allotted at a discount.

3.2 The Vendors are the legal and beneficial owners of the Shares free from all charges, liens or encumbrances.

3.3 None of the Shares was, or represents assets which were the subject of a transfer at an undervalue (within the meaning of sections 238 or 239 of the Insolvency Act 1986) within the five years immediately prior to Completion.

4 Subsidiaries and groups

4.1 The Company has not at any time and will not at Completion be the owner or registered holder of any share, loan capital, interest, equity in or other security of any body corporate (wherever incorporated) nor has it agreed to become the owner or registered holder of any such share, loan capital, interest, equity or other security.

4.2 The Company has never had a participating interest in any other company or undertaking.

4.3 The Company has not since its incorporation been a subsidiary of any body corporate (wherever incorporated).

4.4 The Company is not a party to any joint venture agreement or a member of any partnership or unincorporated company or association.

4.5 The Company does not have any branch, place of business, agency or any substantial assets outside the United Kingdom.

4.6 The Company has not at any time had only one member.

5 Share capital

5.1 No shares in the capital of the Company have been issued, nor has any transfer of shares been registered, otherwise than in accordance with the articles of association of the Company in force at the relevant time.

5.2 All necessary permissions for each issue and transfer of shares has been validly obtained and any stamp duty or other Tax payable upon such issue or transfer has been paid.

5.3 The Company has not at any time:

    5.3.1 purchased or redeemed or agreed to purchase or redeem any shares of any class of its share capital;

    5.3.2 otherwise reduced or agreed to reduce its issued share capital or any class of its share capital; or

    5.3.3 issued any shares for a consideration payable or otherwise than in cash.

5.4 No person has the right (whether exercisable now or in the future and whether contingent or not) to call for the issue of any share or loan capital of the Company under any option or other agreement (including, without limitation, conversion rights).

5.5 There are no rights or pre-emption over or restrictions relating to the transfer of the Shares (whether contained in the Company's articles of association or otherwise) which could apply on the sale of the Shares to the Purchaser.

6 Directors

6.1 The only directors of the Company are the persons listed in Schedule 2.

6.2 No person is a shadow director of the Company but is not treated as one of its directors for all the purposes of the Companies Acts.

7 Accounts and financial matters

7.1 The Accounts, true copies of which are annexed to the Disclosure Letter:

    7.1.1 comply with the CA and all other relevant statutes;

    7.1.2 have been prepared in accordance with generally accepted accounting principles and practices in the United Kingdom, consistently applied;

    7.1.3 comply with all current financial reporting standards adopted or issued by the Accounting Standards Board applicable to a United Kingdom company;

7.1.4   make full provision for all liabilities of the Company as at the Accounts Date;

7.1.5   make full provision for or include a note of all capital commitments and contingent, unquantified or disputed liabilities of the Company as at the Accounts Date;

7.1.6   make full provision for all bad or doubtful debts of the Company as at the Accounts Date;

7.1.7   show a true and fair view of the state of affairs of the Company as at the Accounts Date;

7.1.8   show a true and fair view of the trading and profit of the Company for the financial period ended on the Accounts Date.

7.2   [Full provision or reserve has been made in the Accounts for all Tax assessed or liable to be assessed on the Company, or for which the Company is accountable, in respect of:

7.2.1   profits, gains or income earned, arising, accruing or received (or deemed to arise, accrue or to have been earned or received for any purpose);

7.2.2   transactions effected or deemed to have been effected;

7.2.3   distributions made or deemed to have been made;

in each case as at the Accounts Date.

7.3   Full provision has been made in the Accounts for deferred Tax in accordance with generally accepted accounting principles and practices in the United Kingdom.]

7.4   The stock in trade and work in progress of the Company have been valued in the Accounts at the lower of cost or net realisable value, on the basis of a physical stock count. Full provision has been made in the Accounts for all damaged, obsolete and slow-moving items.

7.5   The results shown by the Accounts were not materially affected by:

7.5.1   transactions of a nature not usually undertaken by the Company;

7.5.2   transactions or circumstances of an extraordinary, exceptional or non-recurring nature;

7.5.3   charges or credits relating to prior or subsequent financial period;

7.5.4   any change in the accounting policies or practices from those applied in the preparation of previous audited financial statements of the Company.

7.6   No commitments on capital account were outstanding at the Accounts Date.

8   Business since the Accounts Date

Since the Accounts Date:

8.1   the business of the Company has been carried on in the ordinary and usual course as a going concern;

8.2   the Company has not incurred or agreed to incur any liability otherwise than in the ordinary course of business;

8.3   there has been no adverse change in the turnover, the financial or trading position or prospects of the Company;

8.4   the value of the Company's net assets has not been reduced below that shown in the Accounts;

8.5   the Company has not incurred any expense or made any payment otherwise than in the ordinary course of business and all payments received by the Company have been paid into the Company's bank account and appear in the appropriate books of account;

8.6   the Company has not borrowed any money which it has not repaid, otherwise than borrowing on an overdrawn current account incurred in the ordinary course of business within limits agreed with the Company's bankers; nor has the Company lent any money which has not been repaid to it;

8.7   the Company has not entered into or agreed to enter into any capital transaction as vendor, purchaser, lessor or lessee or otherwise undertaken any transaction on its capital account or acquired or disposed of any capital assets;

8.8   no property of the Company has been (or agreed to be) transferred, leased, mortgaged, sold, encumbered or made the subject of any dealing, option or agreement, other than current assets purchased and sold in the ordinary course of trading;

8.9   the Company has not paid or declared any dividend or other distribution, whether of capital or income;

8.10   no resolution of the members of the Company has been passed;

8.11   the Company has paid its creditors in the ordinary course of business;

8.12   no supplier to or customer of the Company has ceased or indicated an intention to cease to supply, be a customer of or continue to deal with the Company;

8.13   no part of the business of the Company has been materially affected by any abnormal factor not affecting similar businesses to a similar degree;

8.14   the Company has not acquired or agreed to acquire any real property;

8.15   there has been no increase in the rate of remuneration of the officers and/or employees of the Company;

8.16   no loan to or loan capital of the Company has been repaid, in whole or in part, or has become due and payable or liable (with or without notice or lapse of time or both) to be declared due and payable;

8.17   no payments have been made by the Company to or on behalf of any of the Vendors (or their connected persons) other than the payment of salaries in the ordinary course of business and the rates set out in the Disclosure Letter.

9 Management Accounts

9.1   The Management Accounts, true copies of which are annexed to the Disclosure Letter:

    9.1.1   have been prepared with due care and attention;

    9.1.2   have been prepared in accordance with good management accounting practice on a basis consistent with previous management accounts prepared by the Company and the Accounts;

    9.1.3   make full provision for all liabilities of the Company as at the Management Accounts Date;

    9.1.4   make full provision for or note all capital commitments and contingent, unqualified or disputed liabilities of the Company as at the Management Accounts Date;

    9.1.5   make full provision for all bad or doubtful debts of the Company as at the Management Accounts Date;

    9.1.6   [accurately reflect/reflect with reasonable accuracy] the state of affairs of the Company as at the Management Accounts Date;

    9.1.7   [accurately reflect/reflect with reasonable accuracy] the trading and profit of the Company for the period from the Accounts Date to the Management Accounts Date.

9.2   The results shown by the Management Accounts were not materially affected by:

    9.2.1   transactions of a nature not usually undertaken by the Company;

    9.2.2   transactions or circumstances of an extraordinary, exceptional or non-recurring nature;

    9.2.3   charges or credits relating to any prior or subsequent period;

    9.2.4   any change in the accounting policies or practices from those applied in the preparation of previous management accounts of the Company.

10 **Litigation and compliance**

10.1 The Company is not at present engaged, whether as plaintiff, defendant or otherwise, in any legal action, proceedings or arbitration. There are no circumstances of which the Vendors are aware which might reasonably be expected to give rise to any such claim, legal action, proceedings or arbitration.

10.2 So far as the Vendors are aware, there is no claim, legal action, litigation, arbitration, prosecution or investigation (whether governmental or not) pending, current or threatened by or against the Company, to which the Company is or may become a party or in respect of which the Company is or may become vicariously liable or liable to indemnify any party concerned nor:

10.2.1 has the Company been concerned or involved in any act, event or omission which will or may give rise to such matters after the date of this Agreement; and

10.2.2 are there any circumstances which may or are likely to lead to such matters.

10.3 The Company is not subject to any order or judgement given by any court or governmental agency and has not been a party to any undertaking or assurance given to any court or governmental agency which is still in force.

10.4 Neither the Company nor, so far as the Vendors are aware, any officer or employee of the Company has committed any criminal, illegal or unlawful act or breach of any legislation.

10.5 Neither the Company nor, so far as the Vendors are aware, any officer or employee of the Company, has made or received any:

10.5.1 commercial bribes; or

10.5.2 payment upon the understanding that rebates or refunds will be made through a third party in contravention of the laws of any jurisdiction.

10.6 The Company has not sold, supplied or manufactured any product or provided any service which was or may become defective or faulty in any respect or which do not comply with warranties or representations expressly or implicitly given by it. The Company has not received and is not likely to receive a prohibition notice, a notice to warn or a suspension notice under the Consumer Protection Act 1987.

10.7 The Company has at all times carried on its business and conducted its affairs in compliance with:

10.7.1 its memorandum and articles of association;

10.7.2 all other agreements, contracts and arrangements to which it is or has been a party; and

10.7.3 all applicable laws and regulations of the United Kingdom or any other appropriate jurisdiction.

10.8 The Company has the power and is duly qualified to carry on business in all jurisdictions in which it carries on business.

10.9 There has been no violation of or default with respect to any statute, regulation, order, decree or judgement of any court or governmental agency, whether within the United Kingdom or any other jurisdiction in which the Company trades or which could have an adverse effect on the business of the Company.

10.10 All necessary licences, consents, permits and authorities (public and private) have been obtained by the Company to enable it to carry on its business properly and effectively in the places and in the manner in which it is now carried on. Full details of all such licences, consents, permits and authorities are included in the Disclosure Letter.

10.11 The Company is not in breach of any of the terms or conditions of any licences, consents, permits and authorities held by it; all such licences, consents, permits and authorities are valid and subsisting and the Vendors know of no reason why any of them should be suspended, cancelled, revoked or not renewed when necessary.

11 Contracts

11.1 No action or transaction has been effected in consequence of which:

11.1.1 the Company may be liable to refund in whole or in part any investment or other grant; or

11.1.2 any such grant for which application has been made by the Company will or may not be paid or will or may be reduced.

11.2 There are annexed to the Disclosure Letter copies of:

11.2.1 all material contracts to which the Company is a party, whether or not in the ordinary course of business;

11.2.2 details of all orders received by the Company which are in any respect outstanding;

11.2.3 tenders, quotations or offers made by the Company which are or will become capable of giving rise to a contract by the issue of an order or acceptance by any other party.

11.3 No tender, quotation or offer has been made by the Company otherwise than in the ordinary course of business on terms calculated to yield a gross profit margin consistent with the prudent conduct of the business of the Company.

11.4 The Company is not a party to any contract, agreement, transaction or arrangement or subject to any liability which:

11.4.1 is of an unusual, onerous or abnormal nature;

11.4.2 is outside the ordinary and proper course of business:

11.4.3 is for a fixed term of more than six months or for an indefinite term incapable of termination in accordance with its terms on not more than six months' notice served by the Company at any time;

11.4.4 is of a long-term nature (that is unlikely to have been fully performed in accordance with its terms within six months of the date on which it was entered into);

11.4.5 involves an aggregate outstanding expenditure by the Company of more than £[   ];

11.4.6 cannot be readily performed by the Company without undue expenditure or application of money, effort or personnel;

11.4.7 is with any trade union or any other body or organisation representing its employees;

11.4.8 is in the nature of a partnership, joint venture or consortium;

11.4.9 involves payment by any party by reference to fluctuations in the index of retail prices or any other index or in a currency other than sterling;

11.4.10 is for a loan, guarantee, indemnity or suretyship;

11.4.11 is of a loss making nature (that is known to be likely to result in a loss to the Company on completion of the Company's obligations);

11.4.12 is a consultancy agreement;

11.4.13 includes a power of attorney granted by or to the Company;

11.4.14 is a contract for hire or rent, conditional sale lease, hire purchase or purchase by way of credit sale (other than normal trade credit) or periodical payment;

11.4.15 involves, or is likely to involve, the supply of goods or services the aggregate sales value of which will be more than 5% of the Company's turnover for the preceding financial year;

11.4.16 has resulted in any anti-competitive practice or price fixing or which might be regarded as a cartel;

11.4.17 involves, or is likely to involve, other obligations or liabilities which ought reasonably to be made known to an intending purchaser of the Shares.

11.5 The Company is not in default under any of the contracts, agreements, transactions or arrangements to which it is a party and, so far as the Vendors are aware, no third party is in default under any of them.

11.6 None of the contracts, agreements, transactions or arrangements entered into by the Company:

11.6.1 is terminable, whether automatically or by the service of notice, lapse of time or otherwise;

11.6.2 provides for any variation in the rights, obligations or liabilities of any person;

in each case by reference to any change in the shareholders or directors of the Company.

11.7 The Company has not been party to any contract, transaction or arrangement (whether or not legally binding) nor has the Company incurred any liability of any nature, whether actual or contingent, with or to any of:

11.7.1 the Vendors (or their connected persons);

11.7.2 any officers of the Company or their connected persons.

11.8 The Company has not been a party to a transaction to which sections 320 or 330 of CA apply.

12 Trading

12.1 The Company does not carry on business under licence or otherwise than as principal.

12.2 True and complete particulars of the terms of all agency, distributorship, purchasing, marketing or licensing contracts or arrangements entered into by the Company at the date of this Agreement, or which have subsisted within the previous [*insert time, eg 36*] months, are set out in the Disclosure Letter.

12.3 There is no dispute with any present or former agent of the Company arising out of their agreement with the Company or its termination. As far as the Vendors are aware, there are no matters which may lead to any such dispute or any other liability under such agreement.

12.4 No agent, distributor, representative, supplier or other party (not being an employee) is entitled to any fixed or varying payment or credit in connection with the Company's business past, present or future.

12.5 No customer or supplier to the Company has given notice that it no longer intends to deal with the Company or indicated any intention to reduce materially the level of its dealings with the Company.

12.6 No supplier to the Company is entitled to charge interest in respect of any monies owed to it by the Company. The Company has no liability (whether actual or contingent) for unpaid interest in respect of the late payment of any invoice or other liability paid or settled prior to Completion;

12.7 The Company is not dependent upon any one:

12.7.1 customer for more than 5% by value of its sales;

12.7.2 supplier for more than 5% by value of its purchases.

13 Debts

13.1 No book or other debts owing to the Company which was included in the balance sheet to the Accounts or which has arisen since the Accounts Date has been realised for less than its full face value or is now considered by the Vendors to be irrecoverable in whole or in part.

13.2 All book and other debts owed to the Company at Completion will realise their full face value in the ordinary course of business and, in any event, within [*insert time, eg 90*] days of Completion.

13.3 No book or other debt owed to the Company is subject to any factoring, invoice discounting or similar agreement.

13.4 No book or other debt owed to the Company has arisen otherwise than as a result of the supply of goods and/or services by the Company in the ordinary course of its business.

14 Ownership and condition of assets

14.1 All assets used by the Company are its absolute property. None of the assets owned or used by the Company is the subject of any:

14.1.1 mortgage, debenture, charge, lien, hypothecation, pledge or other security interest; or

14.1.2 hire, rental, conditional sale, lease, hire purchase, credit sale (other than normal trade credit), or similar contract;

nor is there any agreement or commitment to enter into any such arrangement.

14.2 All plant, machinery, vehicles and equipment owned or used by the Company:

14.2.1 are in a good and safe state of repair and condition and are in full working order;

14.2.2 have been regularly and properly maintained in accordance with manufacturers' recommendations;

14.2.3 are not expected to require replacement, enhancement, addition and/or repair within [*insert time, eg 12*] months of Completion;

14.2.4 will be capable of being used efficiently in the business of the Company following Completion;

14.2.5 are in the possession and control of the Company.

14.3 The assets owned by the Company comprise all of the assets necessary for the continuation of its business in the manner and to the extent in which it is now carried on.

14.4 The Company does not use any assets which are owned by the Vendors or their connected persons.

14.5 There are maintenance contracts with independent specialist contractors in respect of all:

14.5.1 material assets of the Company;

14.5.2 assets which the Company is obliged to maintain or repair under any lease, hire, rental, conditional sale, lease, hire purchase, credit sale or similar agreement.

15 Stock

The stocks of raw material, packaging material consumables, work in progress and finished goods held by the Company are:

15.1 not excessive and are adequate in relation to its current trading requirements;

15.2 in good condition and capable of being sold by the Company in the ordinary course of its business in accordance with current prices, without rebate or allowance to a purchaser. None is damaged, slow moving or obsolete;

15.3 included in the books of accounts of the Company at the lower of cost or net realisable value; none of the finished goods included in stock are likely to realise less than their respective book value on sale in the ordinary course of business.

16 **Financial facilities**

16.1 The Disclosure Letter sets out full details of all banking and other financial facilities outstanding or available to the Company immediately prior to Completion and of any limits or restrictions to which they are subject.

16.2 There has been no breach of the terms of any of the banking or other financial facilities available to the Company and, without limitation, the Company does not have any borrowings on any account which exceed that applicable to such account limit.

16.3 No steps for the early repayment of sums outstanding under any banking or other financial facilities available to the Company have been taken or threatened and, as far as the Vendors are aware, no circumstances have occurred which give rise to an obligation to make, or would permit any demand for, early repayment. As far as the Vendors are aware, there are no circumstances which are likely to prejudice the continuation of the banking and other financial facilities available to the Company or give rise to any alteration in the terms applicable to them.

16.4 The Company does not have outstanding, nor has it agreed to create or issue, any loan capital.

16.5 None of the banking or other financial facilities available to the Company is dependent on the guarantee or indemnity of, or any security provided by, a third party.

16.6 The Company has not made a loan or quasi-loan to any person contrary to CA.

16.7 The Company has not made a loan which remains outstanding.

17 **Books and records**

17.1 All necessary and proper accounting records, minute books, registers (statutory or otherwise), papers and other records of the Company (whether required by law to be kept or not) relating to its assets and business:

17.1.1 are in its possession;

17.1.2 have been fully and properly kept;

17.1.3 have been kept in accordance with generally accepted principles relating to all matters recorded in them;

17.1.4 are complete and accurate in respect of what should ordinarily be contained in them;

17.1.5 show a true and fair view of all transactions entered into by the Company and its financial, contractual and trading position.

17.2 None of the Company's record systems, controls, data or information is recorded, stored, maintained, operated or otherwise dependent upon or held by any means which are not under the exclusive ownership and direct control of the Company.

17.3 No notice or allegation has been received or made that any of the statutory books of the Company is incorrect or should be rectified in any respect.

17.4 The computer systems operated by the Company have been properly and fully maintained. The Company has the benefit of the maintenance agreements specified in the Disclosure Letter.

17.5 The computer systems operated by the Company have full capability and capacity for both the Company's current requirements and the projected requirements for not less than three years following Completion for the processing and other functions required to be performed for the purposes of the business of the Company. As far as the Vendors are aware, there is no reason why the computer systems operated by the Company should cease to be so capable.

17.6 Disaster recovery plans are in effect and are adequate to ensure that in the event of a failure of the computer systems operated by the Company or a loss of data, the computer systems operated by the Company can be replaced or substituted with-out material disruption to the business of the Company.

17.7 In the event that any person providing maintenance or support services for the computer systems operated by the Company ceases or is unable for any reason to do so, the Company has all necessary rights to obtain the source code and all related technical and other information to procure the carrying out of such services by the Company's own employees or by a third party.

17.8 The Company owns and has in its possession and control all the up to date manuals, guides, instruction books and technical documents required to operate effectively the computer systems operated by the Company.

17.9 The computer systems operated by the Company have never interrupted or prevented in any way the proper operation of the Company's business. The computer systems operated by the Company have no defect which may interrupt or prevent the proper operation of the Company's business.

17.10 The Company is duly registered as a data user under the Data Protection Act 1998 and particulars of the registrations are set out in the Disclosure Letter.

17.11 The Company has complied fully with the data protection principles set out in the Data Protection Act 1998.

17.12 No individual has claimed, or will have the right to claim, compensation from the Company under the Data Protection Act 1984.

18 Memorandum and articles and resolutions etc

18.1 The copy of the memorandum and articles of association of the Company which is annexed to the Disclosure Letter is true, complete and accurate at the date of this Agreement and contains all documents required to be annexed to it under section 380 of CA.

18.2 The Company has not passed any elective resolution under section 379A of CA and has complied in all respects with sections 381A, 381B and 381C of CA in relation to all written resolutions passed by the Company.

18.3 The Company, its directors, officers and employees have all complied with all the provisions of the Companies Acts in relation to the activities of the Company, and all returns, particulars, resolutions and other documents required by the provisions of the Companies Acts to be delivered on behalf of the Company to the Registrar of Companies or to any other authority, organisation, person or body:

18.3.1 have been properly made, delivered and filed;

18.3.2 were true, complete and accurate;

18.3.3 were submitted within the relevant time period.

18.4 Neither the Company nor any class of its members has passed any resolution at annual general meetings which was special business.

19 Employees

19.1 The Disclosure Letter contains accurate and complete details of the names, ages, dates of commencement of employment, terms of employment and the periods of continuous employment of all the employees and officers of the Company including, without limitation, full details of any profit sharing, commission and discretionary bonus arrangements.

19.2 No officer or employee is remunerated on a profit sharing, bonus or commission basis.

19.3 The Company is under no contractual or other obligation to increase the rates of remuneration of, or make any bonus or incentive or other similar payment to, any of its officers, employees, consultants and/or agents at any future date.

19.4 No change has been made to the terms of employment of any employees in the last 12 months.

19.5   No negotiations for an increase in the remuneration or benefits of an officer, employee, consultant or agent of the Company are current or scheduled to take place within the next 12 months.

19.6   There are no employees of the Company employed under contracts of service or employment (whether in writing or otherwise) which cannot be terminated on 12 weeks' notice or less without payment of compensation (other than the statutory rights to compensation for unfair dismissal or redundancy).

19.7   There is no claim by any past or present officer or employee of the Company pending, threatened or capable of arising against the Company in respect of an accident or injury and any such claim will be fully covered and met by a valid insurance policy maintained by the Company.

19.8   No past employee of the Company has a right to return to work or has or may have a right to be reinstated with or re-engaged by the Company.

19.9   The Company is not liable to make any payment to any former or present officer or employee by way of damages or compensation for loss of office or employment or for redundancy, unfair dismissal, sexual discrimination or racial discrimination. As far as the Vendors are aware, there are no circumstances likely to result in any such claim being made.

19.10 The Company is not aware of any of its officers and employees engaged or involved in any industrial dispute and, as far as the Vendors are aware, there are no circumstances likely to result in any such dispute.

19.11 No officer or employee of the Company:

19.11.1 has given or received notice terminating his office or employment;

19.11.2 is entitled or, so far as the Vendors are aware, is likely to leave his office or employment prematurely as a result of the sale of the Shares.

19.12 The Company has not given to any person any power of attorney or other authority (express, implied or ostensible) which is still outstanding or valid except authorities not exceeding in scope the respective ostensible authorities normally enjoyed by persons holding the like offices and employments in comparable companies.

19.13 No contract of service exists between the Company and any employee in relation to which any relevant requirements including section 319 of CA have not been fulfilled.

19.14 The Company has not agreed to recognise a trade union or done anything which might be construed as granting recognition.

19.15 There are no agreements or arrangements between the Company and a trade union or other body representing employees.

19.16 No undertakings or assurances have been given to the officers or employees of the Company as to the continuance, introduction, increase or improvement of any pension rights or entitlements which the Company would be required to implement in accordance with good industrial practice (whether or not there is any legal obligation to do so).

19.17 The Company has at all times complied in full with all statutes, regulations, orders, decrees or judgements of any court or governmental agency, whether in the United Kingdom or any other jurisdiction in which the Company trades, relating to the employment of its employees and their terms and conditions of employment. All appropriate notices have been issued to all employees of the Company in relation to their terms and conditions of employment.

20 Insurance

20.1 Full, complete and accurate particulars of all insurances maintained by the company have been disclosed in writing to the Purchaser in the Disclosure Letter. All premiums on all such policies of insurance have been duly and punctually paid.

20.2 All assets of the Company capable of being insured are insured in amounts representing their full replacement or reinstatement value against all such risks as are normally insured by businesses similar to that of the Company and the Company is and has at all material times been fully insured against all risks and in such sums as a prudent company carrying on a similar business to the Company would insure against in such sums.

20.3 No claims have been made by the Company on any insurance policy which could have the effect of causing future insurance premiums to be higher than would otherwise be the case nor, so far as the Vendors are aware, have any circumstances occurred which have caused, or may cause, any such insurances to be rescinded, vitiated or avoided.

20.4 The Company has not at any time been refused any insurance or only offered an insurance policy at a cost substantially higher than the normal market rate for such insurance.

20.5 The Company has never received a report or recommendation from its insurance brokers or other advisors which has not been implemented in full.

20.6 The Company has not failed to disclose to an insurer in relation to any insurance policy any information which such insurer would consider to be material for disclosure.

20.7 There is no claim outstanding under any policy of insurances maintained by the Company nor, as far as the Vendors are aware, are there any circumstances likely to give rise to such a claim.

20.8 The Company has not acquired any benefit under any policy of assurance otherwise than as original beneficial owner.

21 Environmental Matters

21.1 The activities of the Company are and have at all times been carried on in compliance with all relevant Environmental Laws.

21.2 The Company has obtained all Environmental Licences. All fees payable in relation to any such Environmental Licence have been paid and there has been no default in the observance of the Environmental Licence by the Company, its officers, employees, consultants and/or agents. No application for an Environmental Licence is pending.

21.3 No steps have been taken for the revocation, cancellation, withdrawal, variation or surrender of any Environmental Licence and, as far as the Vendors are aware, no circumstances exist which could give rise to any revocation, cancellation, withdrawal, amendment, variation or restriction upon transfer of any Environmental Licence or which would prevent compliance with any of its terms.

21.4 Full details of all Environmental Licences are set out in the Disclosure Letter, together with all amendments to or variations from such licences. No other Environmental Licences are required by the Company.

21.5 The Company has not received any claim, notice, requirement or complaint from any person, regulatory body, court or competent organisation in respect of Environmental Matters which:

21.5.1 might prevent the continued use of any part of the Property in the manner and for the purpose for which it is now being used;

21.5.2 requires any remedial work to the Property or the clearance or removal from the Property of any Relevant Substance; or

21.5.3   alleges any breach of Environmental Laws;

and, as far as the Vendors are aware, there is no act, omission or circumstances which might give rise to any such claim, notice, requirement or complaint.

21.6   There has been no deposit, keeping, tipping, storage, treating, importing, exporting, transporting, processing, manufacture, collection or production of any Relevant Substance at, above, upon, in, under, to or from the Property.

21.7   The Company has received no notice or complaint of leaching or migration of any Relevant Substance into any land adjoining the Property or of any unauthorised emission, release or discharge of any Relevant Substance from the Property.

21.8   There is, and has been, no underground storage tank at the Property.

21.9   As far as the Vendors are aware, no property in the vicinity of the Property has been used as a landfill nor has there been any release, discharge or disposal of any Relevant Substance by any person in the vicinity of the Property.

21.10   No process or activity has been carried on at the Property which has caused, will cause or may cause pollution of the environment or harm to human health (in each case within the meaning of the EPA) or will result in a legally enforceable obligation on the Company in respect of such pollution or harm to human health.

21.11   No process or activity has been carried on at the Property which has resulted in any water standing on or running through either the Property or any site adjacent to the Property (whether a natural or man-made watercourse or by percolation).

21.12   The Property is not, and has not been, affected by any surface or subterranean working of mines and minerals. The ground conditions of the Property are not unsuitable for the construction and development of the structures of the type and size of the structures now erected on the Property or any other structures.

21.13   The Company currently satisfies the conditions attaching to authorisations required under section 6 of the EPA. The Vendors are not aware of any changes likely to occur in the foreseeable future to such conditions.

21.14   No works have been carried out at the Property in relation to Environmental Matters by any statutory authority in respect of which such authority is entitled to recover its costs.

22   **Intellectual Property**

22.1   The Disclosure Letter contains full details of all Intellectual Property owned by the Company or used by it in connection with its business. The Company does not own or use any other Intellectual Property, other than copyright arising in the ordinary course of business.

22.2   The Company does not use any Intellectual Property belonging to any third party.

22.3   The Company is the sole and absolute legal and beneficial owner of all Intellectual Property owned by it or, as far as the Vendors are aware, used by it in connection with its business. Where such Intellectual Property is capable of protection by registration in any territory the Company has been duly registered as the sole proprietor of it in all territories where the Company:

22.3.1   carries on or intends to carry on its business;

22.3.2   exploits or intends to exploit such Intellectual Property; and

22.3.3   has licensed such Intellectual Property to any third party.

22.4   Full details of all registrations (and applications for registration) of any Intellectual Property in any territory are contained in the Disclosure Letter.

22.5   Where the Company is registered or applying to be registered as the proprietor of any Intellectual Property, all fees, expenses, charges, duties and other payments have been promptly paid in full and are up to date and there is no:

22.5.1 outstanding obligation which might affect the validity of any such registration or application; or

22.5.2 procedural step, payment or other obligation which falls due to be made or performed within three months of Completion.

22.6 The Company has not licensed or authorised any other person, firm, company, and/or organisation to use, in any way, the Intellectual Property owned by or licensed to the Company.

22.7 The Company has not disclosed any of its Intellectual Property to any other person, firm, company and/or organisation otherwise than in the ordinary course of business, having obtained valid confidentiality undertakings from the recipient.

22.8 The Company has not entered into any agreement for the provision or acquisition of technical information or assistance.

22.9 The Disclosure Letter contains full details of all agreements relating to Intellectual Property to which the Company is a party. All such agreements are valid and binding upon all parties to them and there has been no act, omission or event which would or might (with or without the giving of notice) constitute a default or breach by any of the parties to them.

22.10 None of the processes, products or activities of the Company infringe in any way the Intellectual Property of any other person, firm, company or organisation or involves the unlicensed use of information confidential to third parties.

22.11 None of the Intellectual Property owned, used and/or licensed by the Company is the subject of (and there are no grounds which might give rise to) any claim, dispute, action, opposition, infringement or other restriction or arrangement of any nature in respect of the Intellectual Property used, owned and/or licensed by Company.

22.12 As far as the Vendors are aware, no other person uses any of the Intellectual Property owned, used by and/or licensed to the Company.

22.13 The Company is entitled to use, without payment or other consideration, all know-how and technical information used by it in connection with its business and all information concerning the products, methods and processes used by the Company.

23 **Real Property**

23.1 Copies of all the leases and licences, if any, affecting, benefiting or subject to which the Property is held are annexed to the Disclosure Letter.

23.2 There are appurtenant to the Property all rights and easements necessary for its existing and continued use and enjoyment.

23.3 Any right or easement appurtenant to the Property is held by the Company in fee simple. No right or easement appurtenant to the Property is terminable by any third party.

23.4 The Company has a good and marketable title to the Property with full title guarantee.

23.5 The Company is sole proprietor of the Property registered at HM Land Registry with absolute title.

23.6 The Property is owned by the Company free from any mortgage, debenture, charge (whether specific, floating, legal and/or equitable), rent charge, lien or other encumbrance securing the repayment of monies or other obligation or liability of the Company and/or any other party.

23.7 The Property is not subject to any right of pre-emption, right of first refusal, option, restrictive covenant, stipulation, easement, wayleave, licence, overriding interest (as defined in section 70 of the Land Registration Act 1925), or other similar rights vested in third parties which would inhibit its existing use.

23.8 There is no person in possession or occupation of, or who has or claims any right or interest of any kind in, the Property (whether adversely to the interests of the Company or otherwise) and the Company is entitled to and has exclusive vacant possession of the Property.

23.9 The Property is free from any Local Land Charge, caution, inhibition or notice and no matter exists which is capable of registration against any of the Property.

23.10 Where title to the Property is unregistered, no event has occurred in consequence of which registration should have been effected at HM Land Registry.

23.11 The use of the Property is the permitted use for the purposes of the Planning Acts and the existing permitted use is not temporary or personal or subject to planning conditions of an onerous or unusual nature.

23.12 Planning Permission has been granted or is deemed to have been granted for the purposes of the Planning Acts in respect of any development, alteration, extension or other improvement of the Property which has been carried out prior to Completion. No such Planning Permission relating to the Property is of a personal or temporary nature or subject to unusual or onerous conditions. Building regulations consent has been obtained with respect to all developments, extensions, alterations and improvements to the Property.

23.13 No Planning Permission which has been obtained in relation to the Property has been suspended or called in and no application for Planning Permission is awaiting decision.

23.14 No part of the Property is affected or, as far as the Vendors are aware, is likely to become affected, by:

23.14.1 any outstanding dispute or notice of complaint;

23.14.2 any exception, reservation, right, covenant, restriction or condition which is of an unusual or onerous nature or which affects or might in the future affect the use of the Property for the purpose for which it is now used;

23.14.3 any notice, order or proposal made or issued by or on behalf of any government or statutory authority;

23.14.4 the carrying out of any work upon any building, the modification of any Planning Permission, the discontinuance of any use or the imposition of any building or improvement line;

23.14.5 any compensation received as a result of any refusal of any application for Planning Permission or the imposing of any restrictions in relation to any Planning Permission;

23.14.6 the payment of any outgoings (other than normal rates and taxes);

23.14.7 any commutations of rent or payment of rent in advance of the due dates for payment.

23.15 The Property is not listed as being of specific historic interest or architectural importance nor is it located in a conservation area.

23.16 No licence is required in relation to the current use of the Property.

23.17 The Company does now and has at all times complied in all respects with all permissions, orders and regulations issued under the Planning Acts, any building regulation consent, all agreements under section 106 of the TCPA and section 38 of the Highways Act 1980 for the time being in force with respect to the Property.

23.18 No agreements or undertakings relating to the Property have been entered into or are contemplated under the provisions of:

23.18.1 section 18 of the Public Health Act 1936;

23.18.2 section 104 of the Water Industries Act 1991;

23.18.3 sections 38 and 278 of the Highways Act 1980;

23.18.4 section 106 of the TCPA;

or any similar legislation or earlier legislation of the same nature.

23.19 In relation to or affecting the Property, there are no:

23.19.1 compulsory purchase notices, orders or resolutions or any closing, demolition or clearance orders;

23.19.2 planning contravention, enforcement, breach of condition or stop notices issued by any local planning authority nor has any other enforcement action (including the exercise of any right of entry) been taken by any such authority;

and, as far as the Vendors are aware, there are no circumstances likely to lead to any of the above being made.

23.20 All restrictions, conditions and covenants (including any imposed pursuant to the Planning Acts) affecting the Property have been observed and performed up to date.

23.21 There are no structural defects (latent or patent) affecting the Property.

23.22 The Property is not subject to or affected by rights of common or past or present mining activity.

23.23 There are no disputes with any adjoining or neighbouring owner with respect to boundary walls and fences, or with respect to any easement right or means of access to the Property.

23.24 All building or other works erected upon the Property are in good and substantial repair and condition and, without limitation:

23.24.1 no flooding, subsidence, settlement, electrical defects, infestation, disease, rot or structural or other material defect of any kind affects or has affected the Property;

23.24.2 no building or other works on or comprising the Property contain any high alumina cement, blue asbestos, calcium chloride accelerator, wood wool slabs used as permanent shuttering or any other Relevant Substance or a substance not complying with currently accepted good building practice;

23.24.3 there is currently no dispute over the quality of the construction and/or materials used in the Property;

23.24.4 no building or other material construction work has been carried out upon the Property in the last six years.

23.25 No part of the Property is on or near to an existing or closed landfill site nor has the Property ever been affected by the leaching from adjoining premises or land of chemicals, contaminated water or other liquids or other harmful substances or the migration of gases.

23.26 The Property is not, nor does it include, any reclaimed land.

23.27 The Property is insured:

23.27.1 for its full reinstatement value and associated costs;

23.27.2 against third party and public liability claims to an adequate extent.

23.28 Any fire certificate necessary for the Property has been obtained and complied with in all respects.

23.29 Neither the Company nor any of the Vendors have received an adverse surveyor's, engineer's or other professional's report in respect of any part of the Property.

23.30 The Vendors are not aware of any fact, matter or thing which would, or might reasonably affect, the willingness of a prudent purchaser for value to purchase or take a lease of the Property or to buy the Shares on the terms (including price) of this Agreement.

23.31 The Property enjoys main services of water, drainage, electricity, telephone and gas.

23.32 The principal means of access to the Property are over roads which have been taken over by the local or other highway authority and which are maintainable at public expense and no means of access to the Property is shared with another party or subject to rights of determination by another party.

23.33 The Property comprises all the land and buildings owned by the Company or occupied or otherwise used by the Company or its servants or agents for the purposes of the Company's business.

23.34 The Company is not and has not at any time since the date of its incorporation been the original lessee of any property other than the Property and has not given a guarantee or entered into any direct covenant with either a lessor or assignor of any property.

23.35 The Company has paid the rent and observed and performed the covenants on the part of the tenant and the conditions contained in the leases and/or licences under which the Property is held and:

23.35.1 all such leases and/or licences are valid and in full force;

23.35.2 all licences, consents and approvals required from the landlords or any superior landlords under any leases and/or licences of the Property have been obtained;

23.35.3 the covenants on the part of the Company contained in such licences, consents and approvals have been duly performed and observed.

23.36 There are no rent reviews under the leases of the Property held by the Company currently in progress and none are due in the 12 months immediately following Completion.

23.37 The Company is not for any reason anticipating the expenditure of any substantial sum of money in respect of the Property.

23.38 The Company has not elected to waive the VAT exemption pursuant to paragraph 2 of Schedule 10 VATA, and is not otherwise bound by any election in respect of any part of the Property. No part of the Property is currently standard rated for VAT purposes because of any new building or incomplete or new civil engineering works on the Property within the meaning of Group 1 of Schedule 9 VATA.

24 **Competition**

24.1 The Company, its Directors, agents and/or employees have not at any time done and/or omitted to do anything, nor entered into any agreement or arrangement in respect of the business of the Company which may and/or does:

24.1.1 contravene the Competition Acts 1980 and 1998, the Enterprise Act 2002, the Restrictive Trade Practices Acts 1976 and 1977, the Consumer Credit Act 1974, the Trades Description Act 1968, the Fair Trading Act 1973 and/or the Resale Prices Act 1976 and/or any regulations made under any such Acts;

24.1.2 by virtue of its terms or by virtue of any practice carried on in connection with it, be deemed a consumer trade practice (within the meaning of section 13 of the Fair Trading Act 1973);

24.1.3 infringe Articles 65 or 66 of the Treaty establishing the European Coal and Steel Community, or justify recommendations under Articles 66(7) of that treaty;

24.1.4 infringe Articles 81 or 82 of the Treaty of Rome, infringe any regulation or other enactment giving effect to any of such Articles and/or constitute any other breach of such Treaty;

24.1.5 result in an order being made under any legislation referred to in this clause 24.1; and/or

24.1.6 contravene or infringe any legislation or regulations with similar effect to the matters referred to in clauses 24.1.1 to 24.1.5 above, in any jurisdiction in which the Company has carried or carries on its business and/or is or has been domiciled.

24.2 The Company, its Directors, agents and/or employees have not made any application to the European Commission or any other competition authority for a declaration of inapplicability, for negative clearance, for leniency and/or for a letter of comfort in respect of any agreement, decision or practice relating to the business of the Company.

24.3 The Company, its Directors, agents and/or employees have not been and/or are not subject to any visit, dawn raid, questions, enquiries, investigation, order, undertaking and/or direction by and/or to any competition authority in any jurisdiction.

25 Pensions

Defined Benefits Scheme

25.1 Save as disclosed, no agreement, arrangement, custom or practice (whether ex-gratia or otherwise) exist whereby the Company is under any obligation to provide or pay towards the provision of any relevant benefits (as defined in section 612(1) of ICTA with the omission of the exception to that definition) for any officer or employee or former officer or former employee of the Company or for any dependant of any such person.

25.2 In relation to each Disclosed Scheme (which in this warranty means each agreement, arrangement, custom or practice referred to in clause 25.1 above, details of which have been disclosed to the Purchaser (other than a personal pension scheme) full details of the Disclosed Scheme have been given to the Purchaser including:

25.2.1 true and complete copies of the trust deeds, rules and other documents (including any agreements under which the Company is or may become liable to provide benefits to which clause 25.1 above applies by way of a scheme or arrangement which is not capable of approval by the Board of Inland Revenue under Chapter I Part XIV of ICTA) containing the provisions currently governing the Disclosed Scheme;

25.2.2 copies of the booklet issued to the employees who are or may become members of the Disclosed Scheme and of all announcements or other employee literature issued to such employees which details changes to the provisions of the Disclosed Scheme which are not incorporated in the Disclosed Scheme's formal governing documents;

25.2.3 in relation to a Disclosed Scheme a copy of the Last Actuarial Valuation and of any written actuarial advice given in relation to the Disclosed Scheme subsequent to the effective date of the Last Actuarial Valuation;

25.2.4 a copy of the audited accounts of the Disclosed Scheme for the last three scheme years;

25.2.5 full and accurate details of the past practice under the Disclosed Scheme of providing discretionary increases to pensions in payment and deferments;

25.2.6 a list of the Disclosed Scheme's active members, deferred pensioners and pensioners setting out all information required to determine their entitlement to benefits under the Disclosed Scheme;

25.2.7 full details of any exercise of any power or discretion under the Disclosed Scheme to augment benefits, to provide new or additional benefits which would not otherwise be provided or to admit to membership any person who would not otherwise be eligible for membership;

25.2.8 copies of all insurance policies or contracts effected for the purpose of the Disclosed Scheme;

25.2.9 copies of all investment management, custodianship, data processing and other agreements for the provision of advisory or administration services in connection with the Disclosed Scheme.

25.3 In relation to each Disclosed Scheme under which some or all of the benefits payable thereunder are circulated in accordance with a formula which takes account of (inter alia) the service of a member to retirement and the remuneration of the member averaged over his service or at or close to his retirement or death:

25.3.1 since the effective date of the Last Actuarial Valuation:

25.3.1.1 no payment or repayment of any of the assets of the Disclosed Scheme have been made to any employer participating in it; and

25.3.1.2 contributions have been made to the Disclosed Scheme at a rate or rates not lower than that or those recommended in such valuation or funding review and all such contributions which have fallen due have been paid;

25.3.2 all information supplied for the purposes of the Last Actuarial Valuation was true and complete in all material respects;

25.3.3 the Disclosed Scheme is sufficiently and effectively funded so that all liabilities accrued thereunder at Completion could be secured in full if the Disclosed Scheme were then terminated and also on an on going basis [using the actuarial methods and assumptions adopted in the Last Actuarial Valuation of the Disclosed Scheme/using the Actuarial Assumptions as defined in Schedule 7/using actuarial assumptions which are within the range of accepted actuarial practice in relation to all relevant factors including (without limitation) the assumptions set out in clauses 25.3.3.1 and 25.3.3.2 below] to fund all liabilities of the Disclosed Scheme (whether immediate, prospective or contingent) taking no account of benefits in respect of pensionable service after Completion but making reasonable provisions to reflect the past practice of the Disclosed Scheme with regard to the provision of increases to pensions in payment and deferment; [and assuming:

25.3.3.1 that members in respect of whom benefits are currently, prospectively and contingently payable under the Disclosed Scheme remain in pensionable employment thereunder until their normal pension date subject to reasonable assumptions as to withdrawal, early retirement or death; and

25.3.3.2 that each member's remuneration used for determining benefits under the Disclosed Scheme shall be increased in respect of the period from Completion to the member's normal pension date under the Disclosed Scheme;]

25.3.4 no employer which participated or has participated in the Disclosed Scheme is liable to make any payment to the Disclosed Scheme pursuant to section 144 of the Pension Schemes Act 1993 and regulations made thereunder nor would any such employer be under any such liability if the Disclosed Scheme were wound up at Completion; and

25.3.5 no increase has been made to the remuneration of any member of the Disclosed Scheme which is pensionable under it since the beginning of the scheme's administrative year.

25.4 In relation to each Disclosed Scheme under which the amount of the benefits payable to or in respect of a member (other than any insured lump sum death in service benefits) is based solely on the amount of the accumulated contributions made to the Disclosed Scheme by or in respect of the member together with investment return thereon:

25.4.1 no undertaking or assurance (oral or written) has been made or given to any member of the Disclosed Scheme that any particular level or amount of benefit (other than insured lump sum death in service benefit) will be provided for or in respect of them under the Disclosed Scheme;

25.4.2 contributions are not paid to the Disclosed Scheme in arrears and no contributions to the Disclosed Scheme have fallen due but are unpaid.

25.5 All benefits (other than refunds of contributions) payable under each Disclosed Scheme on the death of a member or during periods of sickness or disability are fully insured under a policy effected with an insurance company of good repute and each member has been covered for such insurance by such insurance company at its normal rates and on its normal terms for persons in good health and all insurance premiums payable have been paid.

25.6 No Disclosed Scheme holds any employer-related investments (within the meaning of section 112 of the Pension Schemes Act 1993) and there are no charges over any of the assets of the Disclosed Scheme.

25.7 No discretion or power under any Disclosed Scheme has been exercised:

25.7.1 to admit to membership or provide past service credits for any person on terms which provided for or envisaged the payment of a transfer value or a transfer of assets from another scheme to the Disclosed Scheme in any case in which such payment or transfer has not been made or has not been made in full; or

25.7.2 since the effective date of the Last Actuarial Valuation to pay a transfer value or make a transfer of assets to another scheme or arrangement the amount or value of which was greater than the cash equivalent to which the person in respect of whom it was made acquired a right under Chapter IV of the Pension Schemes Act 1993.

25.8 Every employee who has been admitted to membership or offered membership of a Disclosed Scheme after 31 May 1989 has been admitted to or offered admission on terms which comply with the requirements of Part 2 of Schedule 6 to the Finance Act 1989 and the substance of such terms have been communicated to each such employee in writing.

25.9 The records of each Disclosed Scheme have been properly and accurately maintained. There has been no breach of the trusts of any Disclosed Scheme and there are not in respect of any Disclosed Scheme any actions, suits or claims (other than routine claims for benefits) outstanding, pending or threatened against the trustees or administrator of the Disclosed Scheme or against the Vendor, the Company or any other employer participating in the Disclosed Scheme and after making due and careful enquiries the Vendor is not aware of any circumstances which might give any rise to any such claims.

25.10 Each Disclosed Scheme is approved or capable of approval as an exempt approved scheme (within the meaning of Chapter I of Part XIV of the Taxes Act) and there is in force in respect of the employments to which the Disclosed Scheme relates an appropriate contracting-out certificate (within the meaning of section 7 of the Pension Schemes Act 1993).

25.11 Nothing has been done or omitted to be done:

25.11.1 which will or may result in any Disclosed Scheme ceasing to be an exempt approved scheme or, if the Disclosed Scheme is not yet approved, the Vendor is not aware of any circumstances which might give the Inland Revenue reasons to withhold such approval; or

25.11.2 which may or will result in any contracting-out certificate held by reference to a Disclosed Scheme being cancelled, surrendered or varied.

25.12 Each Disclosed Scheme has been administered in accordance with all applicable laws, being all relevant statutes and subordinate legislation of the Parliament of the United Kingdom and all relevant provisions of the law of the European Communities.

25.13 In relation to each agreement, arrangement, custom or practice as is referred to in clause 25.1 above which is a personal pension scheme approved or provisionally approved for the purposes of Chapter IV of Part XIV of ICTA to which contributions have been made or are intended to be made by the Company, there has been disclosed to the Purchaser full details of the basis on which the Company has undertaken to contribute to such personal pension scheme including the rate and amount of such contributions made in the three years ending on the date of this Agreement.

25.14 There is no obligation to provide benefits under or pay any contributions to any Disclosed Scheme or personal pension scheme other than as revealed in the document and information disclosed to the Purchaser pursuant to clauses 25.1 and 25.2 above. No undertaking or assurance has been given to any employee or officer, former employee or officer of the Company or their respective dependants as to the continuance or introduction of or increase or improvement to any benefits under any Disclosed Scheme or personal pension scheme which the Company or Purchaser will be required to implement in accordance with good industrial relations practice whether or not there is any legal obligation to do so.

or

Defined Contributions Scheme

25.15 Save as disclosed no agreement, arrangement, custom or practice (whether ex-gratia or otherwise) exist whereby the Company is under any obligation to provide or pay towards the provision of any relevant benefits (as defined in section 612(1) of ICTA with the omission of the exception to that definition) for any officer or employee or former officer or former employee of the Company or for any dependant of any such person.

25.16 In relation to each Disclosed Scheme (which in this warranty means each agreement, arrangement, custom or practice referred to in clause 25.15 above), details of which have been disclosed to the purchaser (other than a personal pension scheme) full details of the Disclosed Scheme have been given to the Purchaser including:

25.16.1 true and complete copies of the trust deeds, rules and other documents (including any agreements under which the Company is or may become liable to provide benefits to which clause 25.15 above applies by way of a scheme or arrangement which is not capable of approval by the Board of Inland Revenue under Chapter I Part XIV of ICTA) containing the provisions currently governing the Disclosed Scheme;

25.16.2 copies of the booklet issued to the employees who are or may become members of the Disclosed Scheme and of all announcements or other employee literature issued to such employees which details changes to the provisions of the Disclosed Scheme which are not incorporated in the Disclosed Scheme's formal governing documents;

25.16.3 a list of the Disclosed Scheme's active members, deferred pensioners and pensioners setting out all information required to determine their entitlement to benefits under the Disclosed Scheme;

25.16.4 full details of any exercise of any power or discretion under the Disclosed Scheme to augment benefits, to provide new or additional benefits which would not otherwise be provided or to admit to membership any person who would not otherwise be eligible for membership;

25.16.5 all insurance premiums due to be paid in respect of each Disclosed Scheme by [target company] or trustees of each Disclosed Scheme have been duly paid.

25.17 The records of each Disclosed Scheme have been properly and accurately maintained. There has been no breach of the trusts of any Disclosed Scheme and there are not in respect of any Disclosed Scheme any actions, suits or claims (other than routine claims for benefits) outstanding, pending or threatened against the trustees or administrator of the Disclosed Scheme or against the Vendor, the Company or any other employer participating in the Disclosed Scheme and after making due and careful enquiries the Vendor is not aware of any circumstances which might give any rise to any such claims.

25.18 Each Disclosed Scheme is approved or capable of approval as an exempt approved scheme (within the meaning of Chapter I of Part XIV of the Taxes Act) and there is in force in respect of the employments to which the Disclosed Scheme relates an appropriate contracting-out certificate (within the meaning of section 7 of the Pension Schemes Act 1993).

25.19 Nothing has been done or omitted to be done:

25.19.1 which will or may result in any Disclosed Scheme ceasing to be an exempt approved scheme or, if the Disclosed Scheme is not yet approved, the Vendor is not aware of any circumstances which might give the Inland Revenue reasons to withhold such approval; or

25.19.2 which may or will result in any contracting-out certificate held by reference to a Disclosed Scheme being cancelled, surrendered or varied.

26 Insolvency

26.1 The Company is not insolvent or unable to pay its debts within the meaning of section 123 of the Insolvency Act 1986.

26.2 No order has been made, petition presented or resolution passed for the winding up of the Company; there are no grounds on which any such order or petition could be made or presented and no such resolution is contemplated by the members of the Company or any of them.

26.3 No distress, execution, statutory demand or other process has been levied and remains undischarged in respect of the Company and there is no outstanding judgement or court order against the Company nor has it stopped payment of its liabilities.

26.4 No power to appoint a receiver has been exercised or has arisen in respect of the business or any of the assets of the Company and there is no unfulfilled or unsatisfied judgement or Court Order outstanding against it.

Schedule 6

Taxation

Schedule 7

Pensions

Specific provisions to be inserted, depending on details of the individual scheme(s) and incorporating comments from pensions advisors and (where appropriate) scheme actuary.

Schedule 8

Completion Accounts

1 **Preparation of Completion Accounts**

1.1   As soon as reasonably practicable after Completion the [Purchaser] shall prepare the Completion Accounts and the statement of the [Net Asset Value/Net Profits]. The Completion Accounts and the statement of [Net Asset Value/Net Profits] shall be delivered to the Vendors as soon as reasonably practicable and in any event on or before the expiry of two months from Completion.

1.2   Subject to paragraph 1.3 the Completion Accounts shall be prepared in accordance with the historical cost convention on the following basis:

1.2.1   in accordance with the accounting policies, principles and practices adopted by the Company in the preparation of the Accounts consistently applied; and

1.2.2   in all other respects in accordance with generally accepted accounting principles and practices in the United Kingdom for companies of similar size carrying on similar businesses to that of the Company.

1.3   The Completion Accounts shall be prepared on the basis of the following principles and practices:

1.3.1   stock, work in progress, consumables and finished goods shall be valued in a proper and consistent manner on the basis of cost (excluding cost of selling, distribution and administration) or market value (which shall itself be taken as the lower of net realisable value and replacement cost), whichever is the lesser. Full provision shall be made for unusable, unsaleable, slow moving or damaged stocks and for any other losses likely to be incurred; the valuation of stocks, work in progress, consumables and finished goods shall be ascertained by reference to a full physical stock take on (or as soon as practicable after) the Completion Date, which shall be attended by representatives of the Vendors and the Purchaser;

1.3.2   full provision shall be made for all Tax, including Tax that would arise on the sale of any asset at the value attributed to such asset in the Completion Accounts;

1.3.3   full provision shall be made for all liabilities, known, actual or contingent (including all contingent liabilities to Tax and to customers and under any undertaking guarantee or other document);

1.3.4   full provision shall be made for all accrued holiday pay;

1.3.5   full provision shall be made for all liabilities, known, actual or contingent of the Company to or in respect of the Disclosed Scheme.

1.4   In the preparation of the Completion Accounts, the Purchaser shall take into account all relevant factors and make proper provision for all liabilities as at Completion which become known to the Company at any time, and not merely those which are known on or before Completion.

2 **Agreement of Completion Accounts**

2.1   The Completion Accounts and the statement of [Net Asset Value/Net Profits] shall be reviewed by the Vendors, who shall be afforded access to all working papers of the Purchaser and all other facilities which are reasonably required to enable them to carry out their review.

205

2.2 Within one month of service on the Vendors of the draft Completion Accounts and statement of the [Net Asset Value/Net Profits], the Vendors shall serve notice on the Purchaser to confirm their agreement to or dispute the draft Completion Accounts and/or the statement of the [Net Asset Value/Net Profits]. If no notice is served on the Purchaser before the expiry of such month, the draft Completion Accounts and statement, of the [Net Asset Value/Net Profits] shall be deemed to have been agreed and shall be final and binding upon both the Vendors and the Purchaser.

2.3 If the Vendors serve notice to dispute any part of the Completion Accounts and/or the statement of the [Net Asset Value/Net Profits], they shall notify the Purchaser of the reasons for such dispute. The parties shall then seek to reach agreement between them to enable the draft Completion Accounts and statement of the [Net Asset Value/Net Profits] to be agreed.

2.4 If the parties are unable to reach agreement within one month of the Vendor's notice served pursuant to paragraph 2.2, the outstanding issues in dispute may be referred by either the Vendors or the Purchaser to the Expert for final determination.

2.5 The Expert shall:
2.5.1 be entitled to require written or oral representations as he sees fit;
2.5.2 act as an expert and not an arbitrator.

2.6 The determination of the Expert shall be final and binding upon both the Vendors and the Purchaser.

2.7 The costs of the Expert shall be borne as the Expert may determine or, if no determination is made as to costs, as to 50% by the Vendors and as to 50% by the Purchaser.

SIGNED and **DELIVERED** as a **DEED** by [   ] in the presence of:

Witness Signature

Witness Name

Witness Address

Witness Occupation

SIGNED and **DELIVERED** as a **DEED** by [   ] in the presence of:

Witness Signature

Witness Name

Witness Address

Witness Occupation

EXECUTED and **DELIVERED** as a **DEED** by [   ] LIMITED acting by a director and its secretary or by two directors

....

Director

....

Director/Secretary

Document 7
Stock Transfer Form

(This form to be printed on white paper)	Certificate lodged with the Registrar
Consideration Money £……………………..	(For completion by the Registrar/ Stock Exchange)

Name of Undertaking	
Description of Security	

Number or amount of Shares, Stock or other security and, in figures column only, number and denomination of units, if any.	Words	Figures (units of)

Name(s) of registered holder(s) should be given in full: the address should be given where there is only one holder. If the transfer is not made by the registered holder(s) insert also the name(s) and capacity (eg Executor(s)), of the person(s) making the transfer	in the name(s) of

I/We hereby transfer the above security out of the name(s) aforesaid to the person(s) named below Signature of transferor(s) 1. …………………………….. ………… 3……………………………………. 2………………………………………….. 4……………………………………..	Stamp of Selling Broker(s), for transactions which are not Stock Exchange transactions, of Agent(s), if any, acting for the Transferor(s). Date

Full name(s), postal address(es) (including County or, if applicable, Postal District number) of the person(s) to whom the security is transferred. Please state title, if any, or whether Mr, Ms, Mrs or Miss Please complete in type or block capitals	

I/We request that such entries be made in the register as are necessary to give effect to this transfer.

Stamp of Buying Broker(s) (if any).	Stamp or name and address of person lodging this form (if other than the Buying Broker(s)).

Reference to the Registrar in this form means the registrar or registration agent of the undertaking, not the Registrar of Companies at Companies House

Form of certificate required for exemption from stamp duty

Instruments of transfer executed on or after 1st May 1987 are exempt from stamp duty when the transaction falls within one of the following categories and will not need to be seen in stamp offices, provided they are certified as below in accordance with the Stamp Duty (Exempt Instruments) Regulations 1987:

(a) The vesting of property subject to a trust in the trustees of the trust on the appointment of a new trustee, or in the continuing trustees on the retirement of a trustee.

(b) The conveyance or transfer of property the subject of a specific devise or legacy to the beneficiary named in the will (or his nominee).

(c) The conveyance or transfer of property which forms part of an intestate's estate to the person entitled on intestacy (or his nominee).

(d) The appropriation of property within Section 84(4) of the Finance Act 1985 (death: appropriation in satisfaction of a general legacy of money) or Section 84(5) or (7) of that Act (death: appropriation in satisfaction of any interest of surviving spouse and in Scotland also of any interest of issue).

(e) The conveyance or transfer of property which forms part of the residuary estate of a testator to a beneficiary (or his nominee) entitled solely by virtue of his entitlement under the will.

(f) The conveyance or transfer of property out of a settlement in or towards satisfaction of a beneficiary's interest, not being an interest acquired for money or money's worth, being a conveyance or transfer constituting a distribution of property in accordance with the provisions of the settlement.

(g) The conveyance or transfer of property on and in consideration only of marriage to a party to the marriage (or his nominee) or to trustees to be held on the terms of a settlement made in consideration only of the marriage.

(h) The conveyance or transfer of property within Section 83(1) of the Finance Act 1985 (transfers in connection with divorce, etc.)

(i) The conveyance or transfer by the liquidator of property which formed part of the assets of the company in liquidation to a shareholder of that company (or his nominee) in or towards satisfaction of the shareholder's rights on a winding-up.

(j) The grant in fee simple of an easement in or over land for no consideration in money or money's worth.

(k) The grant of a servitude for no consideration in money or money's worth.

(l) The conveyance or transfer of property operating as a voluntary disposition inter vivos for no consideration in money or money's worth nor any consideration referred to in Section 57 of the Stamp Act 1891 (conveyance in consideration of a debt, etc.).

(m) The conveyance or transfer of property by an instrument within Section 84(1) of the Finance Act 1985 (death: varying disposition).

Certificate

(1) Insert appropriate category — I/We hereby certify that this instrument falls within category .... (1) in the schedule to the Stamp Duty (Exempt Instruments) Regulations 1987.

(2) Delete if the certificate is given by the transferor or his solicitor — I/We confirm that I/we have been duly authorised by the transferor to sign this certificate and that the facts of the transaction are within my/our knowledge.(2)

Signature(s) .... *Description ('Transferor', 'Solicitor' etc)*
Name(s) ....
Address ....
....
Date .... 20 ....

Form of certificate required where transfer is not exempt but is not liable to *ad valorem* stamp duty (£5.00 fixed duty payable)

Some instruments of transfer are liable to a fixed duty of £5.00 when the transaction falls within one of the following categories for which the certificate below may be completed.

(1) Transfer by way of security for a loan or re-transfer to the original transferor on repayment of a loan.

(2) Transfer, not on sale and not arising under any contract of sale and where no beneficial interest in the property passes: (a) to a person who is a mere nominee of, and is nominated only by, the transferor; (b) from a mere nominee who has at all times held the property on behalf of the transferee; (c) from one nominee to another nominee of the same beneficial owner where the first nominee has at all times held the property on behalf of that beneficial owner. (NOTE – This category does not include a transfer made in any of the following circumstances: (i) by a holder of stock, etc., following the grant of an option to purchase the stock, to the person entitled to the option or his nominee; (ii) to a nominee in contemplation of a contract for the sale of stock, etc., then about to be entered into; (iii) from the nominee of a vendor, who has instructed the nominee orally or by some unstamped writing to hold stock, etc., in trust for a purchaser, to such purchaser).

(1) Insert '(1)' or '(2)'

I/We hereby certify that the transaction in respect of which this transfer is made is one which falls within the category .... (1) above.

(2) Here set out concisely the facts explaining the transaction in cases falling within (1) or (2) or in any other case where £5.00 fixed duty is offered.

I/We confirm that I/we have been duly authorised by the transferor to sign this certificate and that the facts of the transaction are within my/our knowledge.

(2) ....
....
Signature(s)................. *Description ('Transferor', 'Solicitor' etc)*
....
....
....
Date .... 20 ....

Document 8
Interval between Exchange and Completion

(A) Clauses to amend where agreement is conditional

(a) Conditions – insert the following clauses as new clause 5 of the share acquisition agreement immediately after the consideration clause.

5   **Conditions**

5.1   This Agreement is conditional on the following conditions being satisfied or waived:

    5.1.1   the shareholders of the Vendor in general meeting passing a resolution in the agreed terms without amendment to approve the terms of this Agreement;

    5.1.2   the shareholders of the Purchaser in general meeting passing a resolution in the agreed terms to approve the purchase by the Purchaser of the Shares on the terms and subject to the conditions of this Agreement;

    5.1.3   clearance being obtained in terms satisfactory to the Vendor [and the Purchaser] from [*insert name of relevant regulatory body*];

    5.1.4   [*other necessary/desirable consents approvals*].

5.2   The Vendor[s] will use all reasonable endeavours to procure that each condition set out in clauses [*number*] to [*number*] is fulfilled as soon as practicable and in any event before [*insert proposed date of Completion*] provided that if, notwithstanding such reasonable efforts, any of those conditions have not been satisfied by that date then the Vendor[s] will make all reasonable efforts to achieve satisfaction of those conditions as soon as practicable thereafter and in any event not later than [*time*] on [*insert long stop date*].

5.3   The Purchaser will use all reasonable endeavours to procure that each condition set out in clauses [*number*] to [*number*] is fulfilled as soon as practicable and in any event before [*insert proposed date of Completion*] provided that if, notwithstanding such reasonable efforts, any of these conditions have not been satisfied by that date then the Purchaser will make all reasonable efforts to achieve satisfaction of those conditions as soon as practicable thereafter and in any event not later than [*time*] on [*insert long stop date*].

5.4   The Purchaser may at its complete discretion, by notice to the Vendor[s], waive a condition set out in clause [*number*] to [*number*] either in whole or in part [*other than clause [number]*]. The Vendor[s] may at [its/their] complete discretion, by notice to the Purchaser, waive a condition set out in clause [*number*] to [*number*] either in whole or in part [other than clause [*number*]].

5.5   If [any of] the Vendor[s] or the Purchaser becomes aware of any fact or matter that prejudices the satisfaction of a condition, then such Vendor or Purchaser will immediately inform the other parties.

5.6   If a condition set out in clause [*number*] to [*number*] has not been waived and has not been satisfied by [*time*] on [*insert long stop date*], the Purchaser [or the Vendor[s]] may on that date by notice to the Vendor[s] [or the Purchaser (as appropriate)] terminate this Agreement.

5.7   If the Purchaser [or the Vendor[s]] terminate[s] this Agreement in accordance with this clause, none of the parties will have any rights against any other party under this Agreement (other than in respect of any accrued rights).

5.8 Pending Completion the Vendor[s] will ensure that [the Company] [each Group Member] complies with the requirements set out in schedule [*number*].

(b) Completion

Existing clause 5 (Completion) will become clause 6. Delete existing clause 5.1 and replace with the following:

6.1 The Purchaser shall not be required to complete the purchase of the Shares unless all of the Shares are transferred at the same time and all of the Vendors' obligations pursuant to clauses 5.2 and 5.3 are satisfied in full. Subject to this, the sale and purchase is to be completed at the offices of the Purchaser's Solicitors on the later of [*insert date*] and the date which is [7] Business Days after the date (not being later than [*insert long stop date*]) on which the last of the conditions set out at clause 5.1 is satisfied or waived.

(c) Completion Accounts

Clause 6 should be renumbered clause 7.

(d) Warranties

Warranties clause 7 should be renumbered as clause 8.

Insert the following clause 8.2 (existing clause 8.2 (previously 7.2) being renumbered as clause 8.3 and all following clauses in the share purchase agreement being consecutively renumbered):

8.3 The Warranties will be deemed to be repeated immediately before Completion by reference to the facts and circumstances existing at Completion. For this purpose only, where in a Warranty there is an express or implied reference to the 'date of this Agreement' or an equivalent term, that reference is to be construed as a reference to the 'date of Completion'.

(e) Purchaser's rights

Insert new clause 9 (immediately after clause 8 Warranties) and renumber all consequent clauses:

9 Purchaser's rights

9.1 The Purchaser may by notice in writing to the Vendor[s] at any time prior to Completion elect to terminate this Agreement without liability on the part of the Purchaser if any fact, matter or event (whether existing or occurring on or before the date of this Agreement or arising or occurring afterwards) comes to the notice of the of the Purchaser at any time prior to Completion which:

9.1.1 constitutes a breach by the Vendor[s] of any provision of this Agreement (including any breach of the obligations pending Completion in Schedule [*number*]);

9.1.2 would constitute a breach of any Warranty if the Warranties were repeated on or at any time before Completion by reference to the facts and circumstances then existing and on the basis that any reference to 'date of this Agreement' or equivalent term within a Warranty shall be construed as a reference to the time of repetition; or

9.1.3 affects or is likely to affect materially and adversely the financial position or business prospects of the Company [or any other Group Member] (not being an event affecting or likely to affect to a similar extent generally all companies carrying on similar businesses in the United Kingdom).

9.2 If the Purchaser does elect to terminate this Agreement the Vendor[s] will indemnify the Purchaser against all its costs relating to the negotiation, preparation, execution or termination of this Agreement or the satisfaction of a condition set out in clause [3] and each party's further rights and obligations will cease immediately on termination though termination shall not affect a party's accrued rights and obligations at the date of termination.

(f) Announcements

In the event that the Purchaser is raising the cash consideration by way of a share issue and placing, it may need to disclose the transaction as part of the fundraising process and the following clauses, to be inserted in the 'Announcements' clause, allow for this.

The Vendor[s] shall at the request of the Purchaser supply to the Purchaser all such information and reports with regard to [the Company] [each Group Member] as may be required by the Purchaser to enable it to comply with the requirements of the law, any stock exchange or listing authority or the Panel on Takeovers and Mergers regarding the transaction to which this Agreement relates.

From the date of this Agreement the Purchaser and its accountants and agents shall be allowed unrestricted access to the Property and all the books of account and other records of [the Company] [each Group Member] and the Vendor shall promptly supply, and shall instruct the officers and employees of [the Company] [each Group Member] promptly to supply, any information required by the Purchaser or its accountants and agents relating to [the Company] [any Group Member].

(B) Clauses to amend where consideration includes issue of consideration shares

(a) Definitions

The following definitions may be relevant, depending upon which market the shares of the Purchaser are listed on:

'Admission'	EITHER
	[*The admission of the Consideration Shares (i) to the Official List becoming effective in accordance with the Listing Rules issued by the UK Listing Authority, and (ii) to trading on the London Stock Exchange's market for listed securities becoming effective in accordance with the Admission and Disclosure Standards issued by the London Stock Exchange*]
	OR
	[*The admission by the London Stock Exchange of the Consideration Shares to the AIM Market becoming effective upon the issue of a dealing notice by the London Stock Exchange*]
'Consideration Shares'	Ordinary shares of £[*amount*] each in the capital of the Purchaser
'Issue Price'	The average of the middle market quotations for an ordinary share in the capital of the Purchaser on [the Official List of the UK Listing Authority] OR [the AIM Market of the London Stock Exchange] as derived from the Daily Official List at the close of business on the five Business Days prior to Completion
'London Stock Exchange'	London Stock Exchange Limited plc
'UK Listing Authority'	The Financial Services Authority in its capacity as the competent authority for the purposes of Part VI of the Financial Services and Markets Act 2000

(b) Consideration

Delete existing clause 4.1 and clause 4.2 and replace with:

4.1 The consideration for the sale of the Shares will be the allotment and issue to the Vendor[s] of such number of Consideration Shares credited as fully paid as will at the Issue Price have the aggregate value nearest to but not less than £[*amount*].

4.2 The Consideration Shares will rank pari passu and as a single class with the existing ordinary shares of [*nominal amount*] each in the capital of the Purchaser, and will carry the right to receive in full all dividends and other distributions declared, made or paid after the date of the allotment.

4.3 [The Vendor undertakes that if] OR [Each of the Vendors undertakes that such Vendor] will not [without the prior written consent of the Purchaser] for a period of [*period*] after Completion:

4.3.1 dispose of, charge or otherwise encumber any interest in [any] [more than [*number*] per cent] of the Consideration Shares to which [the] [such] Vendor becomes entitled pursuant to this Agreement in any period of [*number*] months; or

4.3.2 without prejudice to the provisions of clause 4.3.1, make any disposal of the Consideration Shares except through such firm of stockbrokers as may from time to time be notified to the Vendor[s] by the Purchaser.

4.4 For the purposes of clause 4.3 [a] [the] Vendor shall be deemed to dispose of a Consideration Share if [such] [the] Vendor ceases in any circumstances whatsoever, other than death, to be the unencumbered absolute beneficial owner of it. Following the death of [a] [the] Vendor the personal representatives of [that] [the] Vendor shall be bound by the obligations of this Agreement as if references to the Vendor[s] were to read references to the personal representatives.

4.5 [The Purchaser reserves the right to pay in cash all or part of the purchase consideration attributable to the Consideration Shares.]

(c) Conditions

Follow the condition wording set out in section A. The following additional conditions may be relevant at clause 5.1.

5.1 The shareholders of the Purchaser in general meeting passing a resolution in the agreed terms to increase the Purchaser's authorised share capital by the creation of, and authorising the Purchaser's directors to allot, [the Consideration Shares] [sufficient ordinary shares] in the capital of the Purchaser to satisfy the Consideration pursuant to clause 4.

5.2 Admission occurring in respect of the Consideration Shares.

(d) Completion

Use the amended completion wording outlined in section A and also consider completion in escrow.

(e) Completion arrangements

The following to be inserted in place of existing clause 5.4 where Consideration Shares are to be allotted:

5.4 The Purchaser will [, conditional only upon Admission taking place,] [procure that a duly convened meeting is held at which the Consideration Shares are [allotted] [and issued] to the Vendors] [and deliver to the Vendors' Solicitors definitive share certificates in respect of the Consideration Shares with a certificate from its stockbrokers as to the Issue Price].

(C) Obligations pending completion

1   The Vendor[s] will procure that [the Company] [each Group Member] will:

   1.1   carry on its business in the ordinary course so as to maintain that business as a going concern and not make any payment other than routine payments in the ordinary and usual course of trading;

   1.2   ensure there is no adverse change in the financial or trading position or prospects of its business;

   1.3   ensure no material adverse change occurs in the assets and liabilities of its business and there is no reduction in the net assets of its business;

   1.4   take all reasonable steps to preserve and protect its assets and minimise its liabilities;

   1.5   not declare, make or pay any dividend or other distribution; not create, allot, issue, grant or agree to grant any option over, acquire, repay or redeem any class of share or loan capital and not vary or agree to vary the rights of, any class of share or loan capital;

   1.6   not do or omit to do, or cause or allow to be done or omit to be done, any act or thing which would result or be likely to result in breach of any of the Warranties at Completion, by reference to the facts and circumstances then existing. For this purpose only, where in a Warranty there is an express or implied reference to the 'date of this Agreement' or an equivalent term, that reference is to be construed as a reference to the 'date of Completion'.

2   [*Consider any specific obligations*]

Document 9
Tax Schedule

Part 1 – Definitions and Interpretation

1 **Definitions**

In this Schedule the following words and expressions shall have the following meanings:

'Accounts Relief'	Any Relief which was:
	(i) treated as an asset of the Company in the [Accounts] [Completion Accounts]; or
	(ii) taken into account in computing (and so reducing) any provision for deferred tax which appears in the [Accounts] [Completion Accounts] or has resulted in no provision for deferred tax being shown in the [Accounts] [Completion Accounts];
	and for this purpose Accounts Relief shall include any Relief which the Company has assumed is available to it and has been utilised in the Accounts whether or not at the time of such utilisation the Company was actually entitled to any such Relief
'ACT'	Advance Corporation Tax
'Auditors'	The auditors for the time being of the Company
['Balance Sheet'	The audited [consolidated] balance sheet of the Company as at the Accounts Date as shown in the Accounts]
'CAA 2001'	Capital Allowances Act 2001
'Claim for Tax'	Any assessment notice, demand letter or other document issued or action taken by or on behalf of a Tax Authority from which it appears that a Tax Liability is to be, or is likely to be, imposed on the Company or the Company is liable or is sought to be made liable to make any payment or is to be denied or is sought to be denied any Relief or any right to repayment of Tax (in whole or in part) which would otherwise have been available to the Company
'Event'	Any act, transaction or omission (whether or not the Company is a party to such act, transaction or omission) and includes (without limitation) the sale and purchase of the Shares pursuant to this Agreement, any change in the residence of any person for the purposes of Tax, the death or dissolution of any person, the accrual or receipt of any income, profit or gains, the declaration or payment of any dividend or other distribution, any transfer, payment, loan or advance, the incurring of any loss or expenditure or any other event which is treated or is otherwise regarded as having occurred for the purposes of Tax
'FA'	The Finance Act for the year by which it is designated
'Group Relief'	Any relief surrendered pursuant to Chapter IV ICTA Part X or any ACT previously surrendered or claimed pursuant to Section 240 ICTA [or any company tax refund surrendered or claimed pursuant to Section 102 FA 1989]

'ICTA'	Income and Corporation Taxes Act 1988
'IHTA'	Inheritance Tax Act 1984

'income, profits or gains' Includes income, profits or gains (including capital gains) of any description or from any source and income, profits, or gains which are deemed to be earned accrued or received for the purposes of Tax Legislation

'Loss' In relation to a Relief, the reduction, modification, loss, clawback, counter-action, disallowance or cancellation of that Relief or right to repayment of Tax or a failure to obtain Accounts Relief or to receive the benefit of a right to repayment of Tax to which the Company was or assumed it was entitled and 'Lost' shall be construed accordingly

'New Relief' Any Relief which arises:

(i) as a result of any Event occurring after [the Accounts Date] [Completion];

(ii) or in respect of any period commencing on or after [date];

'Relevant Person' One or more of the Vendors and any person (except the Purchaser or the Company):

(i) who was before Completion a member of the same group of companies as the Company for any Tax purpose ('Group Person'); or

(ii) with whom, before Completion, the Company or, at any time, any of the Vendors or a Group Person is a Connected Person; or

(iii) [with whom, before Completion, the Company or, at any time, any of the Vendors is a Connected Person;]

(iv) [any person who stands or has stood in a direct or indirect relationship with the Company at any time before Completion such that failure by such person at any time to pay Tax could result in an assessment on the Company under Section 767A or Section 767AA ICTA]

'Relief' Any loss, relief, allowance, exemption, set-off, deduction, credit, right to repayment or other relief available in respect of Tax or in the computation of income profits or gains for the purposes of Tax

'SDRT' Stamp duty reserve tax

'Tax' (i) All forms of taxes, duties, imposts and levies in the nature of taxes whenever created or imposed and whether of the United Kingdom or elsewhere including (without limitation) corporation tax, ACT, income tax or amount equivalent to a tax required to be deducted or withheld from or accounted for in respect of any payment, capital gains tax, any payment under Section 601(2) ICTA, inheritance tax, VAT, landfill tax, stamp duty, stamp duty reserve tax, general or business rates, Customs and Excise duties, national insurance, social security or similar contri-

	butions, and any other taxes, levies, charges or imposts similar to or corresponding with or replaced by any of the above
	(ii) All penalties, fines, charges, surcharges and interest in relation to tax as within paragraph (i) or to any return or information or registration required to be provided for the purposes of any such tax
'Tax Authority'	The Inland Revenue, HM Customs and Excise or other governmental, statutory, state, regional, provincial or local government authority body or official (whether within or outside the United Kingdom) involved in the assessment, collection or administration of Tax
'Tax Claim'	Any claim by the Purchaser under the Tax Covenant or any of the Tax Warranties
'Tax Liability'	(i) Any liability to make an actual payment of or an amount in respect of Tax, whether or not such liability is also or alternatively a liability of or chargeable against or attributable to, any other person and whether or not the Company shall or may have a right of recovery or reimbursement against any other person; or
	(ii) the loss by the Company of a Relief
'TCGA'	Taxation of Chargeable Gains Act 1992.

2 Interpretation

2.1 Reference to the result of an Event or Events on or before [Completion] [the Accounts Date] includes the combined result or results of two or more Events, one of which shall have taken place on or before [Completion] [the Accounts Date].

2.2 For the purposes of this Agreement, where any document is not (or is not properly) stamped, the stamp duty (together with any accrued interest and/or penalties) required to be paid in order that such document be fully and properly stamped shall, notwithstanding that the Company may be under no legal obligation to stamp that document, be treated as a liability of the Company arising on the date when the document was executed and 'Tax Liability' shall be construed accordingly.

Part 2 – Tax Covenant

3 **Vendor's covenant**

3.1 Subject to paragraph 3, the Vendors hereby jointly and severally covenant with the Purchaser to pay to the Purchaser an amount equal to:

   3.1.1 any Tax Liability of the Company:

      3.1.1.1 which has arisen or arises as a consequence of or in connection with any Event which occurred on or before Completion; or

      3.1.1.2 which arises under Section 132 FA 1988 or Sections 179, 189 or 190 TCGA as a result of the combined effect of two or more Events the first of which occurred on or before Completion; or

      3.1.1.3 which arises in respect of or by reference to any income, profits or gains which were accrued or received on or before or in respect of a period ended on or before Completion; or

      3.1.1.4 which arises or is increased as a consequence of the failure of any Relevant Person to pay Tax;

   3.1.2 any Tax Liability of the Company which would have arisen (and in respect of which the Vendor would have been liable under paragraph 3.1.1 but for the setting-off an Accounts Relief or a New Relief against that Tax Liability or (as the case may be) against the income, profits or gains which would have given rise to that Tax Liability;

   3.1.3 any Accounts Relief Lost or (where the Accounts Relief Lost was a deduction from or set-off against income, profits or gains) the Tax which would (on the basis of the rates of Tax current at the date of the Loss and assuming income, profits or gains chargeable to Tax of an amount equal to the Relief) have been saved but for the Loss;

   3.1.4 any liability of the Company to make a payment in respect of Tax under any indemnity, covenant, guarantee or charge entered into by the Company on or before Completion;

   3.1.5 [any liability of the Company to pay or repay an amount in respect of Tax under any agreement or arrangements relating to the surrender of Group Relief, ACT or tax refund entered into before Completion];

   3.1.6 any liability in respect of a chargeable gain which arises as a result of the disposal after Completion of any asset acquired by the Company on or before Completion, to the extent that such liability would not have arisen if the expenditure allowable under Section 38(1)(a) TCGA in respect of the asset (ignoring any other Relief) had not been less than the value of the asset stated in the Accounts or in the case of an asset acquired since the Accounts Date but before Completion, the acquisition cost of the asset;

   3.1.7 any Tax Liability which arises under Section 154(2)(b) TCGA as a result of the Company ceasing after Completion to use a depreciating asset acquired on or before Completion for the purposes of a trade or under Section 154(2)(c) TCGA as a result of the expiry after Completion of a period of ten years beginning with the date of acquisition of the asset; and

   3.1.8 any Tax Liability of a Company or the Purchaser in respect of Inheritance Tax which:

      3.1.8.1 is at or becomes after Completion as a result of the death of any person within seven years after a transfer of value (or deemed transfer of value) on or before Completion, a charge on any of the shares or assets of the Company or gives rise to a power to sell, mortgage or charge any of the shares or assets of the Company; or

3.1.8.2 arises as a result of a transfer of value occurring or being deemed to occur on or before Completion (whether or not in conjunction with the death of any person whenever occurring) which increased or decreased the value of the estate of the Company;

3.1.9 any costs and expenses (including legal costs on a full indemnity basis) reasonably and properly incurred by the Purchaser and/or the Company in connection with:

3.1.9.1 any liability or amount for which the Vendors are liable under any of paragraphs 3.1.1 to 3.1.8 inclusive, including the costs and expenses of investigating, assessing or contesting any Claim for Tax in respect of such liability or amount; or

3.1.9.2 any successful Tax Claim.

3.2 In determining for the purposes of this Schedule whether a charge on or a power to sell, mortgage or charge any of the shares or assets of the Company exists at any time, the fact that any Tax is not yet payable or may be paid by instalments shall be disregarded and such Tax shall be treated as becoming due and the charge or power to sell, mortgage or charge as arising on the date of the transfer of value or other Event on or in respect of which it becomes payable or arises.

3.3 The provisions of Section 213 IHTA shall not apply to any payment falling to be made under this Schedule.

4 Limitations on the Vendor's liability

4.1 The covenants contained in paragraph 3 shall not extend to any Tax Liability or other amount payable by the Vendors under this Tax Covenant to the extent that:

4.1.1 such Tax Liability was paid or discharged on or before [the Accounts Date] [Completion] and such payment or discharge was reflected in the [Accounts] [Completion Accounts];

4.1.2 provision or reserve in respect of that Tax Liability was made in the [Completion Accounts][Accounts];

4.1.3 such Tax Liability would not have arisen but for a voluntary act, transaction or omission of the Company after Completion:

4.1.3.1 otherwise than pursuant to a legally binding obligation entered into by the Company on or before Completion or imposed on the Company by law;

4.1.3.2 which consists of communicating information to any Tax Authority which is required by law; and

4.1.3.3 otherwise than in the ordinary course of business of the Company;

4.1.4 such Tax Liability arises or is increased as a direct result of:

4.1.4.1 any change in Tax Legislation or the published practice of any Tax Authority; or

4.1.4.2 any increase in the rate of Tax;

(in each case first announced and enacted after Completion, whether or not having retrospective effect);

4.1.5 such Tax Liability arises in consequence of an Event which has occurred since the Accounts Date and before Completion in the ordinary course of business of the Company, but for these purposes none of the Events mentioned in Tax Warranty 7 (Events since the Accounts Date) shall be regarded as having occurred in the ordinary course of business.

5 **Credit for Tax Savings**

5.1 If, at the Vendor's request and expense, the Auditors determine that the Company has obtained a 'Tax Saving' (which for the purposes of this paragraph 5 shall mean where the Vendor has made a payment under this Tax Covenant in respect of a Tax Liability which results in the reduction of any other Tax Liability for which the Vendor would have otherwise been liable under this Tax Covenant) the Purchaser shall on demand repay to the Vendor the lesser of:

5.1.1 the amount of the Tax Saving (as determined by the Auditors); and

5.1.2 the amount paid by the Vendor in respect of the Tax Liability which gave rise to the Tax Saving, less any reasonable costs and expenses incurred by the Purchaser or the Company in respect of that Tax Liability.

5.2 The Company will be entitled to use, in priority to any Relief which gives rise to a Tax Saving, any other Relief available to it (including by way of surrender by another company to it) to reduce or eliminate any liability to make an actual payment of corporation tax.

5.3 In determining whether the Company has obtained a Tax Saving, the Auditors will act as experts and not as arbitrators and their determination will (in the absence of manifest error) be conclusive and binding on the parties.

6 **No disclosures**

6.1 Subject to paragraphs 3 to 5 of this Tax Covenant, the Purchaser shall be entitled to make a claim under this Tax Covenant in respect of a Tax Liability notwithstanding that:

6.1.1 the Purchaser had knowledge (whether actual, constructive or implied) on or before Completion of that Tax Liability (or the matter giving rise to the Tax Liability); or

6.1.2 such Tax Liability has been paid or discharged by the Company whether before or after Completion.

7 **No deductions or withholdings**

7.1 Save only as may be required by law all sums payable by the Vendors under this Tax Covenant shall be paid free and clear of all deductions or withholdings whatsoever.

7.2 If any deduction or withholding is required by law to be made from any payment by the Vendors under this Tax Covenant, or (if ignoring any available Relief) the Purchaser is subject to Tax in respect of any payment by the Vendors under this Tax Covenant, the Vendors shall pay such additional sum as is necessary to ensure that the net amount received and retained by the Purchaser (after taking account of such deduction or withholding of Tax) will leave the Purchaser with the same amount as it would have been entitled to receive in the absence of any such requirement to make a deduction or withholding for Tax.

8 **Tax on payments**

If any sum payable by the Vendors to the Purchaser under this Tax Covenant (including without limitation any sum payable under this paragraph 8) is (or but for the availability of any Accounts Relief or New Relief would be) subject to a Tax Liability in the hands of the Purchaser the Vendors shall pay to the Purchaser such sum as would have been required to be paid under paragraph 7.2 had that Tax Liability been a deduction or withholding from the sum payable by the Vendors.

9 **Due date for payment**

  9.1 Where the Vendors become liable to make a payment pursuant to the provisions of this Schedule, the due date for the making of that payment in cleared funds shall be the date falling five Business Days after the date on which the Company or (as the case may be) the Purchaser has notified the Vendors of the amount of the payment required to be made or, if later:

    9.1.1 in the case of a liability within paragraph 3.1.1 the second Business Day prior to the last date on which the payment of Tax in question may be paid to the relevant Tax Authority in order to avoid incurring a liability to interest or a charge fine or penalty in respect of that Tax Liability; or

    9.1.2 in the case of the Loss or set-off of a right to repayment of Tax within paragraphs 3.1.2 or 3.1.3 the date on which such repayment would have been received but for the Loss or set-off; or

    9.1.3 in the case of the set-off of a Relief (other than a right to repayment of Tax) within paragraph 3.1.2 the last date on which the Tax Liability which (but for the set-off) would have been payable could have been paid to the relevant Tax Authority in order to avoid incurring a liability to interest or a charge fine or penalty in respect of that Tax Liability; or

    9.1.4 in the case of a liability within paragraph 3.1.8, the second Business Day before such costs and expenses become due and payable or are otherwise incurred by the Purchaser and/or the Company.

  9.2 The Vendors may at their own expense require the amount of any payment required to be made to be certified by the Auditors (acting as experts and not as arbitrators) and the amount so certified shall (save for manifest error) be conclusive and binding on the parties.

10 **Interest on late payments**

If any payment required to be made by the Vendors under this Tax Covenant is not made by the due date for payment thereof, then that payment shall carry interest from that due date until the date when the payment is actually made at the rate of [ ]% per annum above the base rate from time to time of [the Bank].

11 **Price reduction**

Any payment by the Vendors under this Tax Covenant shall (so far as possible) be treated as a reduction in the consideration paid for the Shares provided that nothing in this paragraph 11 shall limit or exclude the liability of the Vendors under this Agreement.

12 **Claims for Tax**

  12.1 If the Purchaser or the Company shall become aware of any Claim for Tax which is likely to give rise to a liability of the Vendor under this Tax Covenant, the Purchaser shall (or shall procure that the Company shall) as soon as reasonably practicable give notice of such Claim for Tax to the Vendor (but for the avoidance of doubt, such notice shall not be a condition precedent to the liability of the Vendor under this Tax Covenant).

  12.2 If the Vendor shall indemnify and secure the Company and the Purchaser to the reasonable satisfaction of the Purchaser against all losses, costs, damages and expenses (including interest on overdue Tax) which may be incurred as a result, the Purchaser shall (and shall procure that the Company shall), in accordance with any reasonable instructions of the Vendors promptly given by notice to the Purchaser seek to avoid, dispute, resist, appeal, compromise or defend such Claim for Tax provided always that:

12.2.1 the Company shall not be obliged to appeal against any assessment for Tax raised on it if, having given the Vendors notice of the receipt of that assessment it has not, within ten Business Days of service of such notice thereafter received instructions from the Vendors, in accordance with the provisions of this paragraph 12.2 to make that appeal;

12.2.2 the Purchaser and the Company shall not be obliged to comply with any instruction of the Vendors which involves contesting any assessment for Tax before any court or other appellate body (excluding the Tax Authority in question) unless the Vendors furnish the Purchaser with the written opinion of tax counsel of at least five years' call to the effect that an appeal against the assessment for Tax in question will, on the balance of probabilities, be won;

12.2.3 the Purchaser and the Company shall not in any event be obliged to comply with any instruction of the Vendors to make a settlement or compromise of a Claim for Tax which is the subject of a dispute or agree any matter in the conduct of such dispute which is likely materially to increase the future liability of the Company or the Purchaser in respect of Tax or which the Purchaser considers will be materially prejudicial to the business or Tax affairs of the Company on any reasonable ground.

12.3 The Purchaser shall have the right to have any action mentioned in paragraph 12.2 conducted by their nominated professional advisers (provided that the appointment of such advisers shall be subject to the approval of the Vendor, such approval not to be unreasonably withheld or delayed and shall be deemed to be given if the Vendor does not within ten Business Days of request give a fully reasoned written response to a request for approval by the Purchaser).

12.4 The Purchaser shall keep the Vendor fully informed of the progress of any dispute or appeal of any Claim for Tax conducted by the Purchaser at the request of the Vendor and will provide the Vendor with copies of all material correspondence and other documents relating to such dispute or appeal.

12.5 the provisions of this paragraph 12 shall apply mutatis mutandis to any claim by any Tax Authority which is likely to give rise to a claim under the Tax Warranties.

13 Recovery from third parties

13.1 If the Purchaser or the Company recovers from any other person (including a Tax Authority but excluding the Purchaser, any member of the same group of companies as the Purchaser and any officer or employee of any such company) any amount which is referable to a Tax Liability in respect of which the Vendors have made a payment under paragraph 3 of this Tax Covenant, the Purchaser will repay to the Vendors the lesser of:

13.1.1 the sum recovered (less any reasonable costs and expenses incurred by the Company and/or the Purchaser in recovering that sum and any tax payable on the receipt of the same); and

13.1.2 the amount paid by the Vendors under paragraph 3 of this Tax Covenant in respect of the Tax Liability.

13.2 If the Purchaser or the Company becomes aware that it is entitled to recover any amount mentioned in paragraph 13.1, the Purchaser will as soon as reasonably practicable give notice of that fact to the Vendors and provided that the Vendors indemnify and secure the Purchaser or the Company to the reasonable satisfaction of the Purchaser against all losses, costs, damages and expenses which may be incurred thereby, the Purchaser shall procure that the Company shall take such action as the Vendors may reasonably request to effect such recovery.

13.3 The action which the Vendors may request the Company to take under paragraph 13.2 does not include:

    13.3.1 any action which the Purchaser considers to be materially prejudicial to the business or Tax affairs of the Purchaser and/or the Company or to which the Purchaser objects on any other reasonable ground; or

    13.3.2 allowing the Vendors to undertake conduct of any action necessary to effect the recovery of the amount in question.

Part 3 – Tax Warranties

14 Tax returns

14.1 The Company has duly and properly made all claims, disclaimers, elections and surrenders and given all notices and consents and done all other things in respect of Tax, the making, giving or doing of which was assumed to have been made for the purposes of the [Accounts][Balance Sheet]. All such claims, disclaimers, elections, surrenders, notices, consents and other things have been accepted as valid by the relevant Tax Authority and none have been revoked or otherwise withdrawn or are likely to be revoked or otherwise withdrawn.

14.2 The Company has duly and punctually made or submitted all returns, computations, notices, registrations and accounts which ought to have been made for the purposes of Tax (including all returns, documents or information in respect of PAYE and National Insurance) and all such returns (and all other information supplied to any Tax Authority for such purpose) which:

    14.2.1 were at the time when they were submitted correct and up-to-date;

    14.2.2 have not been disputed or resulted in a request for further information by the Tax Authority concerned (other than routine enquiries concerning the corporation tax computations of the Company, all of which have now been satisfactorily answered); and

    14.2.3 so far as the Vendors are aware there are no facts or circumstances likely to give rise to any dispute, discrepancy or claim relating to Tax in respect of any financial period prior to the date of this Agreement.

14.3 The Tax affairs of the Company have never been the subject of investigation or enquiry by any Tax Authority and no Tax Authority has indicated that it intends to investigate the Tax Affairs of the Company. There are no facts or circumstances likely to give rise to any such investigation.

14.4 The Company has duly and punctually paid all Tax which it has become liable to pay and is under no liability to pay any penalty or interest in connection with any Claim for Tax.

14.5 All statements and disclosures made to any Tax Authority in connection with any application for clearance or consent made on behalf of or affecting the Company were made to the appropriate office, section, department or body and fully and accurately disclosed all facts and circumstances material to the decisions of the relevant Tax Authority and any such consent or clearance given remains valid and effective in respect of the relevant transaction for which such consent or clearance was obtained.

14.6 The Company has not been concerned in any transaction to which any of the following provisions have been or will be applied:

    14.6.1 Sections 135 to 137 (inclusive) TCGA;

    14.6.2 Sections 703 to 704 (inclusive) ICTA;

    14.6.3 Section 139 TCGA;

    14.6.4 Section 192 TCGA and Sections 213 to 218 (inclusive) ICTA;

    14.6.5 Sections 219 to 229 (inclusive) ICTA;

    14.6.6 Section 776 ICTA 1988; and

    14.6.7 Sections 779 to 786 (inclusive) ICTA.

14.7 The Company has (to the extent required by law) preserved and retained in its possession complete and accurate records relating to its Tax affairs (including PAYE and National Insurance records, VAT records and records relating to transfer pricing) and has sufficient records relating to past events to calculate the profit, gain, loss, balancing charges or allowances or any reliefs (all for Tax purposes) which would arise on any disposal or on the realisation of any assets owned at the Accounts Date or acquired since that date.

15 Accounts

15.1 The provision or reserve for Tax in the Accounts is sufficient to cover all liabilities of the Company for Tax as at the Accounts Date and all Tax for which the Company may after the Accounts Date become or have become liable in respect of or by reference to:

15.1.1 any income, profits or gains for any period which ended on or before the Accounts Date; or

15.1.2 any distributions made on or before the Accounts Date or provided for in the Accounts; or

15.1.3 any Event occurring on or before the Accounts Date.

15.2 Full potential provision has been made and shown (or disclosed of by way of note) in the Accounts for deferred Tax.

15.3 The Company has duly and properly made all claims, disclaimers, elections and surrenders and given all notices and consents and done all other things in respect of Reliefs the making, giving or doing of which was assumed to have been made for the purposes of the [Accounts][Balance Sheet]. All such claims, disclaimers, elections, surrenders, notices, consents and other things have been accepted as valid by the relevant Tax Authority and none have been revoked or otherwise withdrawn, or are likely to be revoked or otherwise withdrawn, and there are no claims, disclaimers, elections or surrenders the time limit for the making or doing of which expires within three months after the date of this Agreement.

16 Deductions and withholdings

The Company has made all deductions and withholdings in respect of, or on account of, any Tax (including amounts to be deducted under the PAYE and National Insurance systems) from any payments made by it which it is obliged or entitled to make and (to the extent required to do so) has accounted in full to the relevant Tax Authority for all amounts so deducted or withheld and has (to the extent required by law) duly provided certificates of deduction of tax to the recipients of payments from which deductions have been made.

17 Overseas elements

17.1 The Company has never been resident or had a branch, agency, place of business or any permanent establishment (within the meaning of the OECD Model Double Taxation Agreement) and has never carried out any trading activities outside the United Kingdom for the purposes of any Tax Legislation.

17.2 The Company has never been (nor is it liable to be) assessed to Tax as the agent or representative of any person not resident in the United Kingdom.

17.3 The Company does not have and has not in the last seven years had any interest in:

17.3.1 a controlled foreign company within the meaning of Section 747 ICTA (imputation of chargeable profits or creditable tax of controlled foreign companies); or

17.3.2 a material interest in an offshore fund within the meaning of Chapter V of Part XVII ICTA.

17.4 The Company has not entered into any transaction to which the provisions of Schedule 28AA ICTA could apply.

17.5 The Company has never been involved in a transaction to which Sections 765(1) or 765A ICTA would or could apply.

17.6 The Company does not and has never held shares in a company which is not resident in the United Kingdom and which would be a close company if it were resident in the United Kingdom, in circumstances that any chargeable gain accruing to that other company could be apportioned to the Company under Section 13 TCGA.

18 Close companies

18.1 The Company is not and has not at any time been a close company (within the meaning of Section 414 ICTA) in respect of any accounting period.

18.2 The Company is not and has not at any time been a close investment holding company within the meaning of Section 13A ICTA.

18.3 The Company has not at any time during the period of seven years ending on the date of this Agreement made any payment which falls to be treated as a distribution under Section 418 ICTA (distribution to include certain expenses of close companies).

18.4 The Company has not made any loan, advance or payment or given any consideration which could fall to be chargeable to tax under Sections 419 to 422 ICTA and which have remained outstanding at any time during the period of seven years ending on the date of this Agreement and the Company has not released or written off or agreed to write off the whole of any such loans or advances.

18.5 The Company has not made any transfers of value (as specified in Section 94(1) IHTA) and there has been no variation in the Company's share or loan capital within Section 98 IHTA.

19 Capital gains

19.1 The sum which would be allowed as a deduction from the consideration under Section 38 TCGA of each asset of the Company (other than trading stock) if disposed of on the date of this Agreement would not be less than (in the case of an asset held on the Accounts Date) the book value of that asset shown or included in the Accounts or (in the case of an asset acquired since the Accounts Date) an amount equal to the consideration given for its acquisition.

19.2 The Company has never been involved in or connected to any exchange of securities whether or not (by virtue of Section 135 TCGA) Section 127 TCGA applied to the exchange.

19.3 No transaction has been entered into by the Company to which the provisions of Section 18 (transactions between connected persons) TCGA has been or could be applied.

19.4 The Company does not own any depreciating asset in respect of which a held over gain may accrue pursuant to Sections 154(2) and/or 175(3) TCGA.

19.5 The Company has not been a party to or involved in any transaction to which Sections 29 - 34 TCGA may be applicable.

20 Events since the Accounts Date

20.1 None of the following events have occurred in relation to the Company since the Accounts Date:

20.1.1 a deemed (as opposed to actual) acquisition disposal or supply of assets, goods, services or business facilities;

20.1.2 a disposal or supply of assets, goods, services or business facilities by the Company for a consideration which is treated for the purposes of Tax as less than the actual consideration;

20.1.3 a distribution within the meaning given by Part VI ICTA (company distributions, tax credits etc) or within Section 418 ICTA (expenses treated as distributions);

20.1.4   an Event in respect of which a liability under Part XVII ICTA (tax avoidance) arises;

20.1.5   an Event giving rise to a balancing charge.

20.1.6   the Company ceasing or being deemed to cease to be a member of any Group or associated with any other Company for the purposes of Tax.

20.1.7   an Event which results in the Company being liable for Tax for which it is not primarily liable.

20.2   For the purposes of this paragraph 20 'business facilities' means business facilities of any kind including but not limited to a loan of money in a letting, hiring or licensing of any tangible or intangible property.

21 Distributions

21.1   The Company has not in the period of three years ending on the date of this Agreement made (nor is it deemed to have made during such period) any distribution within the meaning of ICTA except dividends properly authorised and disclosed in its audited accounts.

21.2   The Company has not made or agreed to make any repayment of share capital to which Section 210(1) ICTA applies.

21.3   The Company has not issued or agreed to issue any share capital as paid up or otherwise than by receipt of new consideration within the meaning of Part VI ICTA.

21.4   The Company has not elected under Sections 246A and 246B ICTA for any dividend paid or to be paid by it to be treated as a foreign income dividend for the purposes of Chapter V A ICTA and the Company has not made any distribution which may be treated as a foreign income dividend pursuant to Schedule 7 FA 1997.

22 Concessions

The Company has not entered into an arrangement with any Tax Authority (whether general or specific to the Company) which affects the amount of Tax chargeable on the Company or which purports to modify or provide exemption from any obligation to make or submit any computation, notice or return to any Tax Authority.

23 Loan relationships

No liability to Tax or non-trading deficit would arise from the loan relationships to which the Company is partly being repaid to the extent of the amounts shown in respect of such loan relations in the books of the Company at the date hereof.

24 Capital allowances

24.1   No balancing charge in respect of any capital allowances claimed or given would arise if any asset of the Company were to be realised for a consideration equal to the amount of the book value of such asset as shown or included in the Accounts (or, in the case of any asset acquired since the Accounts Date, for a consideration equal to the consideration given for the acquisition).

24.2   So far as the Vendors are aware, all necessary conditions for the availability of all capital allowances claimed by the Company (or, where computations are made for capital allowances' purposes for pools of assets, all the assets in that pool) have at all material times been satisfied and remain satisfied.

25 Secondary liability

So far as the Vendors are aware, no Event has occurred in consequence of which the Company is or may be held liable to pay or bear any Tax which is primarily chargeable against or attributable to some person, firm or company other than the Company.

26 **Stamp duties**

    26.1   The Company has duly paid all stamp duty for which it is or has been or may be made liable and without limitation:

        26.1.1   all documents in the enforcement of which the Company is or may be interested have been duly stamped; and

        26.1.2   there are no documents outside the United Kingdom which if they were brought into the United Kingdom would give rise to a liability to stamp duty payable by the Company.

    26.2   The Company has duly paid all SDRT for which it is or has become liable and the Company has not been party to any transfer of chargeable securities (within the meaning of Section 99 FA 1986) in respect of which the Company could become liable to pay any SDRT.

    26.3   The Company has not been party to any transfer of chargeable securities (within the meaning of Section 99 FA 1986) in respect of which the Company could become liable to pay any SDRT.

    26.4   The Company is not liable to any penalty in respect of any stamp duty or SDRT.

27 **Anti-avoidance**

    27.1   The Company has not in the period of three years ending on the date of this Agreement been party to any non-arm's length transaction.

    27.2   The Company has not in the period of three years ending on the date of this Agreement been party to or otherwise involved in any scheme or arrangement the main purpose or one of the main purposes of which was to avoid Tax.

28 **Value added tax**

    28.1   The Company is registered for VAT in the United Kingdom under schedule 1 VATA and has not at any time in the last six years been treated as (nor applied to be) a member of a group of companies for VAT purposes.

    28.2   In relation to VAT:

        28.2.1   the Company is (and for the last six years has been) a member of a VAT group of which [*name of representative company*] is the representative member ('the Representative Member');

        28.2.2   the Company is not liable nor will it become liable to make any payment or further payment to the Representative Member in respect of VAT.

        References to 'the Company' in the following paragraphs of this paragraph 28 include references to the Representative Member in so far as supplies treated as made by or to the Representative Member relate to the business of the Company.

    28.3   The Company is a taxable person for VAT purposes, has complied with all the requirements of VATA and all applicable regulations and orders, and has fully maintained complete, correct and up-to-date records, invoices and other necessary documents.

    28.4   The Company has not made any exempt supplies in consequence of which it is or will be unable to obtain credit for all input tax paid by it during any value added tax quarter ending after Completion.

    28.5   The Company has not been a party to a transaction to which Article 5 of the Value Added Tax (Special Provisions) Order 1995 (transfer of business as a going concern) has (or has purported to have been) applied.

    28.6   The Company does not have an interest in any new or uncompleted buildings or civil engineering works within the meaning of Group 1 Schedule 9 VATA.

    28.7   The Company has not been engaged in any transaction which has resulted or could result in the Company being treated as making any supply to itself for VAT purposes.

28.8 The Company is not registered (nor required to be registered) for local VAT or its equivalent in any other State other than the United Kingdom.

28.9 No circumstances exist whereby the Company would or might become liable for VAT pursuant to the provisions of Sections 47 or 48 VATA.

28.10 The Company has not made and is not otherwise bound by any election made pursuant to paragraph 2 of Schedule 10 VATA.

29 Duties

All value added tax payable upon the importation of goods and all customs and excise duties payable to HM Customs & Excise in respect of any assets (including trading stock) imported or owned by the Company have been paid in full.

30 Groups

30.1 The Company is not, nor has it at any time in the last seven years been:

30.1.1 a member of a group of companies as defined by Section 170 TCGA; or

30.1.2 a 51% subsidiary of any company as defined by Section 838 ICTA and the Company does not have (and never has had) any 51% subsidiary as so defined; or

30.1.3 owned by a consortium (as defined in Part X Chapter IV ICTA) and the Company is not nor has it ever been a member of a consortium.

30.2 The Company does not have and has not had at any time in the last seven years any associated company within the meaning of Section 13 ICTA.

30.3 The Company has not in respect of the period of six years ending on the date of this Agreement surrendered or claimed, nor will it be obliged to surrender or claim any amount by way of group relief under the provisions of Section 402 ICTA or any ACT under the provisions of Section 240 ICTA.

30.4 No Tax is or may become payable by the Company pursuant to Section 190 TCGA in respect of any chargeable gain accruing prior to Completion.

30.5 The Company is not liable (and will not after Completion become liable pursuant to arrangements entered into before Completion) to make:

30.5.1 any payment for group relief (within the meaning of Section 402(6) ICTA) or any payment for ACT (as mentioned in Section 240(8) ICTA) or any payment for a tax refund (as mentioned in Section 102(7) FA 1989); or

30.5.2 any refund (in whole or in part) of any such payment received by the Company before Completion;

save (in each case) any payment or refund to another Company.

30.6 The Company has not at any time within the period of six years ending on the date of this Agreement acquired any asset other than as trading stock from any other company which at the time of acquisition was a member of the same group of companies as the Company (as defined in Section 170 TCGA) and no member of any group of companies of which the Company is or has at any material time been the principal company (as defined in Section 170 TCGA) has so acquired the asset.

30.7 The Company has not in the last seven years ceased to be a member of a group of companies for the purposes of Section 179 TCGA.

30.8 The Company has not carried out or participated in any depreciatory transaction relating to the shares or securities of the Company which are in its beneficial interest.

30.9 The Disclosure Letter contains particulars of all elections made by the Company under Section 247 ICTA which are still in force.

31 **Share and bonus schemes**

The Company has not established (nor is it a participant in) any bonus, share option, profit related pay or other scheme or arrangement, whether or not approved by the Inland Revenue, for the benefit of its current or former officers or employees or any of them.

32 **Continuity of trade**

32.1   As at the Accounts Date the Company had no trading losses and no surplus ACT available to be carried forward.

32.2   Within the period of three years ending on the date of this Agreement:

32.2.1   the Company has not discontinued any trade or business or made a major change in the nature or conduct of a trade or business carried on by it;

32.2.2   the scale of activities in any trade carried on by the Company has not become small or negligible;

32.2.3   no change in ownership of the Company has taken place.

32.3   In this paragraph 32 references to 'the Company' include any predecessors to the Company within the meaning of Section 434 ICTA.

33 **Inheritance Tax**

33.1   So far as the Vendors are aware the Company is not and will not become liable to be assessed to Inheritance Tax as donor or donee of any gift or as a transferor or transferee of value (actual or deemed) nor as a result of any disposition, chargeable transfer or transfer of value (actual or deemed) made by or deemed to be made by any other person.

33.2   There is no unsatisfied liability to Capital Transfer Tax or Inheritance Tax attached or attributable to the assets of the Company or the shares of the Company and neither such assets nor such shares are subject to an Inland Revenue charge.

33.3   So far as the Vendors are aware, no person has the power under Section 212 of IHTA to raise any Inheritance Tax by sale or mortgage of or by a terminable charge on any of the Company's assets or shares.

Document 10
Disclosure Letter

[Name and address of the Purchaser]

Dear Sirs

[ ] LIMITED

We refer to the agreement of even date made between [ ] and others (1) and [ ] (2) ('Sale Agreement').

1 **Introduction**

1.1 Words and expressions defined in the Sale Agreement shall bear the same meanings in this letter.

1.2 In addition the following definitions will apply:

'[]'   []
'[]'   []
'[]'   []
'[]'   []

1.3 This letter, together with the copy documents annexed to this letter ('the Disclosure Bundle'), is the Disclosure Letter for the purposes of the Agreement.

1.4 Save where expressly stated otherwise any disclosure made in this letter with reference to any particular Warranty is not to be treated as limited in its application to that particular Warranty, but shall be deemed to have been made in relation to any of the Warranties to which the disclosure in question is or may be relevant.

1.5 Any disclosure of any matter or document shall not imply the existence of any warranty, representation, undertaking, indemnity or other obligation of the [Warrantor][Vendor] not expressly set out in the Agreement, nor shall it be taken as extending the scope of the warranties, representations, undertakings, indemnities and other obligations of the [Warrantor][Vendor] in the Sale Agreement.

1.6 If there is an inconsistency between the facts set out or referred to in any of the documents in the Disclosure Bundle and the facts stated in this letter, the provisions of this letter are to be taken as correct. Where one of those documents includes an expression of opinion, no representation or warranty is given as to its accuracy.

1.7 Any reference in this letter to an 'Annexure' is a reference to the relevant Annexure forming part of the Disclosure Bundle.

2 **General**

The following matters are disclosed generally:

2.1 All information and matters disclosed by virtue of the express provisions of the Sale Agreement and the documents entered into pursuant to the Sale Agreement.

2.2 All matters specifically provided for, disclosed or noted in the Accounts.

2.3 All matters affecting each Group Company which would be revealed by a microfiche search against the register of the relevant Group Company at Companies House and dated [ ].

2.4 The contents of and matters referred to in the documents in the Disclosure Bundle.

2.5 The contents of the memorandum and articles of association of each Group Company.

2.6 All matters appearing in the statutory registers and minute books of each Group Company as at the date of this Disclosure Letter.

2.7   All matters revealed by the replies to pre-contract enquiries relating to each Group Company and prepared by the Vendor's Solicitors, a copy of which is attached (Annexure [ ]).

2.8   All matters affecting the Property which would have been disclosed by the making of searches and enquiries of:

     2.8.1   the relevant Local Authority on form Con 29;

     2.8.2   any Register which relates to the Property and which is open to public inspection at HM Land Registry;

     2.8.3   British Coal;

     2.8.4   the Registers of Common Land Rights held by the relevant County Councils or London Borough in relation to each of the Properties;

     2.8.5   the Environment Agency;

     2.8.6   the Health & Safety Executive;

     2.8.7   any other person, corporate body or authority of whom a prudent purchaser and its professional advisers would make enquiry.

2.9   All matters revealed by the contents of the replies to enquiries and requisitions on title relating to the Property, a copy of which is attached (Annexure [ ]).

2.10   All matters which are or should be apparent from the title deeds or any other documents relating to the Property which were made available or copies of which were supplied to the Purchaser's Solicitors and listed in the Disclosure Bundle.

2.11   All matters appearing on the files of each Group Company at the Trade Mark Registry, the Patents Office, European Patent Office or the European Trade Mark Offices on [ ].

2.12   All matters which would or should be disclosed by a physical inspection of each of the Properties, the plant and machinery, vehicles, office equipment and other tangible assets in the possession of or under the control of each Group Company as would have been made by a prudent purchaser and its professional advisers.

2.13   The contents of:

     2.13.1   the accountants' report prepared for the Purchaser and [ ] Limited and [ ] Bank plc by [ ] dated [ ]; and

     2.13.2   the survey report prepared for the Purchaser and [ ] Limited and [ ] Bank plc by [ ] and dated [ ]; and

     2.13.3   [any other reports].

2.14   All matters in the public domain.

3   **Specific disclosures**

We now make the following specific disclosures which, for convenience only, follow the numbering in Schedule [ ] to the Sale Agreement.

[]   []

[]   []

Yours faithfully

....

[ ]

on behalf of the [Warrantor][Vendor]

We hereby acknowledge receipt of the original letter of which this is a copy, together with a complete copy of the Disclosure Bundle, and confirm that we do not require any further information in respect of any matter referred to in the Disclosure Letter.

....

[   ]

INDEX OF DOCUMENTS

1

2

Document 11
Warranty Limitations

1   The aggregate liability of the Warrantors in respect of the Warranties and the Taxation Covenant shall be limited to £[   ] provided always that the aggregate liability of each individual Warrantor in respect of the Warranties and the Taxation Covenant shall be limited to the amount of the consideration received by them.

2   No claim shall be brought by the Purchaser nor shall the Warrantors be liable in respect of any claim:

   2.1   made under or in respect of this Agreement unless:

      2.1.1   the claim exceeds £[   ] in amount; and

      2.1.2   where the amount of the claim exceeds £[   ] ('a relevant claim') the amount of the relevant claim when added to the aggregate amount of all other relevant claims exceeds £[   ] and in such event the Warrantors shall be liable for the whole of such relevant claims not merely the excess;

   2.2   made under or in respect of the Taxation Covenant unless the aggregate of such claims exceeds £[   ] and in such event the Warrantor shall be liable for the whole of such claims not merely the excess.

3   No claim shall be made by the Purchaser against the Warrantors under this Agreement (including the Warranties) or the Taxation Covenant or otherwise:

   3.1   in respect of any warranty, representation, indemnity, covenant, undertaking given or otherwise arising out of or in connection with the sale of the Shares except where it is expressly contained in this Agreement or the Taxation Covenant;

   3.2   in respect of any matter or information disclosed or noted or referred to or provided for in the Accounts or in the audited accounts of the Company for the two consecutive accounting periods prior to that to which the Accounts relate and the accompanying reports of the directors and the auditors;

   3.3   in respect of any liability or other matter or thing if that liability, matter or thing would not have arisen or occurred but for an act omission or transaction done, made or carried out by the Purchaser or the Company or any of their respective directors, employees or agents after Completion other than as required by law or pursuant to a legally binding commitment of the Company created on or before Completion and otherwise than in the ordinary course of business of the Company as carried on immediately before Completion;

   3.4   in respect of any matter resulting from a change in the accounting or taxation policies or practices of the Purchaser or any related company of the Purchaser or the Company (including the method of submitting taxation returns) introduced or having effect after Completion (unless such change is required to correct an accounting policy or practice of the Company prior to or up to Completion which did not comply with requirements of the Companies Acts or generally accepted accounting principles);

   3.5   in respect of any event, fact, matter, occurrence, omission or other breach unless notice in writing thereof (specifying, so far as is practicable from the information then available to the Purchaser, the details and circumstances giving rise to the claim and (without creating any limitation) estimating the total amount of such claim) is given to any one of the Warrantors prior to:

      3.5.1   the seventh anniversary of the date of this Agreement in the case of any claim under the Taxation Covenant or the Tax Warranties; and

3.5.2   [three years] in the case of any other claim;

provided always that legal proceedings are commenced against the Warrantors either within a period of six months after expiry of the relevant period referred to in clauses 3.5.1 to 3.5.2 above in the case of claims for which the liability is not contingent and is quantified or, in the case of claims which are contingent or not quantifiable within a period of six months after expiry of the date on which a contingent liability ceases to be so and an unquantifiable liability becomes quantifiable;

3.6   in respect of any liability or other matter or thing to the extent that it occurs as a result of or is otherwise attributable to:

   3.6.1   any legislation not in force at the date hereof or any change of law or administrative practice having retrospective effect which comes into force after the date hereof; or

   3.6.2   any increase hereafter in the rates of taxation in force at the date hereof (including any effect such increase may have on any provision or reserve made in the Accounts which were prepared in good faith prior to such increase); or

   3.6.3   the Purchaser or the Company disclaiming any part of the benefit of capital or other allowances against the taxation claimed or proposed to be claimed on or before the date hereof;

3.7   in respect of a liability which is contingent only unless or until such contingent liability becomes an actual liability and is due and payable, but this clause 3.7 shall not operate to avoid a claim made in respect of the contingent liability within the applicable time limits specified in clause 3.5.2 above;

3.8   in respect of any matter or liability provided for or taken account of in the Accounts or Management Accounts;

3.9   in respect of any loss for which the Purchaser or the Company is entitled to claim under a policy of insurance or for which the Purchaser would have been indemnified if at the relevant time after Completion there had been maintained valid and adequate insurance cover of a type in force in relation to the Company (or the subsidiaries) at the date of this Agreement;

3.10   in respect of any payment of tax prior to Completion.

4   Notwithstanding any other provision of this Agreement the Warrantors (or any of them) shall have no liability whatsoever under the Warranties in respect of:

4.1   any matter or disclosure referred to in the Disclosure Letter or the documents referred to therein;

4.2   any defect or deficiency whether patent or latent relating to the physical state, condition or qualities of any structure or building upon the Property unless notice of the same has been received by the Company prior to Completion and such notice is not disclosed in the Disclosure Letter.

5   The Warrantors shall be entitled to require the Purchaser (in the name of the Company if the Warrantors so request) or the Company at the expense of the Warrantors to take all such reasonable steps or proceedings as the Warrantors may consider necessary in order to avoid, dispute, resist, mitigate, compromise, defend or appeal against any relevant third party claim (that is to say any claim by a third party against the Company which will or may give rise to a claim under this Agreement) and the Purchaser shall act or shall procure that the Company shall act in accordance with any such requirements subject to the Purchaser and/or the Company being properly indemnified by the Warrantors to the reasonable satisfaction of the Purchaser against all reasonable costs and expenses incurred or to be incurred in connection with the taking of such steps or proceedings.

6 For the purpose of enabling the Warrantors to avoid, dispute, resist, mitigate, compromise, defend or appeal against any relevant third party claim or to decide what steps or proceedings should be taken in order to do so, the Purchaser shall:

6.1 give written notice to the Warrantors within 14 days of any relevant third party claim or any circumstances giving or likely to give rise to a relevant third party claim coming to its notice or to the notice of the Company;

6.2 disclose in writing to the Warrantors all information and documents relating to any claim or matter which may give rise to a claim and, if requested by the Warrantors on reasonable notice give the Warrantors and their professional advisers reasonable access during normal working hours to the personnel of the Purchaser and/or the Company as the case may be and to any relevant premises, chattels, accounts, documents and records within the power, possession or control of the Purchaser and/or of the Company which relate to such claim to enable the Warrantors and their professional advisers to interview such personnel, and to examine such claim, premises, chattels, accounts, documents and records and to take copies or photographs thereof at their own expense;

6.3 not make any admission of liability, agreement or compromise with any person, body or authority in relation thereto without prior consultation with the Warrantors;

6.4 if the Warrantors so request, delegate entirely to them the conduct of any proceedings of whatsoever nature arising in connection with the third party claim and, in that event, give or cause to be given to the Warrantors all such assistance as they may reasonably require in disputing the claim and instruct such Solicitors or other professional advisors as the Warrantors may nominate to act in accordance with the Warrantors' instructions on their behalf or on behalf of the Company.

7 The Warrantors shall reimburse to the Purchaser or the Company (as the case may be) all reasonable costs, charges and expenses incurred by it in complying with its obligations under clauses 4.1 to 4.2 inclusive of this Agreement.

8 The Purchaser shall reimburse to the Warrantors an amount equal to any sum paid by the Warrantors in relation to any claim under the Warranties or under the Taxation Covenant which is subsequently recovered by or paid to the Purchaser or to the Company by a third party.

9 Payment of any claim by a third party shall to the extent of such payment satisfy and preclude any other claim which is capable of being made against the Warrantors in respect of the same subject matter to the intent that the Purchaser shall not be entitled to recover more than once in respect of the same sum.

10 Nothing herein shall in any way diminish the Purchaser's or the Company's common law obligation to mitigate its loss.

11 Any liability of the Warrantors under the Agreement or the Taxation Covenant in respect of any matter shall be computed after taking into account and giving credit for any corresponding increase in the value of the net assets of or other saving by or benefit to the Purchaser or its successors in the title or the Company resulting from the same matter including without limitation any saving of taxation.

11.1 If the Warrantors shall have made any payment in respect of the claim under the Agreement or the Taxation Covenant and the Company shall receive a benefit or refund which the Warrantors can demonstrate was not taken into account in computing the liability of the Warrantors in respect of the claim and would have reduced the liability had this been so, the Purchaser shall forthwith repay to the Warrantors a sum corresponding to such benefit or refund as the case may be.

11.2 If:

    11.2.1 any provision (whether for taxation or any other matter) in the Accounts or in any previous accounts of the Company shall prove to be an over-provision; or

    11.2.2 any sum is received by the Company which has previously been written off as irrecoverable in the Accounts of the Company,

    then the amount over-provided or, as the case may be, the sum so received shall be set off against the liability (if any) of the Warrantors under this Agreement or the Taxation Covenant.

12 The Purchaser hereby agrees with the Warrantors that in respect of any matter which may give rise to a liability under this Agreement and also under the Taxation Covenant:

    12.1 such liability shall not be met more than once;

    12.2 any liability with respect to such matter under the Taxation Covenant shall be deemed to be satisfied by the satisfaction of the liability with respect to such claim under this Agreement and vice versa.

13 Any payment made by the Warrantors pursuant to any claim under this Agreement or the Taxation Covenant shall be deemed to constitute a repayment of and a reduction in the aggregate consideration payable by the Purchaser for the Shares.

Document 12
Earn-out Protection Clauses

1 In this Schedule the following expressions shall have the following meanings unless inconsistent with the context:

'Auditors'	The auditors for the time being of the Company
'Independent Accountant'	A single independent chartered accountant or an independent firm of chartered accountants to be agreed upon between the Vendors and the Purchaser or (in default of such agreement) to be selected (at the instance of either of them) by the President for the time being of the Institute of Chartered Accountants in England and Wales
'Year One'	The financial year of the Company ending on [date]
'Year One Profits'	The profits for Year One determined in accordance with this Schedule
'Year Two'	The financial year of the Company ending on [date]
'Year Two Profits'	The profits for Year Two determined in accordance with this Schedule

2 If Year One Profits exceed £[*amount*] the Purchaser shall pay to the Vendors a sum equal to the greater of:

2.1 [*number*] times the excess; and

2.2 £[*amount*]

3 If Year Two Profits exceed £[*amount*] the Purchaser shall pay to the vendors a sum equal to the greater of:

3.1 [*Number*] times the excess; and

3.2 [*amount*].

4 The Year One Profits and the Year Two Profits shall mean the [consolidated] profits (less losses) as shown by the [consolidated] profit and loss account of the Company (agreed or reported on in accordance with paragraph 9) for Year One and Year Two respectively, such profit and loss accounts to be prepared in accordance with [the accounting policies and principles set out in appendix [*number*] to this Schedule and, subject to that, with] the same bases and policies of accounting applied for the purposes of EITHER [the Accounts] OR [the audited [consolidated] accounts of the Company for the [*state period*]], and with (to the extent not inconsistent with the foregoing) accounting principles generally accepted in the United Kingdom, provided that they shall be adjusted so far as necessary to take account of the following matters:

4.1 any taxation on profits shall not be deducted;

4.2 profits and losses shall be calculated after exceptional items and before extraordinary items;

4.3 any profit or loss on the disposal of any fixed assets (including, without limitation, any Intellectual Property Rights or any interest in the Property) shall be excluded;

4.4 the effects, including any increased depreciation charges, of any revaluation of any fixed assets shall be excluded;

4.5 any management, administration or like charge made by the Purchaser [save for any charge in respect of services which are reasonably required and are provided on an arm's length basis,] shall not be deducted [(and in this Schedule 'Purchaser' shall where the context permits be deemed to include any holding company for the time being of the Purchaser and/or any subsidiary other than the Company for the time being of the Purchaser or of any such holding company)];

4.6 any costs or expenses incurred in complying with any financial reporting or other similar requirements of the Purchaser [to the extent that such reporting or other similar requirements are more onerous than those to which [the Company] [any Group Member] presently adheres,] shall not be deducted;

4.7 [the fees, remuneration and pension contributions in respect of any director or officer of [the Company] nominated by the Purchaser, not being a full-time employee, shall not be deducted [unless such payment is properly related to services provided by such director or officer]];

4.8 any compensation of other payment for loss of office or employment to any officer of [the Company] shall not be deducted [save where the loss of office or employment arises as a result of a breach by the officer of his or her terms of engagement or employment];

4.9 in respect of a transaction between the Purchaser and [the Company] which is not at arm's length, there shall be substituted terms which are at arm's length, and 'transaction' shall include without limitation:

4.9.1 the lending or borrowing of money, and/or being party to any bank netting arrangement for the purposes of calculating interest;

4.9.2 the payment of remuneration or fees to any person who does not work full time on the affairs of [the Company];

4.9.3 the granting of assistance and facilities, including the secondment of employees and the sharing or leasing of premises.

4.10 the effect of any interest rate differentials as on borrowers arising by virtue of the Company becoming a subsidiary of the Purchaser shall be excluded;

4.11 there shall be included any amounts which would have been included but for any breach by the Purchaser of paragraph 5;

4.12 in the event of any adjustment being made pursuant to the provisions of this paragraph in respect of an amount received or paid by [the Company] [any Group Member] there shall be included in the calculation of the adjustment national interest on the relevant amount at the rate set out in clause [10] of the Agreement from the date of such receipt or payment to the date of the relevant accounts;

4.13 any other adjustment as may be agreed in writing between the Vendors and the Purchaser shall be made.

5 The Purchaser covenants with the Vendor[s] that during the period commencing on Completion and ending on [*date*] the Purchaser will procure [so far as it is able] that none of the following will occur in respect of [the Company] [unless otherwise agreed in writing by the Vendor[s]]:

5.1 the removal [of any] of the Vendor[s] from [their respective] office and employment as directors and employees of the Company [save in accordance with the service contracts executed by each of the Vendors with the Company on the date of this Agreement];

5.2 the appointment of any executive director (other than [any of] the Vendor[s]) to its board;

5.3 any material change in its trade or business;

5.4 the sale or other disposal of the whole or any [substantial] part of its undertaking or assets (other than on the advice of a licensed insolvency practitioner);

5.5 the purchase of any material assets outside the normal course of its business [save that such purchases may be made in accordance with the capital expenditure programme agreed between the parties hereto] and initialled by them for the purpose of identification;

5.6 the presentation of a petition for its liquidation or the passing of any resolution for its winding up unless in the reasonable opinion of the directors of the Purchaser the Company is insolvent and such action is necessary to ensure that all directors of the Company comply with their obligations under the Insolvency Act 1986;

5.7 the appointment of a receiver or receiver and manager or administrator over the whole or any part of its assets or undertakings but subject to the requirements and duties of any director under the provisions of the Insolvency Act 1986;

5.8 the sale or other disposal of the legal or any other interest in the whole or any part of its issued share capital (apart from a nominee shareholding), or the allotment or issue of any shares, or the grant of any option or right to subscribe for shares, or any other alteration or reorganisation in respect of its share capital;

5.9 the payment of any amount standing to the credit of any share premium account or capital redemption reserve fund;

5.10 a change of its name;

5.11 making of any borrowing whatsoever apart from normal trade credit and borrowing from bankers at commercial rates of interest then prevailing;

5.12 the giving of any guarantee, indemnity or security in respect of the obligations of any person other than the Company;

5.13 any transaction with the Purchaser which is not at arm's length;

5.14 any change in its accounting reference date or a change in the accounting policies normally adopted by it save for such change as may be required from time to time to comply with legal requirements of Statements of Standard Accounting Practice;

5.15 the declaration of any dividend or the making of any other distribution;

5.16 the diversion of any order or business opportunity from the Company to the Purchaser or any company in the Purchaser's group of companies;

5.17 any act or omission which [would have the effect of diminishing] [would intentionally diminish] the First Year's Profits or the Second Year's Profits.

6 The Purchaser shall procure that:

6.1 as soon as reasonably practicable [but, in any event within [*number*] Business Days] following each of Year One and Year Two the Auditors will prepare and deliver to the Vendor[s] and the Purchaser a calculation of Year One Profits or Year Two Profits (as the case may be) showing the application of the foregoing provisions of this Schedule. The Vendor[s] and the Purchaser will then endeavour in good faith to agree in writing the amount of Year One Profits or Year Two Profits (as the case may be). [The Vendor[s] will have the right to consult [*name of Vendor's[s'] accountants*] in relation to the calculation will be borne by the Purchaser.] In the absence of agreement between the Vendor[s] and the Purchaser as aforesaid within [*number*] Business Days after the Auditors may by notice in writing to the other require Year One Profits or Year Two Profits (as the case may be) to be reviewed and reported upon by the Independent Accountant (whose costs shall be paid as he or they shall direct and shall act as expert (and not as arbitrator) in connection with the giving of such report, which shall be binding except in the case of manifest error);

6.2 The Vendor[s] and the Vendor['s][s'] professional advisers shall have the right to such access to and copies (at their own expense) of the books and accounts of [the Company][each Group Member] and such other relevant information as will be requested by the Vendor[s] to enable them to assess the calculations referred to in paragraph 6.1.

7   The Additional Consideration in respect of Year One and Year Two will in each case be paid in cash, in the same manner as specified in clause [4] to the Vendor[s] [in the same proportions as specified in Schedule 1] within [number] days of the agreement as to determination of the Additional Consideration. If such payment is made after [*date*] (in the case of Year One) or [*date*] (in the case of Year Two) the Purchaser shall pay interest on the relevant amount from such date to the date of actual payment at the rate set out in clause [10] of the Agreement.

8   If the Additional Consideration in respect of Year One or Year Two is not agreed between the Vendors and the Purchaser and is required by either party to be reported on by an independent accountant or an independent firm of accountants, either the Purchaser or the Vendor[s] may by written notice to the other require that (notwithstanding any other provisions of this Agreement) a payment on account of such Additional Consideration be made on the following basis:

8.1   the amount to be paid shall be such Additional Consideration as would be payable if the relevant calculation made by the Auditors were correct, and shall be paid within [*number*] days after the giving of such written notice by the Purchaser or the Vendor[s] (as the case may be);

8.2   within [*number*] days after the amount of such Additional Consideration has been finally determined the appropriate adjustment shall be made by cash payment by the Purchaser to the Vendors or (as the case may be) by the Vendors to the Purchaser, together in either case with interest on the amount of such cash payment at 4% per annum above the base rate for the time being of [Bank] from [*date*] (in the case of Year One) or [*date*] (in the case of Year Two), as the case may be, to the date of actual payment.

Note: definition of and references to Additional Consideration need to be added to the main agreement.

Document 13
Loan Note

LOAN NOTE INSTRUMENT CONSTITUTING 200[ ]-200[ ]
GUARANTEED UNSECURED LOAN NOTE

DATE: 200[ ]

PARTIES:

(1) [ ] LIMITED (company number: [ ]) whose registered office is situate at [ ];

(2) [ ] whose registered office is situate at [ ].

RECITALS:

The Company has, [pursuant to its Memorandum and Articles of Association,] by resolution of its board of directors passed on [ ] created £[ ] 200[ ]-200[ ] Variable Rate Guaranteed Unsecured Loan Notes to be constituted as provided for in this Instrument, subject to and with the benefit of the Conditions.

AGREEMENT:

1   Definitions

In this Instrument the following definitions will apply:

'Act'	The Companies Act 1985
'Agreement'	An agreement of even date made between [ ] (1) and [ ] (2) for the purchase of the entire issued share capital of [ ] Limited
'Bank'	[ ]
'Business Day'	Any day, other than a Saturday or Sunday, on which banks are generally open for business in the City of London
'Certificate'	A certificate in the form set out in Schedule 1
'Company'	[ ] Limited
'Conditions'	The conditions pursuant to which the Notes are issued, as set out in Schedule 2
'Directors'	The directors of the Company from time to time
'Election Date'	For each Note, the date on which notice is served pursuant to Clause 5.4
'Election Period'	For each Note, the period commencing six months from the date of issue of such Note and ending 30 Business Days before the Repayment Date
'Guarantee'	The guarantee given by the Bank in the form contained in Schedule 4
'Interest Payment Dates'	[ ]
'Interest Period'	A three month period ending on an Interest Payment Date
'Interest Rate'	A rate per annum [ ]% [above/below] the base lending rate of the Bank
'Notes'	The £[ ] 200[ ]-200[ ] [Variable/Fixed Rate] Guaranteed Unsecured Loan Notes constituted by this Instrument or (as the case may be) the aggregate principal amount of such Notes for the time being outstanding
'Noteholders'	The persons for the time being entered in the Register as the holders of the Notes

242

'Register'	The register of the holders of Notes maintained by the Company pursuant to Condition 9
'Repayment Date'	For each Note, the date on which it is to be repaid pursuant to Clause 5.1
'Repayment Notice'	A notice in the form set out in Schedule 3

2   **Interpretation**

2.1   The headings and table of contents in this Instrument are inserted for convenience only and shall not affect its interpretation or construction.

2.2   References in this Instrument to Clauses and Schedules are, unless otherwise stated, references to the Clauses of and Schedules to this Instrument.

2.3   The Schedules form part of this Instrument and shall have the same force and effect as if expressly set out in the body of this Instrument.

2.4   Words and expressions defined in the Companies Act 1985 shall, unless they are otherwise defined in this Instrument or the context otherwise requires, bear the same meaning in this Instrument.

2.5   References to statutes shall include any statutory modification, re-enactment or extension of such statute and any orders, regulations, instruments or other subordinate legislation made pursuant to such statute.

2.6   In this Instrument, references to:

2.6.1   the masculine gender shall include the feminine and neuter and vice versa;

2.6.2   the singular shall include the plural and vice versa; and

2.6.3   'persons' shall include bodies corporate, unincorporated associations and partnerships.

3   **Amount of the Notes**

The principal amount of the Notes constituted by this Instrument is limited to £[   ]. The Notes may be issued in denominations of £1 nominal amount or multiples of £1 to such persons at such times and on such terms pursuant to the Agreement as the Directors shall determine.

4   **Status of the Notes**

The Notes when issued shall rank pari passu equally and rateably without discrimination or preference and as an unsecured obligation of the Company.

5   **Repayment of Notes**

5.1   The Notes shall be repayable on the earlier of:

5.1.1   the date specified pursuant to Condition 1.1 following the service of a Repayment Notice in accordance with the Conditions; or

5.1.2   [ ] 200[ ].

5.2   No Note shall be repaid before the expiry of six months from the date of issue of such Note.

5.3   As and when the Notes, or any part of the Notes, become repayable in accordance with this Instrument, the Company will, against surrender by the Noteholder of the relevant Certificate, pay to the Noteholders entitled to them at the registered office of the Company, or at such other place in the United Kingdom as the Company may consider appropriate, the full principal amount of the Notes due to be repaid together with any accrued interest.

5.4   A Noteholder may, by notice in writing to the Company given at any time during the Election Period, elect that all the principal amount of the Notes then outstanding and due to be repaid shall be repaid in US dollars, in which case the Company shall, on the Repayment Date and in full discharge of its obligation to repay the Notes, pay to the Noteholder an amount in US dollars obtained by converting the principal amount outstanding of the Loan Note into US dollars at the spot rate for the purchase of US dollars with sterling certified by the Bank as prevailing at or about 11.00 am on the Election Date (or where the Election Date is not a Business Day on the immediately preceding Business Day) provided that:

    5.4.1   if the amount payable in US dollars pursuant to this Clause 5.4 would otherwise exceed an amount in US dollars obtained by converting 100.2% of the sterling principal amount outstanding of the Note into US dollars at the spot rate for the purchase of US dollars with sterling certified by the Bank as prevailing at or about 11.00 am on the Repayment Date, the latter amount shall be substituted as the amount payable;

    5.4.2   if the amount payable in US dollars pursuant to this Clause 5.4 would otherwise be less than the amount in US dollars obtained by converting 99.8% of the sterling principal amount outstanding of the Loan Note into US dollars at the spot rate for the purchase of US dollars with sterling certified by the Bank as prevailing at or about 11.00 am on the Repayment Date, the latter amount shall be substituted as the amount payable.

6   Interest on Notes

6.1   Until such time as the Notes are repaid in accordance with the provisions of this Instrument, the Company will pay to the Noteholders, in respect of each Interest Period, on each applicable Interest Payment Date, accrued interest on the principal amount of the Notes outstanding at the [applicable] Interest Rate, save that the first payment of interest shall be in respect of the period from the date of issue of the relevant Note to the next Interest Payment Date.

6.2   Without prejudice to any other right of the Noteholders, if the Company fails to pay any amount payable under this Instrument on the due date for payment, the Company shall pay interest on such overdue amount from the due date for payment to the actual date of payment, after as well as before judgement, at a rate of [ ]% above the Interest Rate, such default interest to accrue on a daily basis compounded monthly on the last day of each month.

6.3   Interest will accrue on a daily basis, assuming a 365-day year.

6.4   Interest will be paid net of any taxation which the Company is required to deduct, and any other withholding which the Company is legally required to make. If taxation is deducted from any interest paid to the Noteholder, the Company will:

    6.4.1   deliver to the Noteholder any voucher to which it is entitled evidencing the deduction of taxation on payment of the interest; and

    6.4.2   promptly account for such taxation deducted to the appropriate taxation authority.

7   Events of default

7.1   [Subject to Clause 5.2 the][The] whole of the amount outstanding under the Notes, together with all accrued interest, shall become immediately repayable by the Company upon the occurrence of any of the following events:

    7.1.1   if the Company fails to pay any interest or principal on the Note on the due date for payment; or

    7.1.2   failure by the Company to observe or perform any of its obligations (other than its obligations to pay principal and interest on the Notes) under this Instrument if such failure is not remedied for 21 days after written notice has been given by any Noteholder requiring remedy; or

    7.1.3   if an administrative or other receiver or similar officer is appointed over the whole or part of the assets of the Company or the Company requests any person to appoint such a receiver or similar officer; or

7.1.4   if any order is made or an effective resolution is passed for:

7.1.4.1   the making of an administration order against the Company; or

7.1.4.2   the winding up, dissolution or liquidation of the Company, other than for the purpose of a solvent reconstruction or amalgamation; or

7.1.5   if the Company proposes any composition, scheme of arrangement, compromise or arrangement involving the Company and its creditors generally.

7.2   Any Noteholder may exclude all (but not some only) of the Notes held by him from becoming immediately repayable under the provisions of Clause 7.1 if the grounds on which such Notes would become repayable are:

7.2.1   any such failure by the Company as is referred to in Clause 7.1.1 provided that such Noteholder, within [ ] Business Days of the failure to make payment, serves written notice that he requires the Notes held by him to be so excluded; or

7.2.2   the passing of a resolution for the voluntary winding up of the Company for the purposes of a solvent amalgamation or reconstruction provided that such Noteholder, within [ ] Business Days of his becoming aware of the relevant fact, serves written notice on the Company that he requires the Notes held by him to be so excluded.

8   Covenants by Company

Each of the Noteholders may sue for the performance or observance of the provisions of this Instrument so far as his holding of Notes is concerned.

9   Guarantee

Payment of all principal sums (but not interest or other payments) due on or in respect of the Notes are guaranteed by the Bank on the terms and subject to the Conditions of the Guarantee.

10   Payment

Subject to Clause 6.4, all payments due to be made by the Company to any Noteholder under the Notes shall be made free and clear of any equity, set-off or counterclaim on the part of the Company whether against the original, current or any intermediate holder of the Notes or otherwise.

11   Notices

11.1   Any notice required to be given pursuant to this Instrument shall be in writing signed by, or on behalf of, the person issuing the notice. Notices may be served by personal delivery, prepaid first class post or facsimile transmission to:

11.1.1   in the case of the Company, its registered office for the time being (ref: the Company Secretary); and

11.1.2   in the case of the Noteholders, the respective addresses entered into the Register.

11.2   Notices served in accordance with Clause 11.1 shall be deemed to have been received:

11.2.1   if delivered personally, upon delivery;

11.2.2   if served by prepaid first class post, at the close of business on the second Business Day after posting; and

11.2.3   if served by facsimile transmission, upon receipt of confirmation that the notice has been correctly transmitted (unless such transmission takes place on a day which is not a Business Day or after 5.00 pm on a Business Day, in which case notice will be deemed to have been received at 10.00 am on the next Business Day).

11.3   In proving service by post, it will be necessary only to prove that the notice was properly stamped, addressed and posted.

12 Third party rights

Unless otherwise stated in this Instrument, no person, other than the Company and the Noteholders, may enforce or rely upon this Instrument under the Contracts (Rights of Third Parties) Act 1999. No party to this Instrument may hold itself out as trustee of any rights under this Instrument for the benefit of any third party unless specifically provided for in this Instrument.

13 Entire agreement and variations

13.1   This Instrument contains the entire agreement and understanding in connection with the subject matter of this Instrument.

13.2   No variations to this Instrument shall be effective unless made in writing and signed by all the parties.

14 Governing law

This Instrument shall be governed by and construed in accordance with English law. The Company and the Noteholders agree to submit to the exclusive jurisdiction of the English courts in relation to any claim or matter arising under this Instrument.

IN WITNESS of which the Company has executed this Instrument on the date set out above.

Schedule 1

Certificate No. [ ]

[ ] LIMITED

Company number: [ ]

200[ ]-200[ ] GUARANTEED VARIABLE RATE UNSECURED REDEEMABLE LOAN NOTES

Created and issued pursuant to [the Memorandum and Articles of Association of the Company and to] a resolution of the board of directors of the Company passed on [ ].

THIS IS TO CERTIFY THAT the person(s) set out below is/are the registered holder(s) of the 200[ ]-200[ ] Guaranteed Variable Rate Unsecured Loan Notes in the amount set out below constituted by an Instrument entered into by the Company on [ ] ('the Instrument') and issued with the benefit of and subject to the Conditions and the provisions contained or incorporated in the Instrument

NAME OF HOLDERS	AMOUNT OF NOTES
[ ]	£[ ]

The Notes are repayable in accordance with the terms of the Instrument.

This Certificate must be surrendered before any transfer, whether of the whole or any part of the Notes comprised in it, can be registered or any new Certificates issued in exchange. The Notes are freely transferable. Any partial transfer of the Notes must be in amounts and multiples of £[ ].

DATED:

SIGNED and DELIVERED as a
DEED by [ ] LIMITED acting by [its   ....
duly authorised representative] [a   Director
director and its secretary or by two   ....
directors]   Director/Secretary

Schedule 2

The Conditions

1 **Repayment**

1.1 To demand repayment of the Notes, a Noteholder shall complete and serve on the Company a Repayment Notice stating the amount (being either the whole of the amount of such Notes or integral multiples of not less than £[ ]) required to be paid and the date for repayment of such Notes (which shall be not less than [ ] and not more than [ ] Business Days after the service of the Repayment Notice). [The date for repayment of such Notes must be an Interest Payment Date].

1.2 The Repayment Notice must be signed, dated and lodged with the Certificate for the Notes to be repaid at the registered office of the Company or at such other address within the United Kingdom as the Company may from time to time notify to Noteholders prior to the date of Repayment Notice being served.

1.3 A Repayment Notice given to the Company shall be irrevocable unless the Company gives its consent to the revocation. Immediately upon the expiration of such Repayment Notice the Company shall repay the amount specified in the Repayment Notice together with interest accrued up to and including the Repayment Date.

1.4 If the Notes are converted into US dollars pursuant to Clause 5.4 references in this Instrument to amounts in sterling will be replaced by amounts of US dollars of equivalent value (rounded to the nearest US $5,000) at the exchange rate at which such conversion has taken place.

1.5 Not more than two Repayment Notices may be lodged by each Noteholder in any period of 12 months.

1.6 The Company will be entitled at any time to purchase any Notes by tender or by private treaty or otherwise at any price agreed between the relevant Noteholder and the Company.

2 **Certificate for Notes**

2.1 Each Noteholder shall be entitled to a Certificate to evidence the Notes held by him. Each Certificate shall bear a denoting number and shall be signed by a duly authorised representative of the Company.

2.2 The Notes shall be held subject to the Conditions and the other terms of the Instrument, which shall be binding on the Company and the Noteholders and all persons claiming through or under them respectively.

2.3 The Company shall not be bound to register more than four persons as the joint holders of any Notes and, in the case of Notes held jointly, the Company shall not be bound to issue more than one Certificate for such Notes. Delivery of a Certificate to the first named Noteholder shall be sufficient delivery to joint Noteholders.

2.4 When a Noteholder transfers or has had repaid some of the Notes comprised in a Certificate, the old Certificate shall be cancelled and a new Certificate for the balance of such Notes issued without charge.

3 **Surrender of Certificate**

3.1 Every Noteholder, any part of whose Notes is due to be repaid under any of the provisions of these Conditions, shall not later than the relevant Repayment Date, deliver up to the Company at its registered office for the time being or such other place as the Company may from time to time notify to Noteholders, the Certificate for the Notes which are due to be repaid in order that the same may be cancelled.

Upon such delivery and against a receipt, if the Company shall so require, for the principal monies payable in respect of the Notes to be repaid, the Company shall pay to the Noteholder the amount payable to him in respect of such repayment. Such payment shall be made through a bank on behalf of the Company if the Company shall think fit.

3.2   If any Certificate delivered to the Company pursuant to Condition 3.1 includes any Notes not repayable on the relevant Repayment Date, a fresh Certificate for the balance of the Notes not repaid on that date shall be issued free of charge to the Noteholder.

3.3   If any Noteholder, any part of whose Notes is liable to be repaid under these Conditions, shall fail or refuse to deliver up the Certificate for such Notes at the time and place fixed for the repayment of them or shall fail or refuse to accept payment of the repayment monies payable in respect of them, the monies payable to such Noteholder shall be set aside by the Company and paid into a separate interest bearing bank account and held by the Company in trust for such Noteholder. Such setting aside shall be deemed for all the purposes of these Conditions to be a payment to such Noteholder and the Company shall be discharged from all subsequent obligations in connection with such Notes.

4   Cancellation

4.1   All Notes repaid or purchased by the Company shall be cancelled. The Company may not subsequently re-issue such Notes to any other person.

5   Payment of interest

5.1   Interest on any Notes becoming liable to repayment shall cease to accrue as from the Repayment Date of such Notes, unless payment shall not be tendered by the Company.

6   Modification

6.1   The provisions of the Instrument and the rights of the Noteholders may from time to time be varied, modified, abrogated or compromised in any respect with the sanction of Noteholders holding not less than 75% in nominal value of the Notes and with the written consent of the Company [and the Bank].

7   Dealings

7.1   The Notes shall not be capable of being dealt in on any recognised investment exchange and no application has been or will be made to any recognised investment exchange for permission to deal in or for an official or other quotation for the Notes.

8   Transfer

8.1   The Notes shall be freely transferable. On any transfer of some only of the Notes held by a Noteholder, the Notes shall only be transferable in amounts and multiples of £[ ].

8.2   On the death of a Noteholder (not being a joint holder) his executors or administrators and, in the case of the death of a joint holder, the survivor of such joint holder, shall be the only person or persons recognised by the Company as having any title to the Notes.

8.3   Any person becoming entitled to any Notes in consequence of the death or bankruptcy of a registered Noteholder may upon producing such evidence of his title or interest as the Company shall think sufficient be registered himself as the holder of such Note, and the Company shall be at liberty to retain any interest payable in respect of any Note to which this paragraph applies until such person shall be registered as in the Register of Noteholders.

9 **Company to maintain register**

    9.1   The Company shall at all times keep at its registered office or (subject to the provisions of Section 190 of the Act) at some other place approved by the Noteholder an accurate register showing the amount of the Note for the time being issued, the date of issue and all subsequent changes of ownership of the Note and the name and addresses of the Noteholder.

Schedule 3

Notice of Repayment

To: [ ] **LIMITED**

£[ ] 200[ ]/200[ ] Guaranteed Variable Rate Unsecured Loan Notes

I/We, being the registered holder(s) of the following Notes, hereby give notice that we require repayment of the following amounts on the dates specified

Amount of Repayment (£)	Repayment Date
[ ]	[ ]

I/We enclose my/our Certificate, number [ ], in respect of £[ ] Notes.

Signed: ....
[Noteholder]

Dated: [ ] 200[ ]

Schedule 4

Guarantee

[Insert form of Bank Guarantee]

EXECUTED by [ ] **LIMITED** acting by [its duly authorised representative] [a director and secretary or by any two directors]	.... Director .... Director/Secretary
EXECUTED by [ ] acting by its duly authorised representative	....

Document 14
Letter of Resignation of Director

To   **The Directors**   **Dated [ ] 200[ ]**
        [ ] Limited

Dear Sirs

By this Deed **I HEREBY TERMINATE** my employment (if any) with the Company and **RESIGN** the office of Director of the Company both with immediate effect. I acknowledge and confirm that I have no claim against the Company for loss of office or otherwise howsoever and that there is outstanding no agreement or arrangement under which the Company has any existing or contingent or prospective obligation to me.

SIGNED and **DELIVERED** as a **DEED** by [ ]
in the presence of :

Witness signature

Witness name

Witness address

Witness occupation

Document 15
Completion Agenda

ACQUISITION OF THE ENTIRE ISSUED SHARE CAPITAL OF

[   ] LIMITED

BY

[   ] LIMITED

MEETING TO TAKE PLACE AT

[   ]am/pm on   200[ ]

Document List

	DOCUMENT	RESPONSIBILITY FOR PRODUCTION	STATUS
1	Sale and purchase agreement		
2	Share transfers – stock transfer form and share certificates		
3	Disclosure letter with attached disclosure bundle		
4	Tax deed		
5	Resignations of Directors of Target		
6	Resignation of Auditors of Target		
7	Company documentation in respect of the Company, being certificate of incorporation, change of name certificate, register of members (other statutory registers), minute books, share certificate book and current cheque books		
8	Compromise agreement for departing directors		
9	Service Agreement for key staff		
10	Banking documents: (i) Facility agreement (ii) Guarantee from Target and Purchaser (iii) Debenture from Target and Purchaser (iv) Loan agreement between Target and Purchaser (v) Creditor agreement (vi) Legal charge in relation to Target Properties (vii) Counter indemnity from Target (viii) Deed of Assignment of Keyman Policies (ix) Deed of Priority		

11	Financial assistance: (i) Form 155(6)(a) with annexures (ii) Auditor's statutory report (iii) Auditor's non-statutory report with board memorandum		
12	Board minutes of Target with written resolution		
13	Board minutes of Purchaser with written resolution		
14	Pre-completion Board minutes of the Purchaser		
15	Bank reconciliation statements		
16	Voting powers of attorney		
17	Acknowledgement from Vendor that there are no claims against the Company		
18	New bank mandate		

Order of Proceedings

(a) Pre-completion board meeting of Purchaser

(b) Board meeting of Target including swearing of financial assistance

(c) Board meeting of the Purchaser

Document 16
Completion Board Minutes – Purchaser

[   ] LIMITED

MINUTES of a meeting of the board of Directors held at
on   200[ ] at   am/pm

PRESENT   (In the Chair)

IN ATTENDANCE

---

1   **Quorum**
    The Chairman reported that a quorum was present and declared the meeting open.

2   **Purpose of Meeting**
    It was reported that negotiations had taken place for the purchase by the Company of the
    entire issued share capital of [   ] Limited ('the Target'). The chairman reported
    that the purpose of the meeting was to consider, and if thought appropriate, approve the
    purchase of the Target pursuant to an agreement for the sale and purchase of the entire
    issued share capital of the Target between [   ] and others (1) and the Company (2)
    and to approve matters arising pursuant to or consequent on such agreement.

3   **Declaration of Interest**
    Each of the directors declared to those in attendance their interest in the business to be
    transacted at the meeting. Having done so, it was noted that under the Articles of
    Association of the Company they could vote and count in reckoning a quorum when
    such matters were considered.

4   **Approval of Share Agreement**
    There was produced to the meeting an agreement for the sale and purchase of the entire
    issued share capital of Target between [   ] and others ('Vendors') (1) and the
    Company (2) ('Agreement'). The terms of the Agreement were considered, noting in par-
    ticular that [note principal terms of agreement]. There was produced to the meeting
    signed letters from each of the Vendors acknowledging that they and their families have
    no claims against Target. **IT WAS RESOLVED** that:
    4.1   the terms of the draft Agreement were approved it being in the best commercial
          interests of the Company;
    4.2   any director of the Company was authorised to approve amendments to the draft
          which were not considered by him to be material; and
    4.3   any two directors or any director and secretary was authorised to execute the
          Agreement as a deed on behalf of the Company.

5   **Taxation Deed**
    It was reported that one of the requirements for completion of the Agreement was the
    delivery by the Vendors to the Company of a deed in favour of the Company in respect of
    certain potential tax liabilities of Target ('the Deed'). Two engrossments of the Deed were
    produced to the meeting. **IT WAS RESOLVED** that:

5.1   the form of the Deed be approved;

5.2   any two directors or any director and secretary be authorised to execute the Deed on behalf of the Company;

5.3   the Deed be exchanged with the Vendors.

6   **Disclosure Letter**

There was produced to the meeting a disclosure letter from those of the Vendors giving the warranties set out in the Agreement ('Warrantors') setting out general and specific disclosures against the warranties ('Disclosure Letter'). The terms of the Disclosure Letter were considered noting in particular the specific disclosures. **IT WAS RESOLVED** that the Disclosure Letter be approved and any director be authorised to acknowledge receipt on behalf of the Company.

7   *[Produce to the meeting other documents, consider their terms and approve them].*

8   **Announcement**

There was produced to the meeting an announcement regarding the acquisition in the form agreed between the Vendors and the Company ('Announcement'). **IT WAS RESOLVED** that the Announcement be released to relevant persons immediately following completion of the Agreement.

9   **Close**

There being no further business the meeting then terminated.

....

Chairman

Document 17
Completion Board Minutes – Target

[   ]LIMITED

MINUTES of a meeting of the board of Directors held at
on   200[ ] at   am/pm

PRESENT   (In the Chair)

IN ATTENDANCE

---

1 **Quorum**
The Chairman reported that a quorum was present and declared the meeting open.

2 **Purpose of Meeting**
It was reported that an agreement between the shareholders of the Company and
[ ] Limited ('Purchaser') had been entered into for the sale and purchase of the entire
issued share capital of the Company and the matters contained in these minutes related to
completion of the agreement.

3 **Declaration of Interests**
Each of the directors declared to those in attendance their interest in the business to be
transacted at the meeting. Having done so, it was noted that under the Articles of
Association of the Company that they could vote and count in reckoning a quorum when
such matters were considered.

4 **Transfer of Shares**
There was produced to the meeting the following duly executed transfer of shares of the
Company, together with the relevant share certificates or deeds of indemnities in respect
of lost share certificates, as appropriate.

Transferor	Transferee	Number of Ordinary Shares
[insert names of Vendors]	[Purchaser]	

IT WAS RESOLVED that subject to stamping:
4.1   the transfers be approved;
4.2   the names of the Transferee be entered in the register of members;
4.3   share certificates be sealed and issued accordingly.

5 **Appointment of Directors**
IT WAS RESOLVED that [   ] and [   ] be appointed as directors of
the Company. The secretary was instructed to file at Companies House form 288a.

6 **Close**
There being no further business the meeting then terminated.

....

Chairman

Document 18
Financial Assistance Board Minutes – Target

[ ] LIMITED

MINUTES of a meeting of the board of directors of the Company duly convened and held at [ ] on [ ] 200[ ] at [ ]am/pm

PRESENT	[ ]	(Chairman)
	[ ]	
	[ ]	
	[ ]	

1 **Quorum**
The Chairman reported that a quorum was present and declared the meeting open.

2 **Purpose of Meeting**
The Chairman announced that the purpose of the meeting was to consider, and if thought appropriate, approve certain matters arising pursuant to an agreement for the sale and purchase of the entire issued share capital of the Company between [ ] ('Vendors') (1) and [ ] ('Purchaser') (2). A copy of the agreement for the sale and purchase ('Share Agreement') was produced to the meeting.

3 **Declaration of Interests**
Each of the directors declared to those in attendance their interest in the business to be transacted at the meeting. Having done so, it was noted that under the Articles of Association of the Company they could vote and count in reckoning a quorum when such matters were considered.

4 **Financial Matters**
The Chairman reported that, in connection with the acquisition of the Company by the Purchaser, it was proposed that the Company would enter into:
4.1 a guarantee in favour of [ ] ('Bank') to secure certain facilities to be made available by the Bank to the Purchaser; and
4.2 an unlimited debenture in favour of the Bank, securing all liabilities of the Company to the Bank (including those arising pursuant to the guarantee referred to above).

5 **Security Documents**
The following documents ('Security Documents') were produced to the meeting:
5.1 a guarantee ('Guarantee') to be entered into by the Company in favour of the Bank. It was noted that, pursuant to the Guarantee, the Company was to guarantee to the Bank the due and prompt payment of all monies now or at any time due, owing or incurred to the Bank by the Purchaser; and
5.2 a debenture ('Debenture') to be entered into by the Company in favour of the Bank. It was noted that, pursuant to the Debenture, the Company was to create a fixed and floating charge over all of its assets and undertaking in favour of the Bank as security for all monies now or at any time due, owing or incurred to the

Bank by the Company. It was noted that these liabilities included liabilities arising pursuant to the Guarantee.

6 **Financial assistance**

6.1 The Chairman reported that the execution of the Security Documents by the Company would constitute financial assistance given by the Company for the purpose of the acquisition by the Purchaser of the entire issued share capital of the Company. Accordingly it would be necessary for the requirements of sections 155-158 of the Companies Act 1985 ('Act') to be complied with before the Company could execute, deliver and perform its obligations under the Security Documents.

6.2 It was noted that, under the Articles of Association, the Company had the power to provide financial assistance for the acquisition of its shares.

6.3 The Chairman stated that one of the requirements of the Act was that, before financial assistance could be given, the directors would have to be satisfied that:

6.3.1 the Company had net assets as defined by section 154(2) of the Act (that is that the total assets of the Company exceed the total of its liabilities as such assets and liabilities are stated in the Company's accounting records immediately before the financial assistance is given. It was noted that, for this purpose, 'liabilities' included amounts retained as reasonably necessary for the purpose of providing for any liability or loss which is either likely to be incurred or certain to be incurred but uncertain as to amount or as to the date on which it will arise); and

6.3.2 the giving of the financial assistance would not reduce the net assets of the Company or, to the extent that such net assets would be reduced, that the financial assistance in question was to be provided out of the Company's distributable profits (that is the profits of the Company available for distribution to its members).

6.4 The Chairman reported that, prior to the giving of the financial assistance, the directors were required to make a statutory declaration in the form required by the Act (form 155(6)(a)) ('Statutory Declaration') in respect of the financial assistance to be given. It was noted that the form stated that the directors were of the opinion that, immediately following the date on which the assistance was proposed to be given, there will be no ground on which the Company could then be found to be unable to pay its debts in full, and that the Company will continue to be able to pay its debts as they fall due during the year immediately following the giving of the financial assistance. In forming such an opinion the directors were required to take into account the provisions of section 123 of the Insolvency Act 1986, which deems a company to be unable to pay its debts if it is shown that the value of the company's assets is less than the amount of its liabilities, taking into account its contingent and prospective liabilities.

6.5 It was noted that a director who makes a statutory declaration without having reasonable grounds for the opinions expressed in it is committing an offence for which he is liable on conviction to imprisonment or a fine, or both.

6.6 The Chairman reported that it was necessary to annex to the Statutory Declaration a report ('Auditors' Statutory Report') addressed to the directors of the Company from [   ] ('Auditors'), as auditors of the Company, stating that, having enquired into the state of affairs of the Company, they were not aware of anything to indicate that the opinion expressed in the Statutory Declaration was unreasonable in all the circumstances.

6.7 The Chairman reported that the Bank also required, in addition to the Auditors' Statutory Report, that a further letter be signed by the Auditors ('Auditors' Non-

Statutory Report'), addressed to the Bank, confirming that, in the opinion of the Auditors, the Company had net assets and that the financial assistance will not reduce the net assets of the Company or, to the extent that the net assets are reduced by the giving of financial assistance, that the financial assistance is given out of distributable profits. The Chairman reported that the Auditors had indicated that they would be prepared to sign the Auditors' Non-Statutory Report but required that the directors sign a memorandum ('Board Memorandum') to confirm the directors' opinions as to the financial position of the Company. Drafts of the Directors' Non-Statutory Report and the Board Memorandum were produced to the meeting and approved.

6.8   The directors considered in detail the available financial information concerning the Company comprising (inter alia):

    6.8.1   the last audited accounts of the Company for the financial year ended [   ];

    6.8.2   unaudited management accounts for the [   ] month period ended [   ];

    6.8.3   cashflow, balance sheet and profit and loss account projections for the Company for the period ending [   ]; and

    6.8.4   their knowledge of the affairs of the Company generally.

6.9   The directors considered the financial position of the Company and the information referred to in Minute 6.8. The directors were of the view and they concluded that:

    6.9.1   at the date of this meeting, the aggregate of the Company's assets (as stated in the accounting records) exceeds the aggregate of its liabilities (as similarly stated);

    6.9.2   at [   ] (the last practicable date for such calculation to be made) the distributable profits of the Company were £[   ] and, since that date (from their knowledge of the affairs of the Company), the distributable profits had not reduced; and

    6.9.3   the obligations proposed to be assumed by the Company under the Security Documents were neither certain nor likely to be called and that accordingly no provisions for all or any part of the liability under the Security Documents ought to be made and no reduction in the net assets of the Company would result from entering into the Security Documents; and

    6.9.4   accordingly it was resolved that the financial assistance as proposed could be given in compliance with section 155 of the Act.

6.10   The Statutory Declaration was tabled and considered by the directors. The directors noted the statements that they, as all of the directors of the Company, had formed the opinion that, as regards the initial situation of the Company immediately following the date on which the assistance was proposed to be given, there will be no ground on which the Company could then be found to be unable to pay its debts in full and that the Company will continue to be able to pay its debts as they fall due during the year immediately following the giving of the financial assistance. All the directors approved both of the statements as regards the Company having taken account of:

    6.10.1   the bank facilities available to the Company; and

    6.10.2   the accounting information referred to in Minute 6.8 above.

6.11   The Auditors' Statutory Report was tabled in support of the Statutory Declaration, confirming that the Auditors had enquired into the state of affairs of the Company and were not aware of anything to indicate that the statements referred to in the Statutory Declaration were unreasonable in all the circumstances. It was confirmed that the Auditors would be able to deliver the Auditors' Statutory Report to the Company if a Statutory Declaration in the form produced to the meeting was made on the same day.

6.12 The directors then signed the Board Memorandum and the Auditors' Non-Statutory Report was delivered to the Company for delivery to the Bank.

6.13 The Statutory Declaration was approved and the meeting adjourned whilst the Statutory Declaration was duly made by all the directors in the presence of a solicitor empowered to administer declarations. The Auditors' Statutory Report was then delivered to the Company.

6.14 It was noted that, pursuant to the Act, the financial assistance [had][did not have] to be approved by the members of the Company by special resolution in general meeting [as the Company was a wholly owned subsidiary]. [There was produced to the meeting a draft notice ('Notice'), convening an Extraordinary General Meeting of the Company to approve the giving of financial assistance and the execution of the Security Documents.]

[6.15 It was resolved that the Notice be approved and that the Extraordinary General Meeting be convened to be held immediately, subject to consent to short notice being obtained.]

[6.16 The meeting then adjourned. When it resumed it was noted that the resolutions set out in the Notice had been duly passed unanimously as a special resolution.]

7 **Approval**

7.1 The Chairman then produced the Security Documents.

7.2 It was resolved that:

7.2.1 the execution of the Security Documents was in the best commercial interests of the Company in that it would provide support to the Purchaser to enable bank facilities to be made available to the Purchaser and its subsidiaries. The directors were of the view that the business of the Company would benefit from being a subsidiary of the Purchaser;

7.2.2 the Security Documents be approved and executed as deeds by the Company.

[8 **Subsidiary Company**

8.1 The Chairman reported that it was a term of the Bank's Facilities being made available to the [Company/Purchaser] that each of the Company's subsidiaries execute guarantees and debentures in favour of the Bank in substantially the same form as the Security Documents ('Subsidiary Security').

8.2 It was noted that, pursuant to the Act, the execution of the Subsidiary Security Documents would constitute the giving of financial assistance for the purpose of the acquisition of shares in the Company and the provisions of sections 155-158 of the Act would therefore apply to the subsidiary company, [   ] Limited ('Subsidiary').

8.3 It was noted that, in addition to the requirements imposed upon the Subsidiary, the Act required the directors of the Company to make a further statutory declaration in the form required by the Act (form 155(6)(b)) ('Subsidiary Statutory Declaration') in respect of the financial assistance to be given by the Subsidiary. It was noted that the form stated that the directors were of the opinion that, immediately following the date on which the assistance was proposed to be given, there will be no ground on which the Company could then be found to be unable to pay its debts in full, and that the Company will be able to pay its debts as they fall due during the year immediately following the giving of such financial assistance. It was noted that the same considerations applied to the Subsidiary Statutory Declaration as applied to the Statutory Declaration.

8.4 It was noted that, pursuant to the Act, the financial assistance to be given by the Subsidiary [did not have/had] to be approved by the members of the Subsidiary by special resolution in general meeting [, as the Subsidiary was a wholly owned subsidiary]. [It was resolved that any director be and is hereby authorised to attend and vote at any general meeting of the Subsidiary or to sign a written resolution of the Subsidiary to pass the necessary special resolution].

8.5 The Subsidiary Statutory Declaration was tabled and considered by the directors. The directors noted the statements that they, as all of the directors of the Company, had formed the opinion that, as regards the initial situation of the Company immediately following the date on which the assistance was proposed to be given, there will be no ground on which the Company could then be found to be unable to pay its debts in full and that the Company will continue to be able to pay its debts as they fall due during the year immediately following the giving of financial assistance. All the directors approved both of the statements as regards the Company having taken account of:

8.5.1 the bank facilities available to the Company; and

8.5.2 the accounting information referred to in Minute 6.8 above.

8.6 An Auditors' Report in substantially the same form as the Auditors' Statutory Report was tabled in support of the Subsidiary Statutory Declaration. It was confirmed that the auditors would be able to deliver such report to the Company if a Subsidiary Statutory Declaration in the form produced to the meeting was made on the same day.

8.7 The Subsidiary Statutory Declaration was approved and the meeting adjourned whilst the Subsidiary Statutory Declaration was duly made by all the directors in the presence of a solicitor empowered to administer declarations. The Auditors' report was then delivered to the Company.]

9 Filing

The secretary was instructed to prepare and file with the Registrar of Companies all documents and forms that were required to be filed in connection with the business transacted at the meeting, including without limitation:

9.1 [notice of the passing of the special resolutions passed by the members];

9.2 155(6)a;

9.3 [155(6)b]; and

9.4 the Auditors' Report.

10 Close

There being no further business the meeting was declared closed.

....

Chairman

Document 19
Notice of EGM

[   ] LIMITED

NOTICE is given that an Extraordinary General Meeting of the Company will take place at [   ] on [] 200[] at [] am/pm to consider and if thought fit to pass the following resolutions as special resolutions.

SPECIAL RESOLUTIONS

1 That in connection with the acquisition of [   ] Ordinary Shares of £1 each in the issued share capital [the entire issued share capital] of the Company by [   ] Limited and in accordance with section 155(4) of the Companies Act 1985 the Company be and is hereby authorised to give the financial assistance (details of which are set out in the statutory declaration (Form 155(6)a) sworn by the Directors of the Company on the date of the meeting, which statutory declaration and the Auditors' Report attached hereto have been considered by the Meeting).

2 That the Company be authorised to execute into a guarantee with [   ] ('the Bank') guaranteeing all liabilities of [   ] Limited to the Bank.

3 That the Company be authorised to execute a debenture in favour of the Bank pursuant to which the Company creates fixed and floating charges over its assets and undertaking as security for all liabilities from time to time due, owing or incurred to the Bank.

Dated   200[ ]

Registered Office: [ ]

                      [ ]

                      [ ]

                      [ ]

....
Secretary

Note: A Member entitled to attend and vote at the meeting convened by the above notice may appoint a proxy (who may be more than one person) to attend and vote in his place. A proxy need not be a member of the Company.

We the undersigned, being the holders of the whole of the issued share capital of the Company, hereby consent to the holding of the meeting convened by the above notice and to the passing of the resolution to be proposed as a special resolution notwithstanding that less than 21 days' notice shall be given.

....

[   ]

....

[   ]

....

[   ]

Document 20
Auditors' Statutory Report

From: Auditors

To: Company   [Date]

Dear Sirs

REPORT OF THE AUDITORS TO THE DIRECTORS OF [   ] LIMITED ('THE COMPANY') PURSUANT TO SECTION 156(4) OF THE COMPANIES ACT 1985 ('THE ACT')

We have examined the statutory declaration of the directors dated [   ] in connection with the proposal that the Company should give financial assistance for the purchase of its own shares.

We have enquired into the state of affairs of the Company so far as is necessary for us to review the basis for the statutory declaration.

We are not aware of anything to indicate that the opinion expressed by the directors in their statutory declaration as to any of the matters mentioned in Section 156(2) of the Act is unreasonable in all the circumstances.

Yours faithfully

[Auditors]

Document 21
Auditors' Non-statutory Report and Board Memorandum

From: Auditors

To: Company

Dear Sirs

REPORT BY THE AUDITORS OF [   ] LIMITED ('THE COMPANY')
TO [   ] ('THE BANK')

This report is given in connection with the proposed arrangement whereby the Company will give financial assistance for the purchase of its own shares, particulars of which are given in the statutory declaration made this day by the directors pursuant to section 155(6) of the Companies Act 1985 ('the Act').

The purpose of this report is to assist the Bank in considering whether the proposed arrangement is permitted under section 155(2) of the Act and it is not intended to be used, quoted or referred to for any other purpose.

We have examined the Board [Minutes/Memorandum] dated [   ] 200[] (a copy of which is attached, initialled by us solely for the purpose of identification) for which the directors were solely responsible and have enquired into the Company's state of affairs so far as necessary for us to review the basis for the Board [Minutes/Memorandum]. Our enquiries may not constitute an audit under the provisions of the Act.

We confirm that, as at the close of business on [   ] 200[] [ie the same date as the Board [Minutes/Memorandum], the aggregate of the Company's assets as stated in its accounting records exceeded the aggregate of its liabilities as so stated.

We are not aware of anything to indicate that the opinion expressed on paragraph [] of the Board Minutes is unreasonable in all the circumstances.

Yours faithfully

[Auditors]

Board Memorandum

[   ] Limited

Memorandum in connection with the proposed arrangement whereby the Company will give financial assistance for the acquisition of its own shares, particulars of which are given in the statutory declaration made by the directors this day pursuant to section 155(6) of the Companies Act 1985 (the Act).

1   As at the close of business on [   ] [the latest practicable date before the Memorandum is signed] the aggregate of the Company's assets as stated in its accounting records exceeded the aggregate of its liabilities as so stated.

2   From our knowledge of events since that date and of the likely course of the Company's business [as described in the accompanying paper], the directors have formed the opinion that the aggregate of the Company's assets will exceed the aggregate of its liabilities immediately before the proposed financial assistance is given and:

EITHER

that the giving of such financial assistance will not reduce the net assets of the Company;

OR

that the amount by which the giving of such financial assistance will reduce the net assets of the Company will not exceed the distributable profits of the Company as determined on the basis of its [last annual] [interim] accounts made up to [   ] (and after taking account of distributions made since that date).

SIGNED ON BEHALF OF THE BOARD   ....

DATED   ....

[Same date as statutory declaration of directors]

Document 22
Companies House Form 155(6)a

G

CHFP087

COMPANIES FORM No. 155(6)(a)

Declaration in relation to assistance for the acquisition of shares

155(6)a

Please do not write in this margin

Pursuant to section 155(6) of the Companies Act 1985

Please complete legibly, preferably in black type, or bold block letter-

To the Registrar of Companies
(Address overleaf - Note 5)

For official use

Company number

Name of company

Note
Please read the notes on page 3 before completing this form.

* insert full name of company

Ø insert name(s) and address(es) of all the directors

*

I/We Ø

SPECIMEN

• •delete as appropriate

§ delete whichever is inappropriate

[the sole director][all the directors of the above company do solemnly and sincerely declare that:

The business of the company is:

(a) that of a [recognised bank][licensed institution]† within the meaning of the Banking Act 1979§

(b) that of a person authorised under section 3 or 4 of the Insurance Companies Act 1982 to carry on insurance business in the United Kingdom§

(c) something other than the above§

The company is proposing to give financial assistance in connection with the acquisition of shares in the [company] [company's holding company

Limited]†

The assistance is for the purpose of [that acquisition][reducing or discharging a liability incurred for the purpose of that acquisition].†

The number and class of the shares acquired or to be acquired is:

Presentor's name address and reference (if any) :

For official Use (02/00)
General Section

Post room

Companies House Form 155(6)a

The assistance is to be given to: (note 2)

The assistance will take the form of:

The person who [has acquired][will acquire]† the share is:

The principal terms on which the assistance to be given are:

The amount of cash to be transferred to the person assisted is £

The value of any asset to be transferred to the person assisted is £

The date on which the assistance is to be given is

269

I/We have formed the opinion, as regards the company's initial situation immediately following the date on which the assistance is proposed to be given, that there will be no ground on which it could then be found to be unable to pay its debts. (note 3)

(a) [I/We have formed the opinion that the company will be able to pay its debts as they fall due during the year immediately following that date]* (note 3)

(b) [It is intended to commence the winding-up of the company within 12 months of that date, and I/we have formed the opinion that the company will be able to pay its debts in full within 12 months of the commencement of the winding up.]* (note 3)

And I/we make this solemn declaration conscientiously believing the same to be true and by virtue of the provisions of the Statutory Declarations Act 1835.

Declared at

Declarants to sign below

	Day	Month	Year
on			

before me

A Commissioner for Oaths or Notary Public, Justice of the Peace or a Solicitor having the powers conferred on a Commissioner for Oaths

---

NOTES

1   For the meaning of "person incurring a liability" and "reducing a discharging a liability" see section 152(3) of the Companies Act 1985.

2   Insert full name(s) and address(es) of the person(s) to whom assistance is to be given; if a recipient is a company the registered office address should be shown.

3   Contingent and prospective liabilities of the company are to be taken into account - see section 156(3) of the Companies Act 1985.

4   The auditors report required by section 156(4) of the Companies Act 1985 must be annexed to this form.

5   The address for companies registered in England and Wales or Wales is:-

     The Registrar of Companies
     Companies House
     Crown Way
     Cardiff
     CF14 3UZ

     or, for companies registered in Scotland:-

     The Registrar of Companies
     37 Castle Terrace
     Edinburgh
     EH1 2EB

SPECIMEN

Document 23
Heads of Agreement and Exclusivity Agreement (Business Acquisition)

[ ] LIMITED

SUBJECT TO CONTRACT (Save for paragraph 2)

This document sets out what has been agreed between [   ] ('[   ]') and [   ] Limited ('the Vendor') for the acquisition of the business and assets of the Vendor comprising [   ]. [   ] will form a new company ('Newco') which will acquire the relevant business and assets.

The principal terms which have, subject to contract, been agreed for the Proposed Acquisition are set out below. Save for the agreement set out in paragraph 2 below, which shall have immediate effect and be binding on the parties hereto, nothing set out herein is intended to or shall operate to create any legally binding obligations between any of the parties hereto.

1   In these heads of Agreement the following words and expressions shall have the following meanings respectively:

'Business'	The business of [ ] carried on by the Vendor
'Completion Accounts'	Amounts to be drawn up in accordance with paragraph 4
'Exclusivity Period'	The period from the date of this Agreement until [ ] and, provided that Newco has prior to [ ] provided evidence satisfactory to the Vendor that it has the funding available to complete the Proposed Acquisition, the period from [ ]
'Net Assets'	The aggregate value of the assets to be acquired less the aggregate value of the liabilities to be assumed under the Proposed Acquisition in each case as shown in the Completion Accounts
'Property'	Leasehold property located in [ ] from which the Business is carried on at present
'Proposed Acquisition'	The proposed acquisition being the subject of these Heads of Agreement
'Transfer Date'	The date the Proposed Acquisition, if completed, will take effect from

2   In consideration of [   ] agreeing to take further steps to investigate and implement the Proposed Acquisition on the terms set out in this letter and in consideration of the sum of £1 (receipt and sufficiency of which is hereby acknowledged) the Vendor hereby covenants and agrees with and represents to [   ]:

2.1   that the Vendor will reimburse all professional fees incurred by [   ] with his professional legal and accountancy advisers in connection with the Proposed Acquisition in the event of the Proposed Acquisition not proceeding because the Vendor withdraws from the Proposed Acquisition during the Exclusivity Period provided that:

2.1.1   the maximum amount payable by the Vendor shall be £[   ] plus VAT should it withdraw at any time prior to the earlier to occur of [   ] and the date upon which the Purchaser has provided evidence to extend the Exclusivity Period to [   ]; and

2.1.2   the maximum amount payable by the Vendor should it withdraw at any time after the date upon which the Purchaser has provided evidence to extend the Exclusivity Period to [   ] shall be £[   ] plus VAT.

2.2 During the Exclusivity Period, neither the Vendor nor its holding company nor their respective management and professional advisers will approach or enter into any discussions with other prospective purchasers for all or part of the Business nor will any of them make information on all or part of the Business available to persons other than [ ] and his advisers.

3 Newco will purchase the business and assets of the Vendor (more particularly described in paragraph 5 below) used or employed in [ ] Limited. The consideration will, subject as follows, be the sum of £[ ] payable in cash on Completion. The target date for Completion is [ ] and all parties shall use their reasonable endeavours to achieve Completion by that date.

4 Accounts ('Completion Accounts') comprising a balance sheet of the Business as at the Transfer Date will be drawn up as soon as possible after Completion on the same basis as the last audited accounts of the Vendor. These Accounts will be prepared by the Vendor and be submitted to Newco for approval. These accounts will be agreed between Newco and the Vendor and if not agreed referred to an independent expert for final determination.

If these Completion Accounts show Net Assets of less than £[ ] (and such shortfall is greater than £[ ]) then the consideration will be reduced and repaid by an amount equal to 70% of the shortfall. If the Completion Accounts show Net Assets of more than £[ ] (and such excess is greater than £[ ]) then the consideration will be increased and Newco will pay an amount equal to 70% of the excess, provided that the consideration shall not exceed £[ ] in aggregate.

5 The assets to be acquired will comprise:
5.1 the Business as a going concern;
5.2 the goodwill of the Business;
5.3 all intellectual property rights including, without limitation, all patents, trade names, trade marks (registered and unregistered), drawings, design rights, and the benefit of all software licences;
5.4 the plant machinery, fixtures and fittings, tooling and vehicles;
5.5 stock and work in progress (a stock take will take place as part of the Completion Accounts process and the Completion Accounts shall make full provision for all unsaleable or faulty stock) in the same manner as provision has previously been made in the accounts of the Business;
5.6 trade debtors and pre-payments to the extent that Newco can enjoy the benefit of pre-payments following Completion;
5.7 the benefit of all outstanding orders; and
5.8 an assignment of the lease or grant of sub-lease to the Property.

Cash in hand and cash at bank is not included in the sale and cash is not to be taken into account for the purposes of calculating the Net Assets.

6 Newco will assume all liabilities of the Vendor which are taken into account in the Completion Accounts and other liabilities specified in the Sale Agreement. The Vendor will provide an indemnity to Newco in respect of any other liabilities of the Vendor arising on or prior to the Transfer Date. Newco will provide an indemnity to the Vendor in respect of all liabilities which it assumes pursuant to the Sale Agreement.

7 Appropriate terms will need to be agreed for participation by Newco in the Vendor's scheme for up to six months in respect of those employees in the Business who are currently members of the Vendor's pension scheme.

8 Appropriate terms will need to be agreed in connection with the release and/or replacement of any performance bonds outstanding in respect of the Business.

9   Appropriate consultation with employees and unions will take place prior to the Transfer Date. TUPE will apply in respect of the employees.

10 The sale contract will contain appropriate warranties and indemnities concerning the Vendor and its business in favour of Newco up to and as at Completion.

11 Following Completion Newco will carry out all warranty work and other work for which provision has been made in the Completion Accounts or which is included in those accounts as a liability in respect of work carried out by the Business prior to Completion at an agreed hourly rate. The Vendor will not be required to reimburse Newco for this cost until such time as the cost of the work carried out has exceeded the provision for such work contained in the Completion Accounts. If the Vendor requests Newco to carry out additional work, Newco will carry out such work at the hourly rate for the time being applied by the Business on such payment terms as shall be agreed.

12 Normal restrictive covenants will be required from the Vendor preventing inter alia any competition with the Business, any engagement in competitive businesses or solicitation of customers or employees for a period of two years after Completion or the use of the [   ] name at any time. In addition normal confidentiality undertakings will be required concerning the confidential information of the business transfer. The Vendor will continue to have the right to use the word '[   ]' in respect of its divisions other than '[   ]' provided that such businesses are not competitive with the Business.

13 Pending completion the Business of the Vendor will continue to be run in the normal course.

14 Completion of the Proposed Acquisition will be subject to:
    14.1 satisfactory finalisation of funding arrangements by Newco;
    14.2 a formal contract being approved between the parties which will be drawn up by the Purchaser's Solicitors, [   ];
    14.3 there being no adverse change in the financial and trading position or prospects of the Business prior to Completion;
    14.4 the satisfactory outcome of the due diligence review by [   ] and on behalf of his financial backers;
    14.5 [   ]'s solicitors being satisfied as to the Vendor's title to all its property and assets.

15 On Completion each of the parties will bear and pay their own legal and professional fees and expenses.

16 Following signature of these heads of terms [   ] and the professional advisors and proposed funders of [   ] will be allowed reasonable access to the premises and employees of the Vendor during normal office hours following prior arrangement.

Confirmation of agreement to the points set out in these Heads of Agreement has been signified by the parties by their signature below. Further by its signature below the Vendor signifies its agreement to be bound by the provisions of paragraph 2 relating to exclusivity and costs.

....

[   ]   For and on behalf of

                                                             [   ] Limited

Dated: Dated:

Document 24
Sample Consultation Letters to Employee Representatives

1 **Sample consultation letter from Transferor**

Dear [insert name of employee representative]

PROPOSED TRANSFER OF THE BUSINESS

I am writing to inform you that it is proposed that the business of the Company will be sold to [insert name of transferee]. In advance of this proposed sale, I am informing you of certain matters as required by Regulation 10 of the Transfer of Undertakings (Protection of Employment) Regulations 1981 (TUPE Regulations).

It is proposed that the transfer will be completed on or around [insert date of transfer].

The reasons for the transfer are [insert reasons].

The legal implications of the transfer are that it is intended that the TUPE Regulations apply to transfer of the main terms and conditions of employment of all employees. This includes continuity of employment.

It is not envisaged that there will be any economic or social implications of the transfer for employees.

One of the main implications of the transfer is that employees' membership of our pension scheme will cease after the transfer, and whilst it is expected that [insert name of transferee] will be able to offer benefits under its pension scheme, some differences will be inevitable.

We are informed that [insert name of transferee] intends no measures will be taken in connection with the transferred employees. I understand you will be contacted by them in due course.

As neither we nor [insert name of transferee] envisage that any measures will be taken in relation to the transfer, it seems no further consultation is necessary, but if that position changes we shall of course let you know.

Please let me know if you have any queries or concerns arising out of this letter.

Yours sincerely

[   ]

2 Sample consultation letter from Transferee

Dear [insert name of employee representative]

TRANSFER OF BUSINESS

I am writing to inform you that on [insert date of transfer], it is proposed that we will acquire the business of [insert name of transferor].

We understand that you have already been informed that this will be a relevant transfer under the TUPE Regulations, and I confirm that the main terms and conditions of your employment, including continuity, will be preserved.

There is further information that I would like to pass to you at this stage, to give you a better idea of what is going.

- Taking on the business of [insert name of transferor] will obviously necessitate some integration of staff between the two businesses. I do not envisage any major disturbance either for new staff or existing staff and no change in terms and conditions of employment is likely to be involved.
- Once staff have been fully integrated, the need may arise for redundancies, but it is hoped this can be avoided or at the very least dealt with on a natural wastage basis. If however the need for redundancies does arise, full consultations will take place and alternative measures will be considered in due course.
- Pension matters are excluded from TUPE, but I envisage that shortly after the transfer you will be invited to join our pension scheme. The pension trustees of your existing scheme will, at your request, make any necessary arrangements for the transfer of any accrued rights capable of transfer into our scheme. I will be letting you have full details in due course.

I am able to assure you that the effect of TUPE is to preserve your continuity of employment when you transfer to us. We will observe and respect your continuity, and the statement of terms and conditions of employment that we will issue to you in due course will show us as your new employer but will confirm that your continued employment runs from the date you commenced work with [insert name of transferor].

Yours sincerely

Document 25
Questionnaire (Business Acquisition)

This questionnaire addresses information needed by [name of Purchaser] to assess its proposed purchase of the [entire] business, assets and undertaking of [name of Vendor] carried on under the name of ('the Business').

Please supply responses as and when the information is available rather than waiting until all the information has been collected.

The questionnaire is to be interpreted as covering not only [name of Vendor] but all other members of the Vendor's group involved in the Business.

Please provide the following information:

1 **Vendor's group structure**
   1.1 Brief description of the Business and the function and location of each place where the Business operates from including locations overseas.
   1.2 Explain how the Business can be identified against other businesses of the Vendor and businesses of other companies in the Vendor's group.
   1.3 Memorandum and articles of association of [name of the Vendor] and all other members of the Vendor's group involved in the Business.
   1.4 Details of all shares owned by Vendor identifying those owned in relation to the Business and details of all other shareholders and their shareholding in such companies.
   1.5 Names of all directors and senior managers of the Vendor and any directors or managers of other group companies involved in the Business.
   1.6 Particulars of the involvement or interests of the persons in question 1.5 above in any business other than the Business and in transactions with the Business.

2 **Accounts and finance**
   2.1 Audited accounts of [the Vendor] for the last three years and audited accounts for the last three years of each company in [the Vendor's] group involved in the Business.
   2.2 Management accounts for the Business.
   2.3 Business plan for the Business for current and next financial year.
   2.4 If appropriate divisional accounts of the Vendor in relation to the Business.
   2.5 Details of all bank accounts operated by or on behalf of the Business and in particular:
      2.5.1 details of all pooled banking arrangements;
      2.5.2 details of agreed overdraft limits and actual overdraft.
   2.6 Details and copies of all mortgages, charges, guarantees, indemnities and other financial commitments undertaken by or in respect of the Business including arrangements within [the Vendor's] group.
   2.7 Details and copies of all loans made to the Business including inter-group loans and staff loans.
   2.8 Details of the basis on which the cost of common group services are apportioned to the Business, eg:
      2.8.1 insurance;
      2.8.2 rental;
      2.8.3 accounting department;
      2.8.4 motor vehicles;

2.8.5　marketing;

2.8.6　research and development;

2.8.7　computer time.

3　**Consents**

3.1　Details of all consents needed by [the Vendor] to transfer the Business; eg consents under:

3.1.1　articles of association of [the Vendor] and its holding company and subsidiaries;

3.1.2　shareholder's agreement governing the conduct of [the Vendor] and its holding company and subsidiaries;

3.1.3　finance arrangements including mortgages, loan notes, term debt and leasing contracts;

3.1.4　stock exchange;

3.1.5　regulatory authorities;

3.1.6　trade contracts;

3.1.7　software licences;

3.1.8　leases.

4　**Contracts and trade**

4.1　Copies of all [material] contracts relating to the Business with customers and suppliers including :

4.1.1　all contracts which require consent to assign;

4.1.2　licences;

4.1.3　agency agreements;

4.1.4　long-term contracts;

4.1.5　franchise arrangements;

4.1.6　hire purchase;

4.1.7　credit sale;

4.1.8　lease agreements;

4.1.9　rental agreements.

4.2　A schedule identifying all customers and the percentage of turnover they represent.

4.3　Copies of all standard forms of contract used.

4.4　A schedule itemising current debtors, period of debt and amount.

4.5　Details of all trade within [the Vendor's] group indicating where and on what basis rates charged are discounted.

4.6　Details of any restrictions on the Business to conduct business in any part of the world.

5　**Employees**

5.1　A schedule or print out containing in respect of all persons employed in the Business:

5.1.1　full name;

5.1.2　name of employee, and sex;

5.1.3　date of birth;

5.1.4　date of commencement of employment;

5.1.5　job description;

5.1.6　salary;

5.1.7　bonus entitlement including profit shares;

5.1.8　pension entitlement;

5.1.9　insurance cover, eg sickness and disability;

5.1.10   notice period;
5.1.11   holiday entitlement.
5.2   Names of the key personnel for the operation and management of the Business.
5.3   Copies of standard terms of employment and any contracts of employment not on standard terms.
5.4   Details of any person engaged in the Business as an independent contractor.
5.5   Details of any recognised trade unions and any relevant agreements with the unions.
5.6   Details of any disputes with employees or contractors in the last four years.

6 **Pensions**
6.1   Details of every pension and life assurance scheme operated by or for the Business including :
6.1.1   copies of the deeds and rules and all amendments;
6.1.2   copy of the latest and preceding actuarial valuation and any investment report;
6.1.3   copies of the latest accounts and trustees' report;
6.1.4   copies of all scheme booklets;
6.1.5   copy of the contracting out certificate;
6.1.6   copy of the Inland Revenue approval;
6.1.7   copy of the memorandum and articles of association of any trustee company;
6.1.8   names of current trustees;
6.1.9   details of any insurance policies;
6.1.10   details of active members;
6.1.11   details of current pensioners;
6.1.12   details of deferred pensions;
6.1.13   details of employer's and employees' contribution rates in the last four years;
6.1.14   details of any discretionary practices;
6.1.15   details of any paid up and closed schemes relevant to the Business.

7 **Insurance**
7.1   Details of all insurances taken out by or operated for the benefit of the Business.
7.2   Details of all insurance claims in the last four years.

8 **Litigation/claims**
8.1   Details of all litigation including arbitration and alternative dispute resolution in which:
8.1.1   the Business has been involved in the last four years;
8.1.2   the Business is involved or which is currently threatened.
8.2   Details of any regulatory investigations of the Business or any known investigations of its competitors in the last four years.

9 **Land**
9.1   Details of all freehold property owned by the Business including copies of title deeds.
9.2   Details of all leasehold properties occupied or owned by the Business including:
9.2.1   copies of leases;
9.2.2   current rent and state of rent review negotiations if any;
9.2.3   title number if registered.
9.3   Details and copies of all licences and leases granted to or by the Business including:
9.3.1   name of current tenant and landlord;

9.3.2   current rent.

9.4   Details of current state of dilapidations of the properties including when liabilities will crystallise.

10 Tangible assets

10.1   Details of all plant and machinery and a copy of the plant register.

10.2   Details of all motor vehicles owned or used by the Business.

11 Intellectual property

11.1   Details of all patents owned by or used in relation to the Business including copies of all registrations and applications.

11.2   Details of all Trade Marks and registered designs owned by or used in relation to the Business and copies of all registrations, applications, licences etc including details of actual use in the last three years.

11.3   Details of all copyright including software owned by or used in relation to the Business including copies of all licences.

11.4   Details of all design rights owned by or used in relation to the Business.

11.5   Details including copies of all business names and logos used in the Business.

11.6   Details of any confidential know-how used in relation to the Business.

11.7   Copies of any confidentiality agreements entered into by the Business.

11.8   Details of any overlap between the intellectual property above and that used in the business retained by [the Vendor].

11.9   Details of any claims by any present or past employees in relation to title to intellectual property used in or by the Business.

11.10 Details of any known infringements by or against the Business.

Dated   200[ ]

Document 26
Business Acquisition Agreement

DATE: 200[   ]

PARTIES:

(1) [   ] of [   ].

(2) [   ], a company incorporated in England (company number [   ]), whose registered office is at [   ].

RECITALS:

(A) The Vendor owns the Business and the Assets.

(B) The Purchaser has agreed to purchase the Business and the Assets on the terms of this Agreement.

NOW IT IS HEREBY AGREED as follows:

1   **Definitions**

In this Agreement and the Schedules the following definitions will apply:

'Accounts'	The unaudited financial statements of the Business for the year ended on the Accounts Date
'Accounts Date'	[ ] 200[ ]
'Agreed Form'	In a form agreed between the Vendor and the Purchaser and, for the purpose of identification only, initialled by each of them
'Assets'	The Claims
	The benefit (subject to the burden) of the Contracts
	The Debts
	The Documents
	The Goodwill
	The Intellectual Property Rights
	Such right title and interest (if any) as the Vendor may have in the Financed Assets to the extent that the same can be assigned
	The Fixed Assets
	The Properties
	The Stock
'Business'	The business of the supply of contract labour carried on by the Vendor under the trading name '[ ]'
'Business Day'	Any day (other than a Saturday, Sunday or public holiday) on which banks in the City of London are generally open for business
'Claims'	All rights which the Vendor may have against third parties relating to the Assets and the Business, including (without limitation) all warranties and representations given by manufacturers and suppliers of goods and services in connection with the Assets and the Business
'Completion'	Completion of this Agreement in accordance with Clause 5

'Completion Statement'	The statement to be prepared in accordance with Clause 6 and Schedule 5
'Connected Person'	Has the same meaning as in section 839 of the Income and Corporation Taxes Act 1988
'Contracts'	The Customer Contracts, the Financing Contracts and the Supplier Contracts
'Creditors'	The book and trading debts owing and the periodic expenses which have accrued for payment by the Vendor in connection with the Business as at Completion (whether due for payment or not), but excluding: – amounts owed to other businesses owned by the Vendor or its subsidiary undertakings; – amounts owed to banks or other financial institutions; and – any liability for Taxation (other than liabilities to account for national insurance contributions and PAYE payable in respect of the Employees and any value added tax in relation to the Business which shall be treated as Creditors)
'Customer Contracts'	All outstanding contracts and orders of the Vendor for the supply of services to customers of the Business
'Debts'	All book and trading debts (including monies payable for services supplied but not invoiced at the date of Completion) and all deferred income due to and the benefit of any prepayment paid by the Vendor in connection with the Business as at Completion other than: – amounts owed by other businesses owned by the Vendor or its subsidiary undertakings; – cash in hand and amounts held in accounts with any bank or other financial institution; and – any right to receive a repayment of Taxation
'Disclosure Letter'	The letter of the same date of this Agreement delivered by the Vendor to the Purchaser which contains certain disclosures against the Warranties
'Documents'	All customer lists, supplier lists, pricing lists, accounting records, information and data, terms and conditions of sale and purchase, advertising material, sales publications, circulars, promotional material, artwork, drawings, designs, technical specifications, operating manuals and computer software relating to the Business including, without limitation: – all documents relating to the Contracts; – all records relating to the Employees; and – the records of the Business which are required to be transferred to the Purchaser pursuant to section 49(1) of the VAT Act
'Employees'	The employees engaged by the Vendor in the Business as at Completion, as listed in the Disclosure Letter
'Excluded Assets'	All cash in hand of the Vendor and amounts held in accounts with any bank or other financial utilisation Any right to receive a repayment of Taxation Amounts owed to the Business by any other business of the Vendor or its subsidiary undertakings

'Expert'	An independent firm of chartered accountants appointed:
	by the Vendor and the Purchaser by agreement; or
	if the Vendor and the Purchaser cannot agree upon an appointee within 14 days of a request served by one upon the other so to do, nominated by the President for the time being of the Institute of Chartered Accountants for England and Wales
'Financed Assets'	The assets used by the Vendor in connection with the Business pursuant to any hire, contract hire, hire purchase, rental, leasing or other similar agreements, details of which are set out in Schedule 2
'Financing Contracts'	The agreements pursuant to which the Financed Assets are used in connection with the Business
'Fixed Assets'	All items of fixed and moveable equipment, furniture, computer hardware, fixtures and fittings used by the Vendor in the Business as at Completion, including (without limitation) the items listed in Schedule 6
'Fully Indemnified'	Fully indemnified from and held harmless against all actions, reasonable costs, claims, demands, expenses, liabilities, losses and proceedings in respect of the matter referred to
'Goodwill'	The goodwill of the Vendor in relation to the Business together with the exclusive right for the Purchaser to represent itself as carrying on the Business in succession to the Vendor and to use all or any trading names used in carrying on the Business
'Intellectual Property Rights'	The patents, trade marks, service marks, registered designs, trade or business names, know-how, copyright, design rights and other intellectual property rights (or any applications for any of such rights) used or owned by the Vendor in the Business
'Lease'	The lease dated [ ] between [ ] (1) and the Vendor (2), pursuant to which the Vendor occupies the Property
'Liabilities'	All liabilities of the Vendor (whether actual or contingent) other than the Creditors
'Management Accounts'	The unaudited management accounts of the Business for the [ ] month period ended on the Management Accounts Date
'Management Accounts Date'	[ ] 200[ ]
'Net Asset Value'	The aggregate value, as at Completion, of:
	– the Assets;
	less the aggregate value of:
	– the Creditors;
	to be calculated in accordance with the provisions of Clause 6 and Schedule 5
'Property'	The leasehold property used in connection with the Business, brief particulars of which appear in Schedule 3
'Purchase Price'	means £[ ] subject to adjustment in accordance with Clause 6.8
'Purchaser'	[ ]
'Purchaser's Solicitors'	[ ]

'Recognised Investment Exchange'	The same meaning as in section 285 of the Financial Services and Markets Act 2000
'Regulations'	The Transfer of Undertakings (Protection of Employment) Regulations 1981
'Restricted Activities'	The provision of contract labour
'Stock'	All stationery, packaging and consumables of the Business at Completion
'Supplier Contracts'	All outstanding contracts and arrangements of the Vendor as at Completion for the supply of goods and services to the Business
'Taxation Or Tax'	Income tax, corporation tax, capital gains tax, inheritance tax, value added tax, customs duty, excise duty, import duty, stamp duty, stamp duty reserve tax, national insurance and social security contributions, general and water rates and all other forms of tax, charge, rate, impost, duty, levy, liability or sum payable or formerly payable in respect of income, profits, distributions, gains, receipts turnover, payroll or documents, the holding or occupation of any land or interest in land or otherwise at the instance of any revenue, customs, excise, central state or local or municipal government or other authority of the United Kingdom, the Republic of Ireland or any part of the United Kingdom, the Republic of Ireland or elsewhere and all penalties, charges and interest relating to any liability for or loss of relief from any of the foregoing
'VATA'	The Value Added Tax Act 1994
'VATO'	The Value Added Tax (Special Provisions) Order 1995
'Vendor'	[ ]
['Vendor's Group'	The Vendor and any company which is from time to time a subsidiary or holding company of the Vendor or a subsidiary of a holding company of the Vendor]
'Vendor's Solicitors'	[ ] of [ ]
'Warranties'	The warranties set out in Schedule 4

2   **Interpretation**

2.1   The headings and table of contents in this Agreement are inserted for convenience only and shall not affect its interpretation or construction.

2.2   References in this Agreement to Clauses and Schedules are, unless otherwise stated, references to the Clauses of and Schedules to this Agreement. References to paragraphs are references to the paragraphs of Schedules to this Agreement.

2.3   The Schedules form part of this Agreement and shall have the same force and effect as if expressly set out in the body of this Agreement.

2.4   Words and expressions defined in the Companies Act 1985 shall, unless they are otherwise defined in this Agreement or the context otherwise requires, bear the same meaning in this Agreement.

2.5   References to statutes shall include any statutory modification, re-enactment or extension of such statute and any orders, regulations, instruments or other subordinate legislation made pursuant to such statute.

2.6   References in this Agreement to:

2.6.1   the masculine gender shall include the feminine and neuter and vice versa;

2.6.2   the singular shall include the plural and vice versa; and

2.6.3   'persons' shall include bodies corporate, unincorporated associations and partnerships.

3 Sale of the Business

3.1 The Vendor agrees to sell and the Purchaser agrees to buy the Assets and the Business as a going concern, free from all liens, charges and encumbrances.

3.2 The Assets and the Business are sold by the Vendor with full title guarantee.

4 Consideration

4.1 The consideration for the sale and purchase of the Assets and the Business shall be the:

4.1.1 payment by the Purchaser of the Purchase Price; and

4.1.2 the assumption and discharge by the Purchaser of the Creditors.

4.2 The Purchase Price is to be apportioned amongst the Assets on the basis set out in Schedule 1.

4.3 Unless otherwise stated, the Vendor authorises the Purchaser to pay all sums due under this Agreement to the Vendor's Solicitors. The receipt of any monies due under this Agreement by the Vendor's Solicitors will give a full and valid discharge to the Purchaser.

4.4 The parties intend that the Assets and the Business are sold as a going concern and that, accordingly, section 49 VATA and Article 5 of VATO shall apply to the transfer of the Assets and the Business. Accordingly it is agreed that:

4.4.1 both parties shall use their reasonable endeavours to ensure that the sale of the Assets and the Business is treated as neither a supply of goods nor a supply of services for value added tax purposes;

4.4.2 the parties will notify HM Customs & Excise as required pursuant to VATA; and

4.4.3 upon Completion, the Vendor will deliver to the Purchaser all of the records of the Business required to be retained by the Purchaser following Completion.

5 Completion

5.1 The Purchaser shall not be required to complete the purchase of the Assets and the Business unless all of the Assets and the Business are transferred at the same time and all of the Vendor's obligations pursuant to Clause 5.2 are satisfied in full. Subject to this, the sale and purchase is to be completed at the offices of the Purchaser's Solicitors immediately following exchange of this Agreement.

5.2 On Completion the Vendor is to deliver to the Purchaser:

5.2.1 such documents as the Purchaser may reasonably require to complete the sale and purchase of the Assets and the Business;

5.2.2 possession of the Assets of a tangible nature (which are to be delivered up at the Property);

5.2.3 vacant possession of the Property;

5.2.4 the title deeds to the Property;

5.2.5 a deed of assignment of the Lease in the agreed form duly executed by the Vendor;

5.2.6 the written consent of any mortgagee or other person whose consent is necessary for the sale of the Assets and the Business together with an appropriate release where necessary.

5.3 On Completion the Purchaser will pay the Purchase Price to the Vendor's Solicitors by means of banker's draft or telegraphic transfer. The receipt of the Vendor's Solicitors will give a full and valid discharge to the Purchaser.

5.4 Title to and risk in the Assets and the Business will pass to the Purchaser upon Completion. Completion will be deemed to have taken place at the close of business on the date of Completion. References in this agreement to Completion will be construed accordingly.

5.5   Following Completion, the Purchaser will ensure that the Vendor and its advisers have full, free and uninterrupted access, during normal business hours and on reasonable notice being given, to the Documents to the extent that such access is necessary to allow the Vendor to comply with its obligations under this Agreement.

6   Completion Statement

6.1   As soon as reasonably practicable and in any event within 90 Business Days of Completion the Purchaser will prepare and deliver to the Vendor a draft Completion Statement.

6.2   The Completion Statement is to be prepared on the basis of the accounting practices, policies and conventions referred to in Schedule 5.

6.3   The Vendor will ensure that the Purchaser and its advisers have full, free and uninterrupted access to any books and records (including bank statements) of the Vendor to the extent that such access is necessary to prepare or review the Completion Statement.

6.4   The Purchaser will ensure that the Vendor and its advisers have full, free and uninterrupted access to the Documents for the purpose of reviewing the Completion Statement.

6.5   Within 30 Business Days of receipt by the Vendor of the draft Completion Statement, the Vendor is to serve notice upon the Purchaser to confirm its agreement to the Completion Statement and the statement as to the Net Asset Value or to identify any matters upon which it disagrees and the reasons for its disagreement. If no notice is served within such period of five Business Days, the draft Completion Statement and the Purchaser's statement of the Net Asset Value shall be deemed to have been agreed and shall become final and binding upon both of the parties.

6.6   If notice is served to identify any disagreement pursuant to Clause 6.5, the Purchaser and the Vendor are to consult together with a view to resolving the matter in dispute. If agreement is not resolved within a further 90 Business Days, then either the Purchaser or the Vendor may refer the matter to the Expert for his decision.

6.7   The decision of the Expert will, in the absence of any manifest error, be final and binding upon the parties. The Expert shall be entitled to determine in his sole discretion the basis upon which he receives evidence and argument from the Purchaser and the Vendor. The costs of the Expert are to be borne as he may direct.

6.8   Within five Business Days of the date of agreement or determination of the Completion Statement and the Net Asset Value:

6.8.1   if the Net Asset Value is more than £[   ], the Purchaser will pay an amount equal to the excess to the Vendor;

6.8.2   if the Net Asset Value is less than £[   ], the Vendor will repay to the Purchaser an amount equal to the shortfall.

Any payment made pursuant to this Clause 6.8 is to be made in cash and is an adjustment to the Purchase Price.

7   Warranties

7.1   The Vendor warrants and represents to the Purchaser in the terms set out in Schedule 4 as at Completion.

7.2   The Warranties are given subject only to those matters which are fully and fairly disclosed in the Disclosure Letter. No other information of which the Purchaser is aware or any investigation carried out by the Purchaser is to prejudice any claim made by the Purchaser or operate to reduce the amount recoverable under the Warranties.

7.3 The Vendor warrants and represents to the Purchaser that the information contained in the Disclosure Letter and the annexures to the Disclosure Letter:

7.3.1 is true and accurate; and

7.3.2 does not omit anything which would make such information untrue, incorrect or misleading.

7.4 Each of the Warranties gives rise to a separate and independent obligation; the interpretation of each of the Warranties is not to be limited by reference to any other Warranty or the provisions of this Agreement.

7.5 All Warranties which relate to the knowledge, information, belief or awareness of the Vendor are given by it after having made due and careful enquiry into the subject matter of the relevant Warranty.

7.6 The Vendor agrees with the Purchaser (for itself and as trustee for the Employees) to waive any right which it may have in respect of any misrepresentation, inaccuracy or omission in or from any information or advice supplied or given by the Employees in enabling the Vendor to give the Warranties and prepare the Disclosure Letter.

7.7 Any payment required to be made by the Vendor pursuant to the Warranties is to be paid in cash and shall be deemed to be a reduction in the consideration for the Assets and the Business.

7.8 No claim may be made against the Vendor for breach of the Warranties unless notice is served on the Vendor within [ ] of Completion. Such notice shall provide sufficient information to enable the Vendor to identify the subject matter of the claim and, where practicable, an estimate of the amount of the claim.

7.9 The Vendor shall not be liable for any breach of the Warranties unless the amount claimed by the Purchaser in respect of such breach or claim exceeds £[ ] and unless, when aggregated with all other claims for breach of the Warranties, the value of such claims exceeds £[ ] (in which case the Vendor will be liable for the whole amount of such claims and not merely the excess above £[ ]).

7.10 The aggregate liability of the Vendor for all claims made for breach of the Warranties shall not exceed the Purchase Price plus the value of the Creditors.

7.11 No claim may be made by the Purchaser for breach of the Warranties to the extent that a claim arises as a result of any change of law occurring after the date of this Agreement.

7.12 Any claim made by the Purchaser for breach of the Warranties shall take into account the extent to which:

7.12.1 the Purchaser has previously recovered compensation from a third party in relation to the subject matter of the claim; or

7.12.2 the Purchaser receives a direct Taxation benefit as a result of the subject matter of the claim.

7.13 No claim may be made under the Warranties to the extent that the Purchaser has previously made a claim and received compensation under the Warranties in respect of the same breach or subject matter.

8 **The Contracts**

8.1 Following Completion the Vendor will provide all reasonable assistance to the Purchaser to obtain any consents and approvals which are needed to transfer the Contracts to the Purchaser. Where assignment of a Contract without the consent of any other party would constitute a breach of such Contract or give rise to a right of termination, this Agreement shall not operate as a formal assignment of such Contract until such consent is obtained.

8.2 The Vendor covenants to the Purchaser that, where the benefit of any of the Contracts cannot be effectively transferred to, or the obligations under any of the Contracts cannot effectively be assumed by, the Purchaser otherwise than pursuant to a formal assignment or novation with, or with the consent of, any third party:

    8.2.1 it shall use its best endeavours to procure the agreement and execution of such documentation or the giving of such consent; and

    8.2.2 unless and until any such documentation is entered into or consent given, it shall do all such acts and things in relation to the Contracts as the Purchaser may reasonably require.

8.3 To the extent that any of the Contracts are not formally transferred to the Purchaser at Completion, the Purchaser will on behalf of the Vendor, but at its own expense and for its own benefit, perform all of the obligations of the Vendor under the Contracts.

8.4 The Vendor will keep the Purchaser fully indemnified in relation to any act, omission or default occurring in respect of the Contracts prior to Completion.

8.5 Save to the extent that such obligations arise solely as a result of any act, omission or default on the part of the Vendor in breach of the Contracts prior to Completion, the Purchaser agrees to discharge all of the obligations of the Vendor pursuant to the Contracts and will keep the Vendor fully indemnified in respect of any failure to do so.

8.6 All monies payable pursuant to the Contracts following Completion are for the account of the Purchaser. If the Vendor receives any payment direct it shall immediately remit it in full to the Purchaser without deduction, counterclaim or set-off.

9 **The Debts**

9.1 Following Completion, the Vendor will co-operate fully with the Purchaser in relation to the collection of the Debts. The Vendor shall, if requested by the Purchaser, execute formal assignments of the Debts in such form as the Purchaser may reasonably require.

9.2 Any monies received by the Vendor in relation to any of the Debts are for the account of the Purchaser. If the Vendor receives any such payment direct it shall immediately remit it in full to the Purchaser without deduction, counterclaim or set-off.

10 **Creditors [and liabilities]**

10.1 The Purchaser will discharge the Creditors as and when the same fall due for payment in the ordinary course of the Business. The Purchaser will keep the Vendor fully indemnified in relation to the Creditors.

10.2 The Vendor will immediately forward to the Purchaser any notices, correspondence or other documentation which it may receive following Completion in relation to the Creditors.

10.3 Nothing in this Agreement will require the Purchaser to assume, satisfy or discharge any liabilities of the Vendor other than the Creditors. The Vendor will discharge all of the Liabilities as and when the same fall due for payment and will keep the Purchaser fully indemnified in relation to all Liabilities following Completion.

11 **The Employees**

11.1 The Vendor and the Purchaser acknowledge that, upon Completion, the Employees are to become employees of the Purchaser. The Vendor and the Purchaser will give to each other such assistance as may be reasonably necessary to comply with the Regulations.

11.2   The Vendor will keep the Purchaser fully indemnified in respect of:

      11.2.1   all sums due to or in respect of the Employees for all periods up to Completion, including (without limitation) salaries, bonuses, expenses, emoluments and any national insurance contributions and PAYE payable in respect of such items;

      11.2.2   any claims for redundancy, unfair, wrongful or constructive dismissal or other payments in respect of any act or omission prior to Completion;

      11.2.3   any failure to inform and consult with the Employees pursuant to regulations 10 and 11 of the Regulations in connection with the sale and purchase of the Business; and

      11.2.4   any person being treated as an Employee for the purposes of the Regulations other than the persons listed in the Disclosure Letter.

12 The Properties

12.1   The Vendor shall sell and the Purchaser shall purchase the leasehold interest of the Vendor in the Property.

12.2   The Property is sold with the benefit of and subject to the matters contained or referred to in the leases and licences particularised in Schedule 3.

12.3   The Property is sold in accordance with the Law Society's Standard Conditions of Sale (Third Edition) varied as follows:

      12.3.1   the rate of interest under standard condition 7.3 shall be that specified in Clause 18;

      12.3.2   standard conditions 2.2 and 9 shall not apply;

      12.3.3   standard condition 5.1 shall not apply and the Property shall be the responsibility of the Purchaser from the date hereof;

      12.3.4   in standard condition 5.2.2 the following is added:

          '(i) must not change the use of the Property nor infringe any statutory provision affecting the Property.'

12.4   The Vendor shall assign all its leasehold or other beneficial interest in the Property by a deed of assignment in the form of the draft which has been agreed between the Vendor and the Purchaser and initialled for the purposes of identification.

12.5   The Vendor shall apply to the reversioner of the Lease ('the Reversioner' which expression shall include all persons entitled to the reversion (whether mediate or immediate) expectant on the termination of the Lease and where reference is made to any licence required from or by a reversioner and where more than one is required such reference is to and all such licences) and use its reasonable endeavours to obtain a licence for the assignment of the Lease to the Purchaser ('the Licence to Assign').

12.6   The Purchaser shall promptly and at its own cost and expense:

      12.6.1   supply all such references and information in respect of the Purchaser as the Reversioner may require in connection with the Licence to Assign;

      12.6.2   deal promptly with all correspondence and documentation relating to the Vendor's application for the Licence to Assign;

      12.6.3   comply with all requirements of the Reversioner in relation to the granting of the Licence to Assign in particular but without prejudice to the generality of the foregoing any provided for in the Lease;

      12.6.4   enter into such direct covenant with the Reversioner as may be required to procure the Licence to Assign;

12.6.5   execute the Licence to Assign within ten working days of the engrossments having been supplied to the Purchaser's Solicitors;

12.6.6   otherwise use its reasonable endeavours to assist the Vendor in obtaining the Licence to Assign.

12.7   The Vendor will permit the Purchaser to occupy the Property upon completion on the terms of standard condition 5.2 (as amended) and on the following additional terms pending completion of the sale and purchase provided for in Clause 13.1 and the obtaining of the Licence to Assign:

12.7.1   occupation is at the Purchaser's risk and in the knowledge that the Reversioner of the Property has not granted the Licence to Assign;

12.7.2   the Purchaser will keep the Vendor fully indemnified against any liabilities, costs, claims and demands which may be incurred as a result of the Purchaser's occupation of the Property or any breach of the terms of occupation set out in Clause 12;

12.7.3   the Vendor is not responsible for any loss or damage which may be done to or suffered by the Purchaser or its employees, agents, visitors or invitees resulting from the physical state of the Property or from any neglect or default of the Vendor or the Vendor's agents, visitors, licensees or invitees or of the owner of the tenants' licences or occupier of any nearby premises;

12.7.4   the Purchaser cannot assign the benefit of the licence hereby granted by the Vendor nor part with or share possession or occupation of the Property during the currency of the Vendor's licence hereby granted;

12.7.5   nothing in these terms of occupation shall create a legal demise or any greater interest than a bare licence and the Purchaser appreciates that it will not obtain any security of tenure under Part II of the Landlord and Tenant Act 1954 by virtue of this Agreement;

12.7.6   so far as is consistent with the terms of this clause the Purchaser's occupation of the Property is on the terms and conditions of the Lease and the Purchaser will not do or permit or omit anything which constitutes a breach of such;

12.7.7   the Purchaser is responsible for and indemnifies the Vendor against all outgoings including rents, licence fees, rates and charges for electricity, gas, water, telephone and other services and any other payments whatsoever payable in respect of the Properties throughout the currency of the Vendor's licence hereby granted.

13 Restrictions on the Vendor

13.1   The Vendor acknowledges the importance to the Purchaser of the Goodwill. Accordingly, it is prepared to enter into the commitments contained in this Clause 13 to ensure that the Purchaser's interest in the Business is properly protected.

13.2   The Vendor undertakes that it will, for a period of three months following Completion, provide such assistance and support as the Purchaser may reasonably require to enable it to achieve a smooth and orderly transition of the Business into the ownership of the Purchaser.

13.3   The Vendor severally undertakes to the Purchaser that it will not (and will procure that no other member of the Vendor's Group will) for a period of two years following Completion:

13.3.1   carry on or be engaged, concerned or interested, directly or indirectly in any of the Restricted Activities within a radius of 50 miles from either of the Properties;

13.3.2 solicit or knowingly accept any orders, enquiries or business in respect of any of the Restricted Activities from any person who was, in the 12 months prior to Completion, a customer of the Business;

13.3.3 interfere in the relationship between the Purchaser and the Business with their respective supplies and customers; or

13.3.4 solicit or entice or endeavour to solicit or entice any of the Employees engaged in a managerial capacity or who have had direct contact with customers in the course of their duties to cease working for Purchaser.

13.4 The Vendor severally undertakes to the Purchaser that it will not (and will procure that no other member of the Vendor's Group will) at any time after Completion:

13.4.1 hold itself out as having any continuing involvement with the Business other than in the course of complying with his obligations under this Agreement; or

13.4.2 disclose or use (or authorise the disclosure or use by any third party of) any confidential information concerning accounts, financial or contractual arrangements or other dealings of the Business save to the extent that disclosure of such information is required to satisfy any obligations imposed by law or the rules of any recognised investment exchange.

13.5 The restrictions contained in Clauses 13.3 and 13.4 shall apply to any action carried out by the Vendor (or any member of the Vendor's Group) on its own behalf or jointly with or as agent, manager, director or shareholder of any other person.

13.6 Each of the restrictions contained in Clauses 13.3 and 13.4 are to be treated as separate obligations, independent of the others.

13.7 The parties consider the restrictions contained in Clauses 13.3 and 13.4 to be reasonable as between themselves and the public interest. If, however, any of them are found by a court to be unreasonable and unenforceable, but would be reasonable and enforceable if certain words were deleted, then the restrictions will apply with those words deleted.

14 Name and Goodwill

14.1 The Vendor undertakes to the Purchaser that it will not (and will procure that no other member of the Vendor's Group will) at any time after Completion use the name '[   ]' (whether as a corporate or trading name or otherwise) or any other name which is identical to or liable to be confused with such name.

14.2 The Vendor will co-operate with the Purchaser to enable the Purchaser following Completion to use any telephone and facsimile numbers used by the Vendor prior to Completion in connection with the Business.

15 Announcements

Save as may be required by law, no announcement relating to the sale and purchase of the Assets and the Business shall be made by the Vendor without the prior written consent of the Purchaser.

16 Further assurance

The Vendor shall do and execute all such further acts, things, deeds and documents as may be necessary or reasonably requested by the Purchaser to give effect to the terms of this Agreement and to vest in the Purchaser title to the Assets and the Business.

17 Notices

17.1 Any notice required to be given pursuant to this Agreement shall be in writing signed by, or on behalf of, the person issuing the notice. Notices may be served by personal delivery, prepaid first class post or facsimile transmission to:

       17.1.1 in the case of the Vendor, the address set out above or such other address within the United Kingdom as he may notify to the Purchaser for the purpose; and

       17.1.2 in the case of the Purchaser, its registered office for the time being.

17.2 Notices served in accordance with Clause 17.1 shall be deemed to have been received:

       17.2.1 if delivered personally, upon delivery (unless such delivery takes place on a day which is not a Business Day or after 5.00 pm on a Business Day, in which case notice will be deemed to have been received at 10.00 am on the next Business Day);

       17.2.2 if served by pre-paid first class post, at the close of business on the second Business Day after posting; and

       17.2.3 if served by facsimile transmission, upon receipt of confirmation that the notice has been transmitted (unless such transmission takes place on a day which is not a Business Day or after 5.00 pm on a Business Day, in which case notice will be deemed to have been received at 10.00 am on the next Business Day).

17.3 In proving service by post it will be necessary only to prove that the notice was properly stamped, addressed and posted.

18 Counterparts

This Agreement may be executed in one or more parts, each of which when executed shall be an original. All counterparts together shall constitute one and the same agreement.

19 Interest

If monies payable pursuant to this Agreement are not paid in full on the due date for payment they will bear interest at a rate 2% per annum above the base lending rate of the Royal Bank of Scotland plc from time to time in force, from the due date for payment to the actual date of payment in full, compounded at monthly intervals.

20 Entire Agreement and variations

20.1 This Agreement (together with the documents referred to in this Agreement) constitutes the entire agreement between the parties with respect to all matters referred to in it.

20.2 No variations to this Agreement shall be effective unless made in writing and signed by all the parties.

21 Costs

Each party shall bear the costs of its own financial, accountancy and legal advice in relation to this Agreement.

22 Survival of certain provisions

This Agreement shall remain in full force and effect after Completion in respect of any matters, covenants or conditions which shall not have been fulfilled or performed prior to Completion and the Warranties and all other obligations given or undertaken shall (except for any obligations fully performed) continue in full force and effect notwithstanding Completion.

23 Governing law

This Agreement shall be governed by and construed in accordance with English law. The parties agree to submit to the non-exclusive jurisdiction of the English courts as regards any claim or matter arising under this Agreement.

IN WITNESS of which the parties have executed this Agreement on the date set out above.

Schedule 1

Apportionment of Consideration

The consideration is to be apportioned as follows:

1	The Contracts	£1
2	The Documents	£1
3	The Intellectual Property Rights	£1
4	The Financed Assets shown	The book value of the Financed Assets as at Completion
5	The Fixed Assets shown Completion	The book value of the Fixed Assets as at
6	The Premises	£1
7	The Stock	The book value of the Stock as at Completion
8	Workshop equipment and Service Vehicles	The book value as at Completion

---

Schedule 2

Financed Assets

Schedule 3

Premises

The premises owned by [   ] and occupied by the Vendor at [   ]

Schedule 4

Warranties

Schedule 5

Completion Statement

Schedule 6

Fixed Assets

SIGNED by [   ] acting by an authorised signatory in the presence of:

Witness signature

Witness name

Witness address

Witness occupation

SIGNED by [   ] acting by an authorised signatory in the presence of:

Witness signature

Witness name

Witness address

Witness occupation

Document 27
Assignment of Intellectual Property Rights

THIS ASSIGNMENT is made the   day of   200[ ]

PARTIES

(1) [   ] **LIMITED**
(Registered in England and Wales No[   ])
whose registered office is at [   ] ('Assignor') ('Company')

(2) [   ] of [   ] ('the Employee').

(3) [   ] **LIMITED**
(Registered in England and Wales No [   ])
whose registered office is at [   ] ('Assignee').

BACKGROUND

(A) [The Principal activity of the Company is the supply of computer software programmes for use in the field of [   ] the particulars of which are set out in the Schedule ('Software').]

(B) [The Software has been developed by or on behalf of the Company and the Company is the proprietor of the copyright anywhere in the world in the Software ('Copyright').]

(C) [The Assignor is the proprietor of the [registered] [trade mark] [patent] details of which are set out in the Schedule ('Trade Mark') ('Patent').]

(D) The Employee has entered into this Assignment to acknowledge and confirm the ownership of the [Copyright] [Patent] [Trade Mark] is vested in the Company and to assign the benefit of any copyright in the Software (if any) which is vested in [].

(E) The [Assignor] [Company and []] have agreed to assign to the Assignee the [Copyright] [Patent] [Trade Mark] upon the terms and conditions of this Assignment.

(F) [The Employee and the Company are referred to in this Deed of Assignment as the 'Assignor'.]

IT IS AGREED as follows:

1 **Assignment**

    1.1 In consideration of one pound (£1.00) paid by the Assignee to the Assignor (the receipt of which the Assignor acknowledges), the Assignor with full title guarantee assigns to the Assignee the [Copyright] [Patent] [Trade Mark] absolutely.

    1.2 To the extent that any of the rights assigned under Clause 1.1 above are not wholly and/or validly assigned, the Assignor shall hold them upon a bare trust for the full and exclusive benefit of the Assignee.

    1.3 The Assignor will at the Assignee's request deliver up to Assignee all documents, material and/or other media which may be in the Assignor's possession, power or control which comprises or contains any part of or information in relation to the [Copyright][Patent][Trade Mark].

2 **Obligations and warranties**

    2.1 The Assignor shall at the request [and entire cost] of the Assignee:

        2.1.1 execute any further documents and/or deeds and do any such things as the Assignee may require to enable the Assignee to secure the delivery of information and the benefit of the rights assigned or held in trust in accordance with Clause 1 above; and/or

2.1.2   take such action as the Assignee may reasonably require to assist the Assignee in bringing or defending any proceedings relating to the [Copyright] [Patent] [Trade Mark].

2.2   The Assignor warrants that:

2.2.1   the Assignor is the proprietor of the [Copyright] [Patent] [Trade Mark] and has the full power to enter into this Assignment;

2.2.2   the Assignor has not granted any licences to use the [Copyright] [Patent] [Trade Mark] which have not been disclosed in writing to the Assignee;

2.2.3   the Assignor has not, either by act or omission, caused and/or permitted anything to be done which might endanger the validity of the [Copyright] [Patent] [Trade Mark];

2.2.4   the Assignor has no knowledge of any circumstances that may endanger the validity of the [Copyright] [Patent] [Trade Mark] [or the ability of the Assignee to register the Assignment];

2.2.5   the Assignor has no knowledge of any potential, pending and/or outstanding actions, proceedings, allegations and/or claims by any third party in respect of the [Copyright] [Patent] [Trade Mark] to the effect that the third party has any interest, whether legal or equitable, in the [Copyright] [Patent] [Trade Mark] or any part of it or that the Assignor has infringed the intellectual property rights of that third party;

2.2.6   the Assignor has no knowledge of any existing infringement of the [Copyright] [Patent] [Trade Mark] by any third party; and

2.2.7   [all fees, duties, payments, charges and expenses have been paid in respect of the maintenance and renewal of the registration of the [Patent] [Trade Mark] and that there are no further payments due and/or payable within [30] days from the date of this Agreement.]

2.2.8   [the Assignor has waived absolutely any right to be identified as the author of the Software, in accordance with section 78(2) of the Copyright Designs and Patent Act 1988 together with any right they may have had to object to the alteration and/or derogatory treatment of the Software granted by section 80 of that Act].

2.3   The Assignor agrees to indemnify and keep indemnified the Assignee against any and all actions, claims, proceedings, costs and damages (including any damages or compensation, compromise or settlement of any claim) paid by the Assignee on the advice of its legal advisors and all legal costs and other expenses reasonably and properly incurred and arising out of any breach of this Assignment by the Assignor [or out of any claims by a third party based on any facts which if substantiated would constitute such a breach].

2.4   If any claim is made or threatened against either party by any third party that the exercise by the Assignee of any rights assigned under this Assignment infringe any rights of any third party, the Assignee shall be given full control of any proceedings or negotiations in connection with the claim or threatened claim and shall be exclusively entitled to appoint and instruct legal advisers and/or counsel in connection with any such proceedings or negotiations and to determine the forum for any such proceedings.

2.5   The Employee hereby acknowledges and confirms to the Assignee [and to the Company] that the Employee does not have any claim against the Company in respect of the ownership of the [Copyright] [Patent] [Trade Mark].

3　General

   3.1   This Assignment is governed by and interpreted in accordance with English law and the parties agree to submit to the non-exclusive jurisdiction of the English courts.

IN WITNESS OF THE ABOVE the parties have Executed and Delivered this Assignment as a Deed on the date written at the head of this Assignment.

Schedule

Particulars of the Software

Schedule

Trade Mark

Mark	Registration No	Classes	Date

Schedule

Patent

Country	Patent No	Date of Grant	Title of Patent

SIGNED and **DELIVERED** as a **DEED** by

[   ] **LIMITED**

acting by:

.... Director

.... Director/Secretary

SIGNED and **DELIVERED** as a **DEED** by

[   ]

in the presence of:

SIGNED and **DELIVERED** as a **DEED** by

[   ] **LIMITED**

acting by:

.... Director

.... Director/Secretary

Index